THE 90-DAY GAME

YOUR PATHWAY TO CREATING WHAT YOU TRULY WANT WHILE ENJOYING THE PROCESS

JOHN FELITTO

Woodwright | Press

PEARL RIVER, NEW YORK

Woodwright | Press
PEARL RIVER, NEW YORK

ISBN: 978-0-9961649-0-0

The Learning Annex and Monopoly are registered trademarks.

Editing and design by Joanne Shwed, Backspace Ink (backspaceink.com).

For information regarding special discounts for bulk purchases, please contact Team@90DayGame.com.

To Joan

The only difference between a fabulous life and something less than a fabulous life is one of attitude, yes indeed, one of perspective. When you realize this, you will know that you are already living your fabulous life ...

CONTENTS

Foreword by Bernie Siegel, MD

The subtitle to *The 90-Day Game*—"Your Pathway to Creating What You Truly Want While Enjoying the Process"—speaks of what John can offer to those who want to participate in the process of life. It reminds me of what a pregnant woman experienced and wrote about, comparing her cancer treatment to her pregnancy. Despite the difficulties of her pregnancy, she said, "Residing within me is new life. Nine months finally pass. I give birth to my child. All the discomfort and pain is now justified." After her chemotherapy and radiation treatment, she said, "Twelve months finally pass. I give birth to myself. All the discomfort and pain is now justified."

The 90-Day Game is about giving birth to your authentic self. It is not about fearing the challenge or being a failure if you don't do it right. It is not about backing away from life's challenges with sentences that begin with, "I can't," "I'll try," "I would if," "I should," "I'm tired," and "What if I fail?" This is not about self-interest but about choosing a life that benefits you and others, and letting John be what I refer to as your "life coach."

Coaches give you the knowledge you need and guide you on how to perform to the best of your ability. But you have to show up for practice, not make excuses, listen to your coach's constructive criticism, and learn to create what you truly want without the process being a negative experience. The best doctors learn from their patients, family, and nurses because, when those people know you care, they tell you when they see ways for you to improve your performance. And when you are willing to listen to them, learn, rehearse, and practice—rather than make excuses—amazing things can happen. The nice part is that this is not a nine-month process but a 90-day journey to rebirthing yourself.

As Jung said, we are all duplex structures. Within us reside intellect (or mind) and intuitive, unconscious wisdom (or soul and spirit). As an attorney said, "I came to a conclusion that was eminently reasonable, totally logical, and completely wrong because, while learning to think, I almost forgot how to feel." I like to refer to it as "letting your heart make up your mind." Unconsciously, we create our future. So, knowing your true inner self is of vital importance in creating your desired life. You need a quiet mind to accomplish this, which I will mention again later.

One of the most significant factors involved in the process relates to your answer to this question: "Did your parents love you?" Those who did not feel loved and who answered "No" have an enormous hurdle to overcome because they lack self-worth and self-esteem and are far more likely to become addicts, refuse to attempt to change, and be self-destructive in their lifestyle. One study showed that 98% of those who felt unloved as children suffered a major illness by middle age versus 25% of those who felt loved. So again, let John's game give you the tools to remove the negative hypnotic messages imposed by the opposite of love: indifference, rejection, and abuse early in your life.

Medicine and science are opening their minds to the importance of emotions and how what goes on in your mind becomes your body's chemistry. The placebo effect resides within us. Actors' immune function and stress hormone levels are altered by the role they play. So, think of the way you act and the role you are playing because it will create your life. You are given a lifetime to learn, rehearse, and practice. *The 90-Day Game* can help you create your true self and desired life. You can help by keeping a journal of your feelings, going back to your childhood, so they are not stored up within you, damaging your body and health. Simply keeping a journal, spending time each day being grateful, meditating, and saying a therapeutic mantra will enhance your health and state of well-being. John's wisdom will guide you on that path.

When you follow his coaching guidelines, you will find that you are having a conversation with your true self and will be able to listen to its desires and needs. Listening to your inner voice is vital for your health and a joyful life. By caring about yourself, you become willing to show up for practice, be coached, and achieve the desired goals you have created for yourself. God loves us all. You need to believe that, no matter what your past was like. I call it "re-parenting ourselves."

The wounded soldier is truly the one who can function in love's service, and you can heal yourself and others by example. The process of creation has endowed all living things with survival mechanisms. Wounds heal, bacteria resist antibiotics, and trees survive insects and more. Nature is speaking to us about our potential, but we have to give our body a live message by loving our life and body. When you get the message, the path to creating what you desire will open up before you. And remember: If God closes one door, like hunger, it can lead you to seek nourishment for your body and soul. You will find that, further down the corridor, another door may be open or you may even find an open window. When going through hell, we can all benefit by stopping and asking ourselves what we are to learn from this experience. Then the curse becomes a blessing, and our problem awakens us to what needs to be changed in our life. Remember not to eliminate yourself but to eliminate from your life what is killing you, and then save your life.

You control only your thoughts and, through them, can take command of your life. However, due to our duplex nature, we must get our intellect and intuitive minds to agree on the course we choose or it will be laden with conflict. I see this when people choose a medical therapy but are in conflict over it within themselves. Then they have all the side effects and more. However, when there is harmony within, they can go through treatments with no side effects because of their acceptance, peace, and beliefs. Our mind is a powerful thing. It creates what we and our body believe to be true.

It will only take you 90 days to reach your commencement. Graduations are called "commencements" because they represent a new beginning, and that is what you will learn from *The 90-Day Game*. You are giving birth to a new self. You can even pick a new name for yourself and for whom you are to become. You can and will become what I call a "respant" (a responsible participant) and empower yourself to be creative. The way to know who you are and what you truly want will come to you through quieting your mind. I liken it to the still pond, which allows you to see that you are not an ugly duckling but a swan. However, if your life is filled with turbulence, which troubles the waters, you will never see your true self. Again, use the process outlined in the following pages and achieve the ability to live with a quiet mind, which can help you to know your authentic self.

Quantum physicists tell us that desire and intention alter the physical world, causing things to occur that would not normally occur if they were not desired. So have faith, step up to the plate, and focus on your potential and not your fear of failure. As Ernest Holmes asked, "What if Jesus was the only normal person who ever lived?"

My last word of advice is to not get upset by interruptions during the process because they are what our work is about. So use them to learn and grow from while on your 90-day journey and forever after. When your work becomes how you handle interruptions, you will start enjoying life and not resenting events. And, when you notice that you are frequently losing track of time, you are on the right path. I have found that, when what you are doing is creative, you lose sense of time, your body doesn't age, and your wounds all heal because you have put yourself into a therapeutic trance state. So, turn the pages and commence your journey through not just *The 90-Day Game* but the 90-year game of life. And take it one day at a time because today is the best day of your life.

—Bernie Siegel, MD

Preface

Typically, the preface to a book is written by its author. I am honored that John has asked me to write this preface to *The 90-Day Game*. (Breaking from tradition is nothing new for him.) I have worked closely with John for over 15 years, have played the game multiple times through its evolution, and jumped at the chance to be in the first group of faciliplayers that John certified. This game is something quite special in the way it recognizes the real potential in each of us, how it teaches us to use what might be considered challenges or obstacles as valuable guides on our journey, and ultimately how it helps us create what we truly desire in our lives.

So, with that said, I'm pleased to offer you an invitation to the game!

Does this sound familiar? You know some basic "principles," and you're pretty sure you know what you need to do—at least to make *some* improvement in your life—but you just can't seem to make it happen. You recognize patterns, situations, or circumstances that seem to repeat in your experience, but you don't seem able to change the ending. Do you sometimes feel like one of many inside your head, where one of you wants to move forward, take action, and make a change, but others don't, and you feel "held back"?

On the one hand, we're told that everything is changing and that change is the only constant; on the other hand, change is scary. There's real comfort in the familiar (the devil, you know). So when we really *do* want to change, all sorts of obstacles appear (for example, we doubt that we can really do it, we think that maybe we're wrong and the change would be a mistake, or we wonder what our family and friends will think).

That's where most of us get stuck. It's why we can feel so energized after hearing a motivational speaker or attending a workshop, and we're sure that *this* time we can make a change; however, after a short while, we find ourselves back in our old, familiar territory.

What's going on? We've developed powerful habits over many, many years, reinforcing the same patterns of thinking, emotion, and behavior, until they are second nature. If we are centered and confident, we can be free of them for a while and, when we are stressed, that's where we've trained ourselves to go. Since a principle cause of stress is change, we've come full circle.

The 90-Day Game can help you break out of this loop.

What exactly is the 90-Day Game? It is an integrated system for improving the quality and enjoyment of your life; a coaching model designed to bridge the gap between where you are and where you'd like to be; a personal development program, based on fundamental principles common to most world religions and spiritual and self-help systems—all embodied in the form of a game, which means that it's meant to be played (more on this later).

While sharing some aspects of other approaches (it has been said that the truth doesn't change anyway), the game is, at the same time, completely different in a number of important ways. It is eminently practical, actionable, and results-oriented. Theory and philosophy are kept to a minimum, key concepts are explained in everyday language with real-world examples, and a rich set of tools, templates, checklists, and exercises help to guide you every step of the way. From the very first day, you'll roll up your sleeves and practice applying these principles in your life, to your own situation, in order to make real what you would like to create for yourself and your loved ones.

While acknowledging the gap you'd like to close, the game doesn't reject anything—not where you are, and not what you think or how you feel. In fact, it celebrates *all* of that by helping you access the valuable information "hidden" in everything you experience and understanding that happiness is to be found nowhere else but in this very moment. It guides you to recognize and appreciate what you already have and to acknowledge your successes—real aspects of your life that are too often ignored by focusing only on what is missing.

Lest you think this is some wispy, feel-good set of platitudes, stop right there. The game is solid and sensible, its legs planted firmly on the ground. It could not be more practical, and it supports you in bravely facing and engaging with all of your thoughts, emotions, and moods—fully, without judgment, and without labels of good/bad or positive/negative. It is an incredible tool to help close a specific gap and create a desired outcome, but it's much more than that. You will develop and strengthen a new set of competencies and capabilities that you can apply to every aspect of your life and, in so doing, create a positive cycle of growth, self-knowledge, and increasing happiness.

You know (you *do*, don't you?) that your well-established patterns and habits have led you to where you are now, and this is where you will remain until they are changed. Effecting that change is often challenging, and it's where the game truly shines. Give yourself the chance to change and to establish a new set of skills, habits, and perspectives that will serve you for the rest of your life.

Are you game?

Great!

Now, just one more thing ...

The principles and concepts underlying the game are helpful to understand and appreciate, but here's the thing. Having an intellectual grasp of theory can be a useful prep for growth and somewhat satisfying, but it doesn't usually lead to real change; that *will* be the result, however, if you engage with the book and *actually play the game.*

It is important to recognize that we've all been practicing our habits and behavior patterns for most of our lives. We've gotten quite good at them, and they have directly contributed to the lives we are experiencing. If you want to experience something different—and I assume that is why you are here—you need to *do* something different. (Notice I didn't say "read" something different.)

Just think about it. If you want to learn to play a musical instrument or learn a craft, reading a book will certainly give you some background and understanding of what's involved. But would you expect to be able to perform having just read about it?

If you care to read through this book, please do so with this perspective and awareness. If you want to create what you truly want, and enjoy the process, then get set for an amazing adventure and *play* the 90-Day Game.

Now we're ready!

—Rand Littlestone, certified faciliplayer

Acknowledgments

It gives me great pleasure to express my deepest appreciation to our faciliplayer team and founding partners Barbara Hawkins, Danielle Felitto, John Beljean, Maria Vizzi, Mary Mitchell, Michael Levine, Mike Murphy, Rand Littlestone, and Rudra Dasgupta. Thank you for your loving support, enthusiasm, belief in the mission; the dedication, commitment, and contributions you make weekly to our team; and the support you freely give to our game players. The depth of your friendship means the world to me.

To Rand Littlestone, my hands-on partner: Thank you for rolling up your sleeves in innumerable ways, particularly with the editing process, and the instrumental role you have played—and are continuing to play—in shaping the guidelines of the faciliplayer certification program. Your commitment and generosity know no limits.

To Matt Felitto: Thank you for your research guidance and suggestions about how to best express the research cited in the book.

To Danielle Felitto, Joan Felitto, Barbara Hawkins, and Rand Littlestone: Thank you for the many passes you have taken in reviewing the manuscript. Thank you for your time, patience, and invaluable feedback.

To Marissa Felitto, our graphic designer: Thank you for the many contributions you've brought to all aspects of the project. I am so grateful for your caring touch, playful spirit, creative input, ideas, and designs found throughout the book, the book cover, the interior design, the game materials, and the website.

To LeAnn Erimli, my virtual assistant: Thank you for your brilliantly efficient work, broad knowledge of tools and resources, and extremely practical and tactical advice.

To Joanne Shwed at Backspace Ink, our editing and book production maven: Thank you for your attentive detail in editing and commitment to excellence. It is amazing the things you notice! You have brought great order, flow, and clarity to the book. You are a consummate professional.

To Rosemarie Monica and Jeff Lewis at Group M, Inc.: Your enthusiasm added so much to the spirit of the project. Even before we were formally engaged, you provided so much value and guidance. Thank you for your enormous generosity and vision. It is no wonder why you are an award-winning public relations and marketing firm.

To my clients: Thank you for educating, motivating, and inspiring me to develop the many coaching models that are imbedded in the game. You have deepened my understanding of how to be a coach.

To the game players, who, over more than a decade, have played in the games: Your participation gave me the insights needed to shape the game into what it has become today.

Thanks to all the authors, too numerous to mention, whom I've read and interviewed: You have seasoned my thinking and influenced the approaches utilized in the 90-Day Game.

To my wife Joan: No words can express the appreciation and love I have for you. In addition to your many manuscript reviews and useful input that you've contributed to the project, you have relentlessly supported me in every choice I have made throughout my life. You truly are a living example of unconditional love.

PART I

Introduction and Orientation

WEEK 1

Welcome to the 90-Day Game

Day 1—What Do You Want to Create?

Since you picked up this book, you obviously have something you want to create in your life. Before we go any further, I'd like you to respond to a few questions to jumpstart the process. I am not asking you to write about what you think is possible, or what someone else thinks is possible, or what society thinks is appropriate for you. I am asking you what your soul is yearning for, what your heart is crying out for, and what's been on your mind for a long time.

Bring that to mind and answer the following jumpstart questions. Take no more than 10 minutes on this. Let it come to you from those deep places of heart and soul. Anything longer will be counterproductive to our aim here. No rational analysis; answer from your gut. This is not a test, and there will be no grades.

Jumpstart Questions
1. What do I want to create?
....
....
....
....

3

Jumpstart Questions
2. What is motivating me to create this?
....
3. What talents and strengths do I have that align with my intention?
....
4. Why is creating this valuable to me?
....
5. How will I and others benefit from my creation?
....

Congratulations! You have completed Day 1 of the 90-Day Game. If you have time, feel free to move on to Day 2 for a little orientation.

Day 2—You Have More Command over Your Life Than You Realize

Chances are you are eager to create something great and are looking for an effective framework to bring it to life. Making it an enjoyable process is likely quite appealing to you as well. In the moment, are you conjangled?

Okay, you are probably wondering—what the heck is "conjangled"? Don't run off to look it up; this word is not found in any dictionary. But, if you are conjangled, you may already know what it is because it sounds a lot like it feels. It's the perfect word to describe that blend of stuckness, frustration, tension, and overwhelm that we all experience at times; where you feel that you have one foot on the gas pedal and one foot on the brake. Split between fuzzy and clear and deeply yearning to move forward. It is a state where you feel entirely out of control, and you sure could use some kind of psychological and/or emotional chiropractic. That's conjangled!

Another way of defining it is by its antonym "congruent"—a harmonious state of being, where your soul is singing hallelujah; your emotions are warm yet exhilarated; your mind is reveling with brilliant, sparkling, confident clarity, able to see the big panoramic view of your plans while taking lots of action with grace and ease and, because of it, you and others really like being with you. That is what the 90-Day Game is all about: to create what you truly want while enjoying the process and the precious, present moment.

In order to enjoy the congruent state mentioned above, you'll need to activate all four of your SEMB resources: Soul, Emotion, Mind, and Behavior. Like a four-engine airplane, it's smooth sailing when all engines are functioning efficiently. A four-engine airplane can fly with fewer than all engines or if a few are not operating at optimal capacity. You too can function with your equipment at less than optimal capacity, although that means less fluidity and a bit more unnecessary conjanglement. Early on, you'll be introduced to four great day game plays, each suited to activate one of your four resources. Play them all as intended, and you'll fly high and far with ease.

The game does not guarantee that you will never ever again find yourself in a conjangled way, but it will increase your awareness of its symptoms. It will also show you how to utilize them in a productive way to stay on course and increase the frequency of joy attacks as you revel in the process of creating.

As a game player, your willingness to try on new approaches will accelerate your progress. We all have preferred styles; this is natural and to be honored. That doesn't mean we can't develop new skills that make the most of the natural gifts we were given. Engaging all the game plays and practices is essential, so get ready. Nothing in the game requires any hard labor; it is all quite simple. But it is also challenging because you will be integrating new behaviors into your established daily routines.

The game is a vehicle for change in just about any aspect of your life and for anything you desire. For example:

- Enjoying better health
- Cultivating a sense of purpose
- Creating greater financial stability and freedom
- Establishing a career track
- Having a more compassionate relationship with yourself
- Developing a significant intimate connection with a person or a higher power
- Establishing habits and internalizing fresh ideas

Even if you don't know what your soul craves right now, you will experience significant progress over the next 60 to 90 days. This method will offer you a track to run on but will not create what you want for you. All you need is already within you, and the game is designed to evoke your greatness.

I make no promises of yachts, palatial houses, or millions of dollars in your bank account. We don't need to rule out those possibilities, but they are not the objective here. Whether you are already quite successful or truly struggling, the aim is for you to recognize that you have more command of your life than you may realize: a profound capability to create what you want and enjoy a peaceful and fulfilling state of being while creating it. Once you have discovered your amazing capacity to enhance your conditions to some degree, you will expand previous boundaries, building faith in yourself and enhancing your conditions to greater and greater degrees. You will discover that you are truly living a fabulous life.

Why a Game?

Whether it inspires you or not, no one is getting out of here alive! Mortal life on this planet is a gift, with a definite beginning, middle, and end. Just like going to a party, you can focus on the music being too loud or too low, the people too classy or classless, the food too rich or too bland, or you can focus on having fun, enjoying the company you are with, making new friends, bringing some life to the party, or just enjoying the moment.

When we put such importance on things or invest in wasteful judgments, we miss out on the party and the gift that life truly is. There is a reason why we have this tendency, which will be explained shortly. With that understanding, you will be free to experience life in a different way.

Aldous Huxley stated that, "The secret of genius is to carry the spirit of the child into old age, which mean never losing your enthusiasm."[1] Making it a game brings an element of light-ness, which is valuable in and of itself. Additionally, it establishes fertile ground for creativity. We have far more expansive and creative ideas when we are light, playful, and enthusiastic. Mind expands and welcomes *Aha!* possibilities.

The intuitive mind is a sacred gift and the rational mind is a faithful servant.
We have created a society that honors the servant and has forgotten the gift.

—Albert Einstein[2]

When we overidentify with our challenges, we experience a different kind of creativity, conjuring up intricate storylines for why we cannot have what we want. We get stuck in our rational mind as it desperately struggles to figure it all out. This tension blocks the intuitive mind's capacity to attract and receive fresh insights.

Don't get me wrong. The rational mind is a faithful servant, and we honor its role in organizing and analyzing information. We make a poor choice, however, when we become overly reliant on this servant for problem solving, as it works with only what is already known. It is the sacred gift's intuitive, imaginative, and creative role that will bring us the fresh data and insights we need for innovative thinking. Then, the faithful servant is in a position to test, verify, and organize these new insights for practical implementation. When we make a game of it, we lighten up and fresh insights come to us.

Do games have challenges? You bet they do. That is where the fun and fulfillment are. Navigating challenges provides the growth only direct experience can offer. Once you get beyond the old-school conditioning of "passing the test" and doing it "just right," you will welcome each challenge as an opportunity for great discovery. Challenges are gifts, valuable guidance information contained within the wrappings of limited perception. Each challenge holds within it a satisfying reward and, when appraised as such, it powerfully advances your confidence. With each obstacle you overcome, you'll register valuable information to create what you want now—and later.

So lighten up! Be playful! Welcome challenges, and you'll learn to bend rather than break. With the objectivity you develop, you'll be surprised how you can become quite comfortable with being uncomfortable, see the perfection within the perceived imperfection, and benefit immensely from it. How you leverage these challenges with the spirit of lightness will be fully addressed in the game, so stay tuned.

Why 90 Days?

Directing attention regularly toward any intention changes your brain—literally. Similar to establishing the hand-eye coordination needed to hit a ball, balance a bike, or gain confidence as a driver, in each case the individual goes through three phases: mechanical, integrated, and assimilated. Establishing any new behavior requires self-compassion. Recognizing the need for patience, the game provides practices that soothe your nervous system and put order to your mental chatter, yielding resilient staying power.

Just as you would not expect a child to hit the ball or ride a bike overnight, don't pressure yourself. Simply follow the game's track, and you'll accomplish great things. You have 90 days, so relax and play.

In the end, it is repetition that effectuates these changes, and this is true of our brains as well. Until recently, it was widely accepted that our brains were hard-wired in beliefs and behaviors that could not be changed. The science of neuroplasticity has shown that repetition of thought, emotion, and behavior does indeed change the brain. For those of you who revel in the details of science, there is a wealth of material at your disposal. In the game, we are going to take a more experiential, pragmatic, light approach. We're interested in creating what you want—not educating you in neuroscience.

Ninety days has proven to be an effective time frame for sufficient repetition of attention and practices for making significant changes in attitude, perspective, and behavior. It also provides adequate time to build momentum and realize considerable progress.

What's Your Playing Style?

Do you prefer to play on your own, with a buddy or a coach, or in a group? The choice is yours. The day-to-day format of the game is designed to produce results for all learning styles. If you are a self-starter who is more comfortable flying solo, go for it. Most find that buddying up with a fellow game player or a coach, or working with a group and facilitator creates structure and accountability, helping them remain in the game. When playing in a group telegame, you will be guided by a 90-Day Game facilitator each step of the way. Additionally, you'll be inspired by your fellow game players' shifts and progress.

You will find buddies, certified facilitators (we call them "faciliplayers"), and teleconference groups at 90DayGame.com.

That's enough for now. Go ahead and have a great day!

Day 3—Make It a Great Day: Your Great Day Game Plan

Think about how powerful our physical senses are. Sight, sound, taste, touch, and smell are our tools for navigating the physical world. These senses are so powerful that they can easily distract us from subtler senses, like thoughts and emotions. Although our external senses are extremely influential, it is these far more subtle senses that actually create what we observe with our more obvious ones.

It can seem as though the thoughts and emotions we experience are caused by the people we encounter and the events we experience, and this is how most of us tend to live: in reaction to these external influences. It may be easier to blame external forces for our conditions, but this is not the pathway to creating what we want—or a fulfilling life.

In order to gain command of your life, you'll need to gain command of your states of mind and being. Attitude, perspective, and emotional responses play significant roles in the quality of your experiences and resulting conditions. When you turn things around—that is, when you take command of your thoughts and emotions—you are no longer victim to the people and events around you.

Understand that taking command of your thoughts and emotions is not controlling them. Thoughts and emotions come up spontaneously; you do not and cannot control them. The way to gain command of them lies in your ability to direct your attention. What you direct your attention on will influence the qualities of your spontaneous thoughts and how you feel about things.

Developing the ability to direct your attention is an art form that requires practice. You will need objects of attention, and the qualities of these focal points are an important consideration as well. In the world, there exists the "divine" and the "diabolic." These are the same forces that capture your attention and, when your attention is captured, so are you. Our aim is to choose where we direct our attention and, with practice, we will become the directors of our life.

The aim is not to deny that darkness exists; we just don't want to get into bed with it. Living in the light allows us to see what's present and available and empowers us to have impact and enhance conditions. Like flipping a light switch on in a dark room, we can see more clearly and take steps that benefit all. As you refine this art form, you'll discover that even the dark and diabolic have value, can motivate you, and be the catalysts for positive change. It simply becomes more valuable information, more grist for your creative mill. To enjoy this point of view, you first need to build a resilient state of mind and being.

What better place to direct your attention than on what you want to create in your life? That will be your primary focus during the course of this game. If you are uncertain as to what you want to create, which is more common than most people realize, let that discovery be your intention for the game.

With this passionate purpose in mind, you will utilize the natural talents, strengths, and skills you've developed during your lifetime and seek complementary resources to support them while remaining awake to the value they will have in your life and in the lives of others.

An airplane pilot or a ship's captain must first direct his attention on where he is presently, determine a desirable destination, and then chart his course toward it. Since unexpected weather often shows up along the way, the captain needs to be an alert observer—one who promptly notices and mindfully responds to the environment with a cool head and a warm heart. The pilot does not complain or blame or surrender his power to the crosswinds and turbulence but instead acknowledges these external forces and regains his chosen course.

That is what experienced players do:

- Observe people and events without reacting to them; instead, they retain command of their state.

- Appraise what is present.

- Like the professional pilot, respond with a cool head and a warm heart, considering what is best for them and all involved.

At least that is the aim. Fact is, you—and even the most seasoned game players—will react to external forces at times and learn from them. Over time, you will eliminate many triggers that cause you to be reactive.

In order to develop this essential command and enjoy the harmonious, congruent flow that will alleviate much unnecessary conjanglement, we begin with four great day game plays. Each is focused on activating and aligning the four SEMB resources (Soul, Emotion, Mind, and Behavior):

1. **Pick a card, any card** is where we begin to develop the power of directed attention. It aligns first with the soul—our soulful, spiritual nature and its deep desire for meaningful purpose.

2. **Your lightness and energy menu** fosters resilient emotions and the foundation for this new responsive relationship with our emotional nature.

3. **Your great day game planner** aligns with our behavioral nature, giving the players a framework for practical action; all four resources are congruent and harmoniously aligned.

4. **Abundant Mind mind game** aligns with the many faculties of the creative, intuitive, imaginative mind as well as the logical, orderly aspects of mind.

Each day, you'll stimulate all of these SEMB resources with an emphasis on one, and you will do it with grace and ease—no hard labor. These great day game plays will be mostly daily as we need not be obsessive or compulsive about it. After all, games need challenges, but they have to be fun too. If not, why would anyone want to play?

Playing with ease means no struggling, no rushing, and no forcing, and that includes each day's plays and practices. We want to take elegantly mindful and refined actions. Simply play the game (about 15 to 20 minutes a day, roughly four or five days a week), and you will develop the ability to be in command of your state and, as a result, in command of your life.

None of the game plays or practices requires more than the time allotted. But, if you feel that you would enjoy engaging more deeply in any particular game play or practice, feel free to go beyond the 15 or 20 minutes. You can even carry it over to the next day. We have free days built into the game for just that reason. But don't get too carried away and find yourself falling way behind pace. In order for you to experience the full impact and benefits from the program, it is essential that you maintain the pace as designed. At too slow a pace, your brain will not experience the rhythm of the day-to-day repetition needed to create the desired changes and habits that you want to develop; at too fast a pace, you will not be able to internalize the content effectively.

Above all, enjoy the process! Just play with the exercises at the designed pace, challenge any perfectionist tendencies, and assume that you are doing them just fine. If you feel that you need a hand, check in with your facilitator, coach, or buddy. If you are flying solo, email us at Team@90DayGame.com, and you'll get what you need to stay in the game.

Congratulations! You have just completed another day. That means 87 days or fewer remain to create what you want. Many game players do create what they want in far less time—some within 60 days and others in as little as 45. This is not a race. Take your time and enjoy the ride, and you'll actually get there faster! You can move onto the next day, if you'd like, or pick it up tomorrow. Your choice!

Day 4—Reminders and Tips of the Week

I t's time to set up for the game. We have allocated three days for this. The game resumes on Week 2, Day 8. If you are playing on your own, or with a buddy, or a coach, who are also ready to play, you can step into Week 2 together at any time.

Get Your Game Gear

Your purchase of this game book entitles you to free access to a card deck PDF file entitled the "Top 10 Spiritual Principles for Evoking Your Greatness" and 10 audio downloads in mp3 format. You'll need these to play the game. Log into 90DayGame.com to download your free game gear now.

When to Play

Whenever possible, first thing in the morning is best. Here's why:

- We are creatures of habit. Once you get into the flow of your well-established routine, it can be challenging to find the needed 15 to 20 minutes.
- The spirit of the game will enhance the quality of your days by kicking them off with an uplifting mindset.
- In the end, it is up to you. Whatever your choice, establish a routine, and you'll find it much easier and more fun!

Breathe

Experience has shown that more than a five-day per week commitment is counterproductive to the game player's success. Having to play every day would create tension between maintaining game commitment and overall life commitments. Going forward, each week you will have:

- Four days focused on game plays and practices;
- One day with reminders and tips; and
- Two free days.

The free days give you room to breathe and enjoy the game plays and practices. Free days also send the message that we need not push our way to success. The lighter your disposition, the more enjoyable the process will be and the better the results. It is also an opportunity to express faith in yourself and your plans.

Feel free to use free days as you wish. You can step away from the game completely, practice the great day game plays, or utilize the time to engage more deeply in one of the exercises. Although free days are numbered at the end of each week, you can take them at any point during the week that is convenient for you.

Play Optimally

Sure, you can play on your own or with a buddy, but playing with a telegame group once a week is the optimal way to go because:

- You tap into the synergy of the group.
- You learn from, and relate to, your fellow game players' wins and challenges.
- You receive direct support by a skilled faciliplayer.
- The groups are small, so every game player can be heard, receive support, and contribute to the team.
- Telegames make it easier to keep pace and maintain a high level of commitment.
- It is simple. If you have a phone, you have all you need.
- If you miss a call, you'll get a recording of the session.
- Your participation fee comes with a 100% unconditional satisfaction guarantee.

Go to 90DayGame.com to find out more.

Have a Player's Attitude

When you get on an airplane, your captain is the pilot in command—not the pilot in control. There are many things out of our control. For the pilot, he is not in control of the weather, crosswinds, or turbulence, but he is in command of the airplane and himself. He steers into the crosswind to stay on course and, when there is turbulence, he seeks an alternate altitude to find smoother air. He keeps a cool head and a warm heart, caring for the safety of his passengers.

Step into the game as a player in command: fully accepting that the idea of controlling everything is pure folly and sure to give the gods a hearty laugh, and that your perspective and attitude are fully within your command. Make it your mission to remain awake to this fact, and you will stay on course and enjoy the trip along the way.

PART II

Great Day Game Plays

Setting the Environment to Flourish

Day 8 (Game Play 1)—Pick a Card, Any Card: The Top 10 Spiritual Principles for Evoking Your Greatness

Our attitudes, perspectives, states of mind, and emotions are like the roots of a plant or a tree. The conditions of these unseen root systems produce what is visible above the soil. The condition of our attitudes, perspectives, states of mind, and emotions are the roots of what we currently see harvested in our health, careers, finances, relationships, and everything else that comprises what we call our lives.

What influences our attitudes, shapes our perspectives, and affects our states of mind and emotions? There are many, but there is one driving force that supersedes all others. This force is largely the cause of our fears, doubts, and worries. It is what causes us to seek approval. It is what makes us tentative and hesitant. It is this force that makes us doubt ourselves and our plans. It causes us to be overly concerned with the what-ifs of life. It is the grip that has us clinging to the familiar when every fiber of our being knows that we need to make a change. It is an impulse always on alert, seeking out potential danger.

This force influences each of us individually and our society collectively. We were raised by parents and directed by teachers and other authority figures, who were equally immersed in it as were all those who went before them. It is a trance that we are all under, to varying degrees, and what I call "the social hypnosis." When in this hypnotic state, we are at the mercy of the attitudes, perspectives, states of mind, and emotions of people around us, who are also in this same trance.

The tones of the social hypnosis are of insecurity, are win-lose oriented, and affirm a belief that we must struggle to make this dog-eat-dog life work. What has become commonplace is a form of camaraderie where we commiserate with our misery—with Blue Mondays, Hump Wednesdays, and Thank God It's Fridays. Oddly enough, the drive behind this hypnosis is not a design flaw by God or Mother Nature. Actually, we owe it a mountain of gratitude because, without it, we would not be here to talk about it. The driving force of this hypnosis is our survival instinct.

Bringing conscious awareness and acceptance to this stealth-like force is where our freedom lies. Holding this awareness gives us the opportunity to temper it in a way that does not dominate us. We can appreciate its role as our protector and its skill at keeping us from becoming overly complacent, and allow it to guide us appropriately rather than control us.

In the absence of this awareness, we tend to get sucked into the social hypnosis and, in doing so, our choices are fear based, full of doubt and worry. Awareness of this fact is what snaps us out of trance, enabling us to make love-based choices, build faith and confidence in ourselves and our plans, and develop full acceptance of who we are without any need to be all things to all people. We can appreciate the fullness of the present while molding tomorrow, affirming a belief that we can create with grace and ease, and that our intentions yield joy and peace of mind for the benefit of all.

We can snap out of this trance, but it is easy to fall back asleep. How can we remain awake and not let the social hypnosis bring our precious perspectives and attitudes down when we really want to lift them up?

The Thrive Instinct

We have another impulse, which I call the "thrive instinct," and stimulating it will support us in remaining awake. When game players direct attention to the Top 10 Spiritual Principles for Evoking Your Greatness in the card deck, most report a natural resonance with them.

We all recognize our desire to love and be loved, see the value in cultivating faith in ourselves and in our plans, and notice the shift in our state when we direct attention to the riches present in our fabulous lives. The thrive instinct is far more accessible as we begin to direct attention to the Top 10 Spiritual Principles for Evoking Your Greatness and other game plays coming up. They will not eliminate your susceptibility to the social hypnosis; rather, they will dampen it from being the dominant state, strengthen a resilient attitude, and set an environment for you to flourish on your own terms.

Like the see-saw in the park, all it takes is 51% of the weight on the side of your choice to tip it. The first of four great day game plays is designed to start tipping that scale from fear, doubt, and worry to love, faith, and gratitude. We do this by applying and strengthening the power we have to direct our attention. Once tipped, things begin to shift, momentum builds, and amazingly everything organizes beautifully.

Our first game play, Pick a Card, Any Card, will begin to tip the scale from the constraints of the social hypnosis to a more expansive view. You will go well beyond that nose-to-the-grindstone conditioning and toward the freedom found in your divine design.

We begin by activating the "S" in SEMB, which is your soul. The urge that brought you to this game is coming from a deep soul level. As you develop effective communication with your soul, you will become increasingly aware of its desires and the means to meet its needs. Your soul comes coded with your perfect blueprint and, as you develop this conversation further, you will be drawn to meet its cravings.

For my left-brain dominant players: Before you write this soulful stuff off as just another airy-fairy walk down wishful lane, reserve judgment and use your intellect to build a rational case for why using more of your capacities is sound reasoning.

For those of you who favor the sacred soulful aspect: You too will be challenged to engage parts of yourself, which may feel less than organically aligned with your natural preferences. Play with it all!

Whether you see them as gifts from your Creator, Mother Nature, or a miracle of biology, you will discover the magnificent interplay and value of all your SEMB resources.

These 10 principles are what we use to open up the conversation with your soul and the game practice, which begins on Day 15. It will offer you a clear structure to refine that communication, unlocking the amazing power of your soul's intent.

Although the primary role these guiding principles play is at this "S" or soul level, they also play supportive roles for the other three resources as well (that is, Emotion, Mind, and Behavior). They are the first of several focal points for developing command of your attention, and increasing your awareness of the influence that your thoughts and emotions have on your behavior and the impact they have on what you create.

By now, you have downloaded your deck of cards entitled the "Top 10 Spiritual Principles for Evoking Your Greatness" from the 90DayGame.com website. If you have yet to do so, go there now. You have free access to the PDF file. The principles are also listed in the appendix in the back of the book.

First, familiarize yourself with the principles and see how they strike you. Some will be deeply moved by these principles while others may at first be bored by them. Whatever your first response may be, consider the merit behind each principle's intent and simply "play" with the framework. Trying on new approaches will activate latent systems, accelerating your progress, reducing conjanglement, and thereby increasing congruent flow.

Appreciating these principles is one thing; understanding them is another, yet I invite you to go beyond just appreciation and understanding. They are to be internalized and lived. Therefore, all game plays and practices are designed to reinforce these principles experientially. You will recognize their impact both subjectively (that is, how you feel about your life) and from the objective results you experience as you live them and create the personal reality of your choice during this 90-Day Game.

As you gain greater familiarity with these principles, you will notice them everywhere and appreciate their relevance in what you value most, how you view your life, and how you choose to mold it going forward.

Simply direct your attention toward one principle per day. These principles are within you already. Your gentle attention will evoke these truths from within your heart and soul, and they will become increasingly present in your daily awareness.

In life's ever-changing environment, having a foundational bedrock of constancy has infinite value. During the game, I encourage you to explore the possibility of using these as guiding principles to live by. They can inspire your days, bring clarity to muddled times, and simplify choice-making.

How to Play: Pick a Card, Any Card

- Each morning, shuffle the deck and select one principle card.
- Read the principle and relate it to whatever is going on in your life in real time.
- Carry this principle in mind as you go about your activities.

Ask yourself the following questions:

- *How does this principle apply to what I am experiencing in my life today?*
- *How does today's principle relate and support what I truly want to create?*
- *How can this principle enhance the enjoyment of my life in the present moment?*

Day 9 (Game Play 2)—Your Lightness and Energy Menu: How to Play and Enjoy Life Today

- Do you believe that life is meant to be enjoyed?
- Do you believe that you are worthy of doing something you enjoy when the spirit moves you?
- Do you believe that you need to first accomplish a goal, task, or outcome before you qualify for some enjoyment?
- Do you feel guilty when you take a moment to enjoy yourself?
- Do you feel that you are being irresponsible when you do enjoy yourself?
- Do you believe that life is to be enjoyed in the moment?

In order to arrive at your desired destination and enjoy the ride along the way, you'll need lots of energy. Enjoying life is energizing.

Societal pressures and old work ethic conditioning can reinforce the limiting belief that you don't have time for these pleasurable activities, they are less important than other activities, or you haven't "qualified" to enjoy such frivolous things. Getting beyond these conditioned responses reaps great rewards! This energetic fueling will take you where you choose to go with greater efficiency and resilience, and you will enjoy yourself along the way.

The social hypnosis carries the belief that work and play do not mix and that they are separate and distinct things. Many report feeling guilty when they are having too much fun while working. We view enjoyable activities as irresponsible distractions. Continually struggling for the actualization of goals divorces us from the enjoyment of life in the moment when, in reality, life can only be experienced in the moment. Anything else but the present is an illusion, a psychological gymnastic of the imagination. In the game, we will make strategic use of the imagination and our capacity for vision, to create wonderful outcomes, yet we will aim to remain awake to the fact that life is happening now. Our pursuits are meaningful and purposeful yet playful and joyful, and our actions will carry that spirit.

Unlike the old-school, nose-to-the-grindstone approach, having a joyful life happens now and is not deferred to some future point in time after you have achieved your goal. The old-school way is to first deprive yourself, and then have a tasty treat to take the bad taste of struggling out of your mouth. Although the game does not advocate overindulgence, it does support the enjoyment of life now while you go about engaging life purposefully, pursuing meaningful intentions filled with passion, purpose, love, and benefits for all. Not one in exception of the other, but both, and both can and will be accomplished joyfully.

Complicating things further is the badge of honor we wear. The busier we are, the more we bemoan our struggle, and the more important we feel. Being perceived as an "important" person in our culture is most seductive. When we get our juice from external validation, we set ourselves up for turbulent ups and downs: "up" if we are acknowledged; "down" if we are met with disapproval. Inner stability comes from self-affirming acknowledgment and inner satisfaction from engaging in our meaningful intentions, while enjoying the precious, present moment. This type of gratification cannot be taken away from you by any person or external force.

The business of wearing this badge of honor, pushing ourselves, and struggling is quite costly; sooner or later, the spirit, mind, and body revolt. The ad men and women of Madison Avenue are quite familiar with our egotistical prowess and addiction to incessant activity, offering us external solutions to just about any ailment. Have an ache? Here's a pill. Not enough time to eat? Here's some fast food. Of course, this soothes the symptom rather than the cause, and the unconscious abuse and damaging behavior continues.

Making no connection between our behavior and what ails us, we make assumptions that back pain is normal and something everyone deals with, high blood pressure is just a function of advancing age, and heart disease or worse is genetically inevitable. With a healthy body and mind, taking action is effortless. In a state of disease, taking action requires far more effort and slows progress, and we struggle when we could be creating with grace and ease.

The social hypnosis continues. All too often, we cope through life, perceiving it as an ongoing burden of undesirable tasks, doing our best to get them done and out of the way, rather than viewing life as a gift that gives us the opportunity to mold and create rich experiences. It is no wonder that drugs, alcohol, sugar, shopping, and other addictions are needed to cope and medicate the pain through this life of burdens. The weekends afford us about 104 days of enjoyment each year. If you factor in a good portion of each Sunday in anticipation of the Blue Monday to follow, you are left with about 52 out of 365 days to enjoy. This is simply madness.

I saw this same sort of coping hypnosis in my employee benefits work. I spoke with many people, including some very young people in their mid-twenties and early thirties, who had a lot of credit card debt, while deferring money into their 401(k) retirement account. The financial services industry leverages our fears of uncertainty with an illusion of security. With visions of our retirement years, playing 18 holes of golf each day, and endless, blissful days on the beach in the tropics in exchange for deferring—not just our money, but our enjoyment of life in the present.

Having been a financial advisor and now a coach, I am an advocate for planning to enhance our conditions. But, when coping replaces happiness in the present for the illusion of an elusive vision of tomorrow, something simply does not add up. To me, this is just another reflection of our society's fears over investing in tomorrow at the cost of today. Our days and weeks are lived this way for far too many people when they could be enjoying the moment, the trip to the weekend, and the journey to the golden years.

Our goals are deemed to be so important, our being busy so revered, and our medications so valued because they distract us from our discomfort in the moment and our uncertainty and insecurity of tomorrow. We have no clue as to how powerful refueling ourselves with the healthy joys of life can be. We defer these activities so much that we rarely, if ever, make time for them. We structure our lives so much around productivity and distraction that we might want to sit down and play the piano for a few minutes, get a good workout, or take a walk in the sun, but the time simply does not seem available. Of course, we all have 24/7, so it is a matter of choice. Since being busy is so well ingrained, implementing the choice can be challenging but not impossible.

Notice how we tend to stop doing the things that bring us energy when we need it the most! If we are frustrated or challenged, we think that we have to try harder. How can we possibly stop and do something enjoyable? When we feel good and engaged in our projects, we keep going and then find ourselves out of gas and out of balance, running around and putting out fires. So, rather than pushing, forcing, and exhausting yourself, engage in several of your favorite activities daily.

What about the feeling of guilt some experience when they engage in what feels like "self-indulgence"? This is a real stopper for some.

One veteran game player and small business owner, Maria, loves her Chihuahuas. She reported that she'd feel too guilty to play with them when she "should be" working. She said that playing the game gave her the permission slip to do it. Getting beyond the sense of guilt, Maria found that having fun with the pooches revitalized her energy during the day, and she came back to her office refreshed and revitalized. She is convinced that this had a positive effect on her mood, her creativity, and productivity in her business. As you will see, Maria is convinced for many sound reasons. We'll revisit this topic again, touch on the research that supports the value of this approach, and expand upon it on Day 52.

Cultivating the habit of daily, healthy, and playful energizing activities has a positive impact on everyone and everything you touch. It is one of the most selfish and selfless things you can do. You shift the energy in the room, you're more patient and present with others, and all the roles you play are engaged at a higher level.

Enjoyable activities produce energy, lighten your emotional state, and broaden your perspective. Increasing your energy refreshes and revitalizes you. When you are enjoying yourself, you are far more creative and tap into possibility thinking. When you invest in activities you enjoy, you invite intuitive insights to dawn on you.

Today, we direct our attention toward fun, playful, and joyful activities that bring us this lightness and energy. Here is a list of energizing and revitalizing activities that I enjoy:

- Playing guitar
- Meditating
- Exercising
- Going flying
- Reading anything on flying
- Watching and listening to my favorite guitarists on YouTube
- Watching flight training tutorials
- Reading and watching inspirational and scientific TEDTalks videos, which relate to my work and avocations

- Engaging in family banter
- Going to the music store with my son Matt
- Doing stuff with my family
- Going out to eat
- Checking in on the telephone at lunchtime with my wife
- Going for a drive
- Walking in the park
- Playing basketball
- Taking a hot shower
- Watching baseball
- Listening to the radio
- Going to a ball game
- Taking family trips and vacations
- Getting together with pals from the old neighborhood

Now it's your turn. At the end of this section, you will be asked to list everything that you enjoy doing. Jot down activities that energize and revitalize you. You can include activities that bring you lightness and energy—not things that you think you "should" be doing but desirable activities that you find attractive and enjoyable. Do the "write" thing, and jot down whatever comes to mind.

On the maiden voyage of the 90-Day Game, we had a player named Cindy, who enjoyed the thrill of riding roller coasters—hardly an activity most can do in the middle of a workday. Yet, it is something she enjoys, and she made time to go out and have fun doing it.

Today, you will begin compiling your list and adding to it as other activities come to mind. Place an asterisk (*) next to activities like Cindy's roller-coaster ride (that is, things you can do more easily on a free day or when you have a nice chunk of time available). My personal menu now has an asterisk next to these activities:

- Going flying
- Going to the music store with my son Matt
- Going to a ball game
- Taking family trips and vacations
- Getting together with pals from the old neighborhood

Hmmm. Which one would I like to get on my calendar now? I do want to pick up a guitar strap, and Matt needs new headphones. Saturday is Matt's day off. I'll ask him if he'd like to go with me then. Now that I think about it, spring is coming. If I want to get back to flying, I'll have to renew my medical certificate. Get the idea?

Albert Einstein said that his laboratory was on his little boat, and his violin was his most valued piece of equipment. This is how he set the environment for his ideas to come to him. So, go ahead and play that piano, get a good workout in, take a walk in the sun, and be a genius.

Today's game plays will include:
• Pick a card, any card
• Your lightness and energy menu

Your Lightness and Energy Menu
Write down 10 or more activities that bring you lightness and energy:

....

....

....

....

....

....

....

....

....

....

Add to the list as other activities come to mind. Make selections daily from your menu based on how you feel in the moment.

Ask yourself:

- *Which of my enjoyable activities will I fuel up on today to bring lightness and energy toward my creation?*
- *How are the enjoyable activities I engaged in today enhancing the quality of my day-to-day life experiences?*

Day 10 (Game Play 3)—Your Great Day Game Planner: What Will Make Today a Fulfilling and Satisfying Day?

- What first comes to mind when you awaken in the morning?
- How do you feel?
- What conversation are you having with yourself in your inner dialogue?
- What is the first action you take?
- Do you react to your environment?
- Do you set the environment by your own choice?

Meet Carl

Carl began a service business about a year ago and is eager to bring his fledgling enterprise from barely making ends meet to a profitable operation. He has specific ideas on how to bring his business to the next level and knows the next steps that need to be taken.

Carl has a morning routine. He awakens by a clock radio tuned to the local news. It is set at a loud volume so that he will most certainly wake up. After a series of slaps to the snooze button, followed by jolts of blaring bad news, he gets out of bed. Groggily, Carl saunters slowly to his computer and opens his email. Stimulated by the reading, he begins to come around to a more conscious state. Before he knows it, he is reacting to the urgency of his clients' demands. Suddenly, it is nearly 11 a.m. and Carl has not yet showered, dressed, or eaten! He takes a hurried shower, throws on his clothes, grabs his briefcase, and tries to make it on time to his first scheduled appointment.

The balance of his day carries the same alarming tone, mirroring the reactive urgencies from which it began. As Carl's day wraps up, a sullen sense of disappointment permeates his spirit. There was little to no time to advance in his plans. His frustration is further exacerbated by weight gain; exercise is nonexistent, his family feels unattended, and he hasn't called his mother in weeks.

Here is his ongoing conversation with himself: "There's not enough time to do what I want to do. There is too much to handle to move my business to the next level. Will my plans ever work out? Who am I kidding? What's the use?"

Allow me to ask you again, "What first comes to mind when you awaken in the morning? How do you feel? What conversation are you having with yourself in your inner dialogue? What is the first action you take? Do you react to your environment? Do you set the environment by your own choice?"

Each spontaneous emotion triggers thought, each thought consciously or unconsciously triggers a belief, and your behavior always follows your beliefs. Your interpretation of your spontaneous emotions, thoughts and beliefs will cause you to behave in ways that directly create your experience. This is largely how life unfolds.

So ask yourself, *Do I react to my environment, or do I set the environment by my own choice?* Now, be certain not to get judgmental with yourself. Permit yourself to honestly appraise what is, without judgment, knowing that you are gathering valuable information that will enhance the quality of your entire life. This is a loving act for your benefit and for the benefit of all the lives you touch. Just know that one of several ways we will learn to set the environment to flourish is by developing the power of directed attention.

We tend to think of attention as a mental faculty and, although this is true, attention includes attending to our soul's yearnings, emotional states, and behaviors as well—all four SEMB resources.

Like Carl, you may have intentions but, without directing your attention toward them, you have little chance to advance your plans and enjoy the process of bringing them to fruition. You, like everyone, have emotions; but, without attending to them, you will not recognize them as the natural guidance system they are, beautifully designed to get your deepest needs met. You have an inner dialogue going on all the time, yet, if you are not observant of it, you lose the opportunity to become aware of the beliefs you are carrying. Your behavior always follows your beliefs. If you are not observing your behavior, you are most likely on automatic pilot, going through rote motions based on conditioned and reactive reflexes.

Perhaps this may all sound like a tall order, but the beauty of the 90-Day Game is that all of this is accomplished through the incredibly simple game plays you have already begun and the practices we will cover. You need not even know the intricacies of the underlying context; all you need to do is play the game as it unfolds to get the desired results.

Our friend Carl has a dream. In order for Carl to live that dream, he will be well served by becoming a compassionate witness of his thoughts, feelings, and behavior. If he continues to have these feelings of disappointment, and continues to reinforce beliefs that there is not enough time and too much to handle, and then doubts his plans and believes he is kidding himself—he will continue to build a rational case, with rational evidence, for why he cannot have what he wants. Additionally, he will do a splendid job of creating that outcome because his behavior will follow his beliefs. He will then experience and gather more rational evidence for why he cannot have what he wants, and the cycle will continue.

I can relate to Carl when I look back at my history. I did quite a good job of affirming what I did not want in my life, and then did an equally good job of ushering it in.

- What if Carl played the 90-Day Game?
- What if he exchanged the tone of the jarring clock radio with a soulful, spiritual principle?
- What if he directed his attention toward engaging in a day peppered with enjoyable activities to look forward to?

- What if he directed his attention on the riches already present in his life: his health, meaningful work he is truly passionate about, and the contribution he is making to his family and the clients he appreciates?

- What if he maps out three priority actions he will take today to advance his dream?

- What then?

When Carl became a game player, he quickly began to discover the power of his directed attention. He started fueling up on the joys of life and the passion for his dreams, which generated uplifting emotions and thoughts in contrast to his self-deprecating and defeating inner conversation. Playing the game stimulated rich emotions and triggered thoughts and beliefs, which were in alignment with his dreams. He began taking action toward their manifestation because his behavior began to follow beliefs congruent with his intentions.

Now, Carl has discovered that he is not a victim to circumstances. He is beginning to respect himself and his needs more. He chooses to shower, dress, and provide himself with proper nutrition first, rather than throw himself into the day. He ends his day with uplifting feelings of his accomplishments. He does the "write" thing and registers what he has learned and how he is advancing his plans.

His conversation with himself now acknowledges that it is no longer a question of whether there is enough or no time; it is now about his choices. By direct experience, he sees that he is handling what needs to be handled, his dark doubts in his plans are now extinguished by the light of a building confidence, and he no longer believes that he is kidding himself. Now, he will continue to build a rational case for why he can have what he wants, and he will do a splendid job of creating that outcome because his behavior will follow his beliefs. He will experience and gather more rational evidence for why he can have what he wants, and that becomes his reality.

I am not suggesting that all of this happened for Carl by Day 10. These great day game plays got him started and pieces of the puzzle began and continue to come together. Like Carl, you will learn how to build powerful intent, and then use your emotions to guide you and reconstruct your beliefs as the game unfolds. Just take it one day at a time, and each day will build on the next, supporting you in an enjoyable process of conscious creation.

Today's game play, like the others, is another simple yet effective step toward congruent flow, increasing alignment and reducing conjanglement.

Make It a Great Day

Before taking off, a pilot needs to know where she is, where she intends to go, and how she is going to get there. Could you imagine your pilot hopping in the airplane, taking off, and then asking, "By the way, where are we going today?" I am certain you would prefer not to even consider that one.

Yet how many of us throw ourselves into the day with little to no sense of direction? It is no wonder we find ourselves reactive to the people and circumstances in our lives, not to mention ending our days like Carl did: feeling far less satisfied and fulfilled, knowing that, with just a little bit more focus, we could have accomplished a great deal more. Just as the pilot has her navigation log and charts well at hand, you will have your map to navigate with and enjoy each day with intentional purpose.

The great day game planner is a simple yet effective tool to track your game plays, target priority actions, and have a great day. It focuses on the B in the SEMB acronym—Behavior—and compliments the other resources as it has soulful purpose, increases emotional satisfaction, and heightens mental focus.

As with the other game plays, this format will be further developed and refined. For now, add this to your daily repertoire and make it a great day.

The great day game planner below begins with an important awareness followed by a question, one Carl initially neglected to ask himself each morning: "It's great to be alive and well! What will make today a fulfilling and satisfying day?"

Today's Great Day Game Planner

It's great to be alive and well! What will make today a fulfilling and satisfying day? Do the "write" thing, and jot down whatever action steps you'd like to take.

....

....

....

....

....

....

Highlight three priority actions. These priority actions will take precedence over all others. Then, time permitting, select others from the planner.

TODAY'S GAME PLAY CHECKLIST

Place a checkmark next to each completed game play:

☐ Today's principle card selected and engaged

☐ Fuel-up activities selected from your lightness and energy menu

☐ Game plan actions entered

Day 11 (Game Play 4)—The Abundant Mind Mind Game: Focus on Your Riches and Successes

The spiritual principle of appreciation states that when you direct your attention on the riches already present in your life and the opportunities before you, you attract and create more and more riches and perpetuate more opportunities. This is the essence of an abundant mentality. By the same token, when you direct your attention on what is missing in your life and the worries of an uncertain tomorrow, you attract and create more lack and perpetuate more worries and insecurity. This is the essence of a scarce mentality.

Without consciously exercising the power we have to direct our attention, two influences will direct our attention by default: (1) our previous conditioning; and (2) the stimuli in our environment, which includes the social hypnosis. Therefore, if we have cultivated an abundant mentality, we will notice more of the riches and opportunities; if we have cultivated a scarce mentality, we will notice more lack and limitations.

Ask yourself, *Do I have an abundant or a scarce mentality?* Chances are that you have a blend of the two but lean predominantly toward one side. Consider the seesaw at the park. Back and forth it goes, depending on how much weight is being distributed at any given moment. Without consciously directing your attention, the stimuli in your environment will tip the scale and influence how you view your present and future conditions.

Do you begin your day focusing predominantly on problems, or do you focus on opportunities to create what you want in your life? The social hypnosis leans more toward problem involving than problem solving; the problems are on the radar screen, and we either address them rationally and creatively, or fight our way through, or retreat from the emotional discomfort the thoughts of problems trigger.

R. Buckminster Fuller—engineer, inventor, and philosopher, among other attributes—was one of the key innovators in the 20th century. Fuller said, "You never change things by fighting the existing reality. To change something, build a new model that makes the existing model obsolete."[3] Similarly, Einstein stated, "We can't solve problems by using the same kind of thinking we used when we created them."[4] Both Fuller and Einstein acknowledged the need for change and the existence of problems, and took action to create new models and solutions. This game play strengthens your ability to acknowledge where your attention is presently, and then direct the power of your attention on what you choose to create.

Let me be clear that the game neither encourages emotional repression nor the denial of present conditions. Rather, it advocates for an increased awareness and engagement of what is, and then appraises it all as valuable guidance information. This appraisal principle will be expanded into two strategic practices where so-called "negative" emotions and thoughts will be catalysts for meeting needs and fortifying empowering beliefs. It is in the engagement where we will bring core needs out from the shadows and into the light of conscious awareness. As light illuminates darkness, problems dissolve within the process of creating.

Abundant Mind Mind Game—How to Play

Ask yourself:

- *Do I tend to lean toward an abundant or scarce view?*
- *Is my attention on problems or on what I choose to create?*
- *How will the quality of my life be enhanced by further developing:*
  - *An abundant mentality?*
  - *My capacity to direct my attention?*
- *Play the Abundant Mind mind game audio.*

While this mind game's main focus is on the M—the resource of Mind—it nicely complements the other three resources by stimulating the S of the Soul's purpose, soothing the E of Emotion by massaging the nervous system with deep breaths, and priming the B of Behavior to take practical action.

You'll consciously tip the scale toward an abundant view by exercising the power of your directed attention. At a highly suggestible state and with a keen awareness of the riches present in your life, you will direct attention and celebrate your previous successes, building confidence in yourself and your capacity to succeed. Your inner voice will affirm, "I have, I can, I will, and I am!" Tuned to the success channel, you will use this calm and focused state to mentally rehearse your day, grateful and expectant for success.

One final note: Even if you believe that you have a highly abundant mentality, do engage in this exercise as this will provide the foundation for other applications and practices as the game unfolds.

The Abundant Mind mind game is a mere four minutes in length, and audio is provided to guide you through a brief series of steps directing your attention toward:

- A highly suggestible and receptive state
- The riches already present within your life
- The acknowledgment of your successes

Your brain and mind are then tuned to the success channel where you can focus dynamically on anything you desire. Since the guided portion is brief, you may want to enjoy this deeply relaxed state further, reflect more on gratefulness and successes, or direct attention on what you want to create during the game. You can mentally rehearse your great day game plan too. You will notice a heighted state of focus, which will continue to strengthen the power you have to direct your attention as you practice this and other mind games to follow.

You'll find the Abundant Mind mind game on your audio CD or online at 90DayGame. com.

Today's Great Day Game Planner

It's great to be alive and well! What will make today a fulfilling and satisfying day? Do the "write" thing, and jot down whatever action steps you'd like to take.

....

....

....

....

....

....

....

Highlight three priority actions. These priority actions will take precedence over all others. Then, time permitting, select others from the planner.

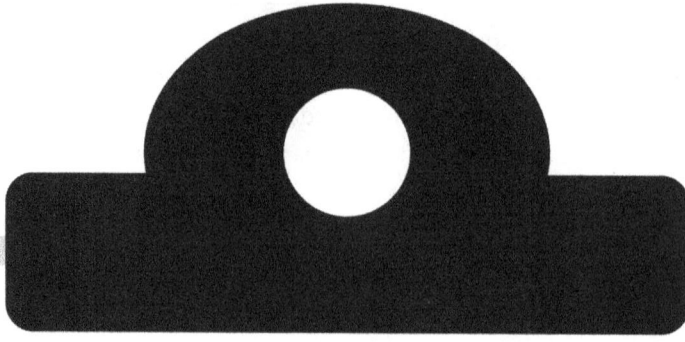

TODAY'S GAME PLAY CHECKLIST

Place a checkmark next to each completed game play:

☐ Today's principle card selected and engaged

☐ Fuel-up activities selected from your lightness and energy menu

☐ Game plan actions entered

☐ Abundant Mind mind game played

Day 12—Reminders and Tips of the Week

Play Them All!

Here are a couple of common comments from game players:

- "I'm loving the principle cards, and I'm back to playing the piano again! This has definitely lightened me up."
- "The simplicity of the great day game planner is making me more effective and efficient, and the mental exercise is keeping me focused on opportunities."

New players tend to gravitate to the game plays they find most appealing. That's natural. When asked if they are playing them all, the response is sometimes "no."

You need to roll the dice, move the iron, have some cash and invest it in some properties if you want a chance at winning Monopoly. If you are missing any of these, your chance of doing well is very limited. To win big in this game, you need to stimulate all four of your SEMB resources.

When combined, the principles' stirring and introspective tones, the joy of play, rejuvenating breaks, abundant perspective, and practical action produce a thriving environment for receptivity and engagement.

I invite you to challenge yourself to play them all and discover how this tips the scale from Blue Monday concerns to waking up and recognizing that you are already living your fabulous life!

Tips for the Card Game

Keep the cards in a convenient place. Here are a few locations to consider:

- Your nightstand
- By the coffeemaker
- On your desk
- By your phone

To Tech or Not to Tech—The Easy Way

Techie or not, the easiest way to get organized is to get the 90-Day Game bundle. It comes complete with the Top 10 Spiritual Principles for Evoking Your Greatness card deck, the playbook and a CD with all the mind game exercises. These items are also sold separately online.

The playbook comes complete with all the forms included in this game book. Additionally, some of these forms can be downloaded separately from the website.

If you're a techie person, you might like to keep your lightness and energy menu and great day game planner on your smartphone, or save the forms in a 90-Day Game folder on your desktop.

Mind Game Audio

Your purchase of this book entitles you to access the mind game mp3 files absolutely free from the website. Save them to iTunes or your desktop. Otherwise, you can buy the mind games CD. Whatever your preference, get set up and organized because more forms and mind games will follow soon. All game materials are available at 90DayGame.com.

With the game plays in play, you are primed to play with the core power practices. You will:

- Create a meaningful intention statement designed to enhance communication with your soul. It will be your guidepost for both thought and action.

- Utilize mind games to further strengthen the power of directed attention.

- Enter Rumi's guest house where you will transform so-called "negative" emotions into valuable guidance information to identify and meet your deepest needs. We call this Rumi-nating.

- Take your so-called "negative" self-talk to court. Utilizing the courtroom exercise, you will develop empowering affirmations to fortify the beliefs needed to bring your soulful intentions into material reality.

Today's Great Day Game Planner

It's great to be alive and well! What will make today a fulfilling and satisfying day? Do the "write" thing, and jot down whatever action steps you'd like to take.

....

....

....

....

....

....

....

Highlight three priority actions. These priority actions will take precedence over all others. Then, time permitting, select others from the planner.

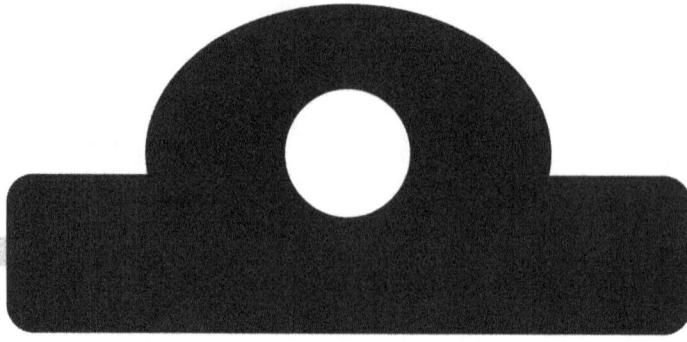

TODAY'S GAME PLAY CHECKLIST

Place a checkmark next to each completed game play:

☐ Today's principle card selected and engaged

☐ Fuel-up activities selected from your lightness and energy menu

☐ Game plan actions entered

☐ Abundant Mind mind game played

Days 13 and 14—Free Day Reminder

If you have not yet taken a day or two off from the game, you can.
You get two free days every week. You need not wait to the end of the
week. Use them freely at your convenience. You can take a game break,
practice the basic game plays, or review any material covered to date.
It's your call.

PART III

The Power of Intent

WEEK 3

The Conversation with Your Soul

Day 15—Your Meaningful Intention Statement: When You Are Clear, the Path Appears

You have within you a powerful force you can draw upon to create anything your soul desires. It is the power of intent. The greater the clarity of intent, the greater this force becomes. Today we will lay the groundwork with key definitions and distinctions for the first of the four core practices—a concise and well-articulated meaningful intention statement, one that will evolve throughout the game as you increase awareness and clarity. This will facilitate an ongoing conversation with your soul and become your guidepost for both thought and action.

Get ready to experience the power of clear intent and how it draws you forward into action. Your ability to meet challenges will strengthen, and each step along the way will become increasingly enjoyable. Emotionally stimulated by your intention statement, you will attract ideas, people, and events into your life in alignment with your intent.

Now is a good time to bring to mind what you truly want and why you came to play this game. Take a moment to read your responses to the jumpstart questions from Day 1 and then continue reading here.

Desire

Let's take a look at several dictionary definitions of the word "desire":

- To wish or long for; want

41

- The feeling that accompanies an unsatisfied state
- Synonyms for desire: covet, crave, wanting, longing, yearning

Wow, desire is not particularly inspiring, eh? Yet everything we create begins there! Desire is the catalyst for action and can also be one for inaction as well. Desire can leave a person feeling saddened by this unsatisfying state and remain frozen in the longing and yearning, which is all about what's missing. Left here, this person's mental screen is flooded with scarcity, causing him to see plenty of evidence for what's missing in his life.

Noticing what's missing can also be motivating and can lead one to take action to fulfill his desires. This core practice will transform desire into intention.

Intention is desire in action, and it is my meaningful intention to help you come to a great realization that you are divinely designed with all the resources needed to fulfill your most heartfelt intentions. Change is uncomfortable for most mortals, and the concern of potential disappointment can cause us to shy away from pursuing what we truly want. I invite you to make the shift and embrace change gracefully. Follow the steps outlined in this game, and you will greatly benefit from the process.

As you may recall from Day 11, we want to tip the scale toward an abundant consciousness that is focused on the riches already present in our lives and the opportunities before us. That is what we want to show up on our radar: an abundance of richness and opportunity all around us.

Inherent in a desire is a reaction to an absence of something you want or a presence of something undesirable you wish to eliminate from your life.

All meaningful intentions create a shift in consciousness from the focus of what is missing to what is available. It is mindfully created and filled with passion, purpose, and love and includes benefits for you and for all involved. You can view it as Einstein's shift in consciousness and Fuller's new model. From awareness of the undesirable, we create the desirable.

Therefore, with intention being defined as "desire in action," we thank desire itself because, without its inherent wanting, yearning, and longing, we would never enhance our conditions. As we choose to transform desire into intention, we opt to convert the unsatisfied state into one of great satisfaction.

Passionately Involved Yet Detached

You may think you know what you want. Your belief is based on finite data—that is, the current information you have stored in the limited database of conscious awareness. Your soul, on the other hand, has infinite information to offer you, and that is one important reason why you must keep communication open with your soul. Be passionately involved, take action, and, above all, watch carefully. Be most observant. Shy away from assumptions and judgments. By being an alert witness, and allowing your soul to guide you, you will satisfy the essence of your intention far more powerfully and with an even deeper level of satisfaction beyond what you first imagined.

In order to do this, you must playfully entertain your yearnings and longings with a fresh perspective, knowing that you can and will fulfill your soul's cravings. This perspective shift from feelings of dissatisfaction to rich enthusiasm has us bumping into another game practice called Rumi-nating, which will support you in welcoming all your emotions as valuable guidance information, but that is for another day. In the end, it may be the greatest gift you gain from playing.

Being passionately involved yet detached leads us to yet another significant distinction: intentional outcomes versus goals.

Stop Chasing Goals and Live the Life You Want Now

It may strike you as odd that I recommend you stop chasing goals. After all, I am a coach. How can I possibly promote the idea of kicking goals out of the game?

Meaningful intentions are filled with passion, purpose, love, and benefits for all. They carry context, which goals rarely do. In my experience in business, and particularly in sales, I participated in many valuable training sessions and benefited greatly from a good number of them. These one-hit wonders, however, lacked connective tissue. One focused on cultivating a vision, another on a mission, and another on goal-setting. There were others too, but rarely were they woven together in any significant way. It is important to note that vision, mission, values, and goals are not the exclusive property of business but of life itself.

Goals can be quite effective in getting stuff done but, independent of such context to vision, mission, and values, they can be empty and unfulfilling.

What I propose is to retain the elements of goals that offer heightened focus, eliminate their impediments, and bring them into this uplifting framework of meaningful intent.

One limitation of goal-setting is its rigidity. The focus can be so high and the commitment to it so great that it puts blinders on the individual. A vision of a man with a machete, hacking away at weeds, comes to mind. He is creating a path to find a clearing. As the camera is raised in an overview shot, evidence of how far he has gone is apparent and, into the scene from the left, just a few feet away, is a vast clearing.

The finite view of rigid goals blocks us from the infinite access of our natural guidance systems, such as intuition. When we get locked on a goal, it blinds us to this divine guidance.

When we take a broader view, we see more possibilities. Often, the most significant turns in life are meetings of chance. Being in a particular place at a certain time, completely unplanned, we may meet someone who influences our course in life. Reflect for a moment on your own life:

- Were most of the noteworthy turns in your life from deliberate plans or from the unplanned?
- How did you meet your spouse?
- What about your other meaningful relationships?

- How did you acquire your jobs?

- How did you come to the town in which you are living?

- I suspect you'll agree that some may have come from plans, some far from your plans, and many from meetings of chance.

Rather than being attached to goals, game players focus on the essence of their intentional outcomes and entertain a broader range of possibilities, which often alters their course. We may see new scenery, cultivate new relationships, create new communities, and at times begin entirely new lives. Reflect on your own life, and you'll find this to be true.

For the man with the machete, his goal was to find a clearing, and he chose a rigid path. His strategic goal kept him persisting in one direction, heading straight ahead. Eventually, he would have succeeded; however, he would have been better served to have looked around.

Perhaps you've had experiences like me and many of my clients who hit goals yet were unsatisfied. That's valuable information! When that happens, chances are that the goal lacked sufficient context to a meaningful intention. Or it may have been calling you toward another intention—one that is more meaningful and better suited to you and your needs and values. That's the significance of learning to listen to your soul, free of judgment, understanding its yearnings, and receiving its guidance.

When we are clear on our purposeful intention, desirable pathways toward our intentional outcomes come clearly into view as well. We are then drawn to take actions to realize them. Can you say that these outcomes are goals too? Yes, but they are goals with context. For the purposes of the game, we will call these goals with context "intentional outcomes," as they will retain the essential integration of vision: purposeful mission in integrity with the values we hold for our intentions.

Another aspect of goals is that they are inherently future-oriented. Our attention is fixated on the goal to such an extent that we are divorced from the present. The present is where life is experienced, and tomorrow is very much an illusion. Overinvesting in these illusions often leads us to conclude that, when we achieve a particular goal, we will be happy. When a goal is obtained, the fleeting moment of success is quickly followed by yet another specific goal to chase.

This leads to another assumption: If I don't reach this goal, I will be unhappy. This lines us up nicely for wasted energy spent in self-judgment (e.g., "If I had reached the goal," "If I had what it takes to reach it," "If I were smart enough to ..." or "good enough to ...") and on and on. Happiness becomes hinged to the goal and even influences our relationship with ourselves.

You might be tempted to say that the "goal" is to revel fully in the moment and in the now. But that too will separate us from the all-important aspect of context, disconnecting us from the rich value found within the passion, purpose, love, and benefits of our meaningful intentions. Therefore, the joy in the present is found in active engagement.

With this in mind, we release ourselves from the folly of attempting to control outcomes and engage a process that is within our command. We set an environment to flourish; a process that is perfectly pleasing to us and so enjoyable that we revel in the moment while we go about molding tomorrow.

We take refined action and accomplish more—not because our goals are so clear but more that our intention is clear and the practical actions we take are therefore perfectly aligned. Joyfully, we meet our needs and live our values while enhancing conditions for all. That is the context.

What is a great life but a succession of great days? So let us focus on having great days, hours, minutes, and seconds. Let us revel in setting the environment to flourish by keeping the great day game plays going, listening to our soul, and allowing it to guide us in the present moment and in the moments to come.

Today's Great Day Game Planner

It's great to be alive and well! What will make today a fulfilling and satisfying day? Do the "write" thing, and jot down whatever action steps you'd like to take.

....

....

....

....

....

....

Highlight three priority actions. These priority actions will take precedence over all others. Then, time permitting, select others from the planner.

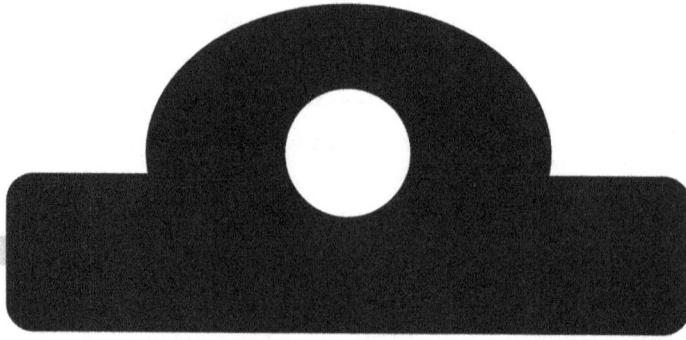

TODAY'S GAME PLAY CHECKLIST

Place a checkmark next to each completed game play:

☐ Today's principle card selected and engaged

☐ Fuel-up activities selected from your lightness and energy menu

☐ Game plan actions entered

☐ Abundant Mind mind game played

Day 16—Your First Step toward Creating a Meaningful Intention Statement: The Five Jumpstart Questions

The power you experience from your meaningful intention statement and the value it will hold as a guidepost for both thought and action are in direct proportion to the value you assign to them, the commitment you have to honoring them, and the level of your engagement. Here's why:

Your brain is much like a short-order cook, continually serving up anything and everything you present to it based on where you are directing your attention. As you move along in this process, you will gain a greater understanding of how your brain works and, with that understanding, you will produce desirable results with great efficiency and ease, and concurrently cease creating more of what you don't want.

Your brain converts every thought, word, and feeling into images. The greater the clarity of your intention, and the value and honor you give it, the more cooperative your brain will be. It will seek and sort all information in alignment with those images so as to actualize what you are presenting to it. In turn, you will become much more sensitive to this information in your environment.

Game players report that it often feels magical when opportunities begin to organize around their intent. This is a product of where you are directing your attention. You then notice more opportunities and are naturally drawn to act on them.

Therefore, your ability to produce the results you want in your life, and the level of enjoyment you experience in creating those results, are based on where you direct your attention. The more respect and honor you have for this conversation with your soul, the more your brain and SEMB resources will support you.

The more engaging the intention, the more easily you will direct the power of your attention toward it and create what you want, and enjoy the precious present moment all the more.

What do you want to create?

- Perfect health?
- An ideal career?
- Financial freedom?
- An intimate relationship?
- A memorable trip?
- Actually live what you learned from that weekend seminar?
- Make a grand contribution?

Maybe you want to discover what it is that your soul is truly yearning for. Perhaps you want to cultivate more trust, faith, ease, or some other subtle state of being. This too is fine fare for the 90-Day Game.

Can you conceive that what you deeply desire is possible for you? Do you find the notion stimulating, or does it create doubt in you or even frighten you? It is quite natural to have these feelings whenever change is entertained because your brain has a love affair with the familiar. Don't let it concern you; rather, pull yourself back to the present moment as your beliefs will be expanded, emotions will be soothed, and confidence strengthened along the course of the game. For now, go freely into this exercise, engage in the sacred gift of your imagination, and permit yourself to dream.

You can start with something simple or dive into your deepest, most heartfelt passion. The choice is yours.

The five jumpstart questions will begin a refining process, enabling you to direct your attention on a clear intention. These are the same questions you responded to on Day 1. This time, however, think in terms of what you want your life to look and feel like at the end of the 90-Day Game. It is best to respond to these five jumpstart questions spontaneously. Shoot from the hip, go from your gut, and express from your heart—whatever your personal style may be. Get a visceral response from your soul's desires.

Let me emphasize an important point by sharing a personal story. I have a vivid recollection of drawing a snowman in first grade. I gave my snowman a black outline, and I absolutely loved how it stood out boldly against the white construction paper. The teacher told me that snowmen don't have black lines around them. This authority figure, whom I respected, effectively told me that what I did was incorrect. I believe that simple comment put a restraint on my creativity and the beginnings of what I call "do it right-itis." More accurately and most importantly, that was the meaning I assigned to her comment. I'm certain many of us have similar memories like this where we were told, in some way or another, that we should not color outside the lines.

From the many tests we've taken, interviews we've been on, criticism from parents albeit with a loving intent in most instances, coupled with the desire to be seen in a good light and accepted by our family, friends, and colleagues, we have a strong urge to do things right. There is a tension associated with this, which cramps free thinking and unbridled expression.

Recognize that the following exercise is not a test. There is no way of doing it wrong nor is this something you need to commit to now. This is an exercise designed to enhance self-communication and stimulate self-awareness. Whatever you write is right for you! It will be perfectly fine, and you will continue to have ongoing opportunities to refine your answers. You also have the permission slip to crumple up and toss out whatever you write.

The ultimate aim is to develop clarity and, when you are clear, your path will appear. Be playful with it. Remember Huxley's words: "The secret of genius is to carry the spirit of the child into old age, which mean never losing your enthusiasm."[5] For these 90 days, simply see it as a game!

The Five Jumpstart Questions Exercise

Directing your attention on a clearly articulated intention is a most important ingredient in attracting anything you desire into your life. Your statement will remain dynamic and alive as a daily conversation with your soul. It will reflect your growth and progress. Responding to these questions is the first step within this process of intentional conscious creation.

Complete this exercise in 10 minutes or less. More than that would be overanalyzing, which is counterproductive to our aim here. However you respond to these questions is fine; there will be plenty of time to refine. Remember, you are tapping into your soul's desire, which is meant to be expressed.

Jumpstart Questions
1. What do I want to create? ....
2. What is motivating me to create this? ....
3. What talents and strengths do I have that align with my intention? ....

Jumpstart Questions

4.   Why is creating this valuable to me?

....

....

....

....

5.   How will I and others benefit from my creation?

....

....

....

....

Today's Great Day Game Planner

It's great to be alive and well! What will make today a fulfilling and satisfying day? Do the "write" thing, and jot down whatever action steps you'd like to take.

....

....

....

....

....

....

....

Highlight three priority actions. These priority actions will take precedence over all others. Then, time permitting, select others from the planner.

TODAY'S GAME PLAY CHECKLIST

Place a checkmark next to each completed game play:

☐ Today's principle card selected and engaged

☐ Fuel-up activities selected from your lightness and energy menu

☐ Respond to the five jumpstart questions

☐ Game plan actions entered

☐ Abundant Mind mind game played

Day 17—Refinement Step 1: State What You Want, Not What You Don't Want

Now that you have responded to the five jumpstart questions, you are but three simple refinement steps away from having a first draft of your meaningful intention statement. The emphasis is on "draft," and it will always remain a draft. This is essential for you to understand. Without change, there is no growth. When you think you've got your meaningful intention statement perfectly complete, you can be certain that you have gone off course. The sooner you recapture your course, the more briskly you will create what you want.

The better you get to know anyone you are in conversation with, the more effective your communication becomes and the more your relationship grows with that party as well. You are about to get more intimately connected with your soul and learn how to communicate effectively with it.

Here's a summary of the three standard refinement steps. Be assured that you will be walked through each step thoroughly:

1. **From "don't wants" to "wants":** First, you will review all responses to be certain that you are stating what you want and not what you don't want.

2. **From future to present:** Then you will take a second pass at your responses, being certain that they are expressed in a present-moment context—not in the future but in the "now."

3. **Complete your first draft:** You'll then drop away the five questions and stream your responses together into one flowing statement.

Let's get to the first refinement of your draft within this framework.

State What You Want

Here are some common responses to the question, "What do you want to create?"

I want to:

- Lose weight.
- Quit my dreadful job.
- Get out of debt.
- No longer be lonely.

None of the above responses answers the "What do you want to create?" question; instead, they answer a "What do you want to get rid of?" question.

You'd never tell your waiter all the things on the menu that you don't want, but we do this routinely when expressing our desires to ourselves. If you find that your thoughts go to what you don't want at first, don't be surprised. That is quite normal. This comes from childhood and social conditioning, which we will address later. Knowing what you don't want however can be useful in identifying what you do want. Simply use the "don't want" responses to formulate the "do want" desires.

For example:

- "Attain my ideal healthy weight" rather than "lose weight."

- "Enjoy a satisfying job/career" rather than "quit my dreadful job."

- "Create financial ease or freedom" rather than "get out of debt."

- "Attract rich friendships and/or a wonderful intimate relationship" rather than "no longer be lonely."

Here's why language is critically important.

Your Obedient Brain

Your brain translates all words into images. Like a good short-order cook, your brain will serve up more of whatever you request. It is obedient and makes no judgments; it simply aims to fill the order based on where attention is presently. In the examples above, one view creates images of weight, dreadful work, debt, and loneliness; the other view creates images of perfect health, a satisfying career, financial ease, and rich relationships.

Now that you understand that your brain translates words into images, and how your brain gravitates to actualizing them, give your brain clear directions, and let it be your partner in creating what you really want.

Let's revisit our friend Carl. You read about him on Day 10. He's the guy who began a business about a year ago, barely making ends meet. He is beginning to recognize that he has gotten into habits that do not serve him. He starts his days agitated and rushed, and ends them quite disappointed in his lack of progress. Thanks to a good friend's suggestion, Carl began playing the 90-Day Game.

Here are his responses to the five jumpstart questions:

1. **What do I want to create?**

I'm tired of starting my days upset, scared, nervous, doubting myself. I'm barely making ends meet. I am not ready to give up. I want to make this business work.

2. **What is motivating me to create this?**

I'm frustrated and tired. I'm beginning to get into some substantial debt. I don't want to go back to work for someone else.

3. **What talents and strengths do I have that align with my intention?**

I'm good at client relationships. I enjoy providing them with solutions to their business challenges. I am trustworthy, honest, and have a strong knowledge base.

4. **Why is creating this valuable to me?**

I know if I can just get things organized and set up a few systems I can really make this business work. I want to make it work.

5. **How will I and others benefit from my creation?**

I always wanted to work for myself. It would be satisfying to see my efforts turn into profits. I'd have money to reinvest in my business, hire an assistant, and be out in the field more. My wife would believe in me again and be less stressed. We would be able to provide the things both of us want for our kids.

Now here are Carl's "don't wants" followed by his rephrased "wants" directly below where applicable.

1. **What do I want to create?**

Don't wants: *I'm tired of starting my days upset, scared, nervous, doubting myself. I'm barely making ends meet. I am not ready to give up. I want to make this business work.*

Wants: *I want to start my days happy, calm, and confident. I want to be profitable and finally have some financial stability. I want to work for myself and make this business a success.*

2. **What is motivating me to create this?**

Don't wants: *I'm frustrated and tired. I'm beginning to get into some substantial debt. I don't want to go back to work for someone else.*

Wants: *I want to feel satisfied and energized. I want to build a financial reserve. I want to enjoy working for myself and growing my business.*

3. **What talents and strengths do I have that align with my intention?**

Don't wants: *I'm good at client relationships. I enjoy providing them with solutions to their business challenges. I am trustworthy and honest and have a strong knowledge base.*

Wants: (No changes needed.)

4. **Why is creating this valuable to me?**

Don't wants: *I know that if I can just get things organized and set up a few systems, I can really make this business work. I want to make it work.*

Wants: (No changes needed.)

5. **How will I and others benefit from my creation?**

Don't wants: *I always wanted to work for myself. It would be satisfying to see my efforts turn into profits. I'd have money to reinvest in my business, hire an assistant, and be out in the field more. My wife would believe in me again and be less stressed. We would be able to provide the things both of us want for our kids.*

Wants: *My wife will believe in me again and be more at ease.* (No other changes needed.)

Tomorrow, it will be your turn to apply Refinement Step 1.

Today's Great Day Game Planner

It's great to be alive and well! What will make today a fulfilling and satisfying day? Do the "write" thing, and jot down whatever action steps you'd like to take.

....

....

....

....

....

....

....

Highlight three priority actions. These priority actions will take precedence over all others. Then, time permitting, select others from the planner.

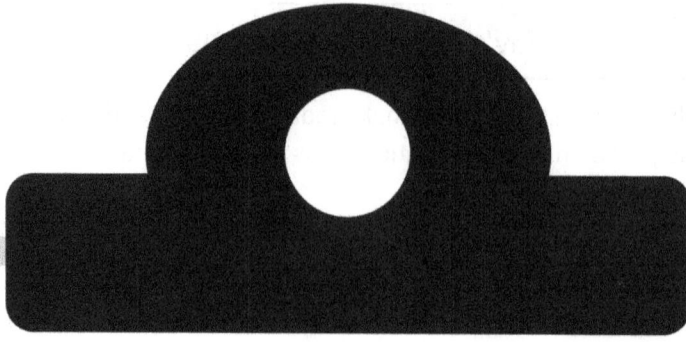

TODAY'S GAME PLAY CHECKLIST

Place a checkmark next to each completed game play:

☐ Today's principle card selected and engaged

☐ Fuel-up activities selected from your lightness and energy menu

☐ Your five jumpstart questions responses reread

☐ Game plan actions entered

☐ Abundant Mind mind game played

Day 18—Refinement Step 1 Exercise: From "Don't Wants" to "Wants"

Refine your responses to the jumpstart questions, changing "don't wants" into "wants." Referring back to Carl's work may be helpful.

Refinement Step 1: State What You Want, Not What You Don't Want
Refine your responses to the jumpstart questions, stating what you want, not what you don't want, or wish to rid yourself of.

1. What do I want to create?

....

....

....

....

2. What is motivating me to create this?

....

....

....

....

3. What talents and strengths do I have that align with my intention?

....

....

....

....

Refinement Step 1: State What You Want, Not What You Don't Want

4. Why is creating this valuable to me?

....

....

....

....

5. How will I and others benefit from my creation?

....

....

....

....

Today's Great Day Game Planner

It's great to be alive and well! What will make today a fulfilling and satisfying day? Do the "write" thing, and jot down whatever action steps you'd like to take.

....

....

....

....

....

....

....

Highlight three priority actions. These priority actions will take precedence over all others. Then, time permitting, select others from the planner.

TODAY'S GAME PLAY CHECKLIST

Place a checkmark next to each completed game play:

☐ Today's principle card selected and engaged

☐ Fuel-up activities selected from your lightness and energy menu

☐ Intention statement—Refinement Step 1 completed

☐ Game plan actions entered

☐ Abundant Mind mind game played

Day 19—Reminders and Tips of the Week

Get Your Hands Dirty

Get used to the idea of being a little sloppy. As you create your meaningful intention statement, cross stuff out and jot stuff down. Kids have no problem with being messy. Be a big kid; be spontaneous. Freely write what comes to mind, knowing that you can make changes whenever the spirit moves you.

This is and will continue to be an ongoing conversation with your soul. You'll be making many changes. As you change and grow, your intention statement will reflect that growth.

If you like neat and orderly, rewrite the sloppy stuff. Rewriting means more attention on your intention, and that's great!

No Shoulds Allowed!

"I should be more positive."

"I should have done 'that' instead of 'this.'"

"I shouldn't feel this way."

"I shouldn't be stuck (or frustrated or tired ...)."

Yes, there sure is plenty of opportunity for "should" stuff, isn't there?

What's going on in your life right now is exactly what is supposed to be going on, and it's up to you—the player—to make sense of it. Without the wanting, longing, and yearning of desire, there is no clear intent. Without so-called "negative" emotions, no deep needs can be met and no significant values can be honored. Without so-called "negative" self-talk, limiting beliefs would go unnoticed and remained misaligned.

The shift from victim to victor is in the awareness, acceptance, and action of these so-called "negative" states. The problem is not in the thoughts or feelings themselves; it is in not knowing what to do with them. Seasoned players know how to work with them.

Your mission is to reappraise them as valuable guidance information.

I'm sure Carl would have preferred not to be upset, scared, nervous, or doubtful of himself. He'd rather not feel frustrated and tired. Yet, through his awareness and engagement, he took all that so-called "negative" stuff and began to use it effectively. He is utilizing it to have a conversation with his soul, crafting his meaningful intention filled with passion, purpose, love, and benefits for all. He's transforming the "negative" into valuable guidance information, and so are you. You have turned your "don't wants" into "wants" and will further refine the conversation during the game and throughout your life.

So when you get conjangled—and you will, just as I do and every human does—let that bring a shine to your eye and a grin on your face, knowing that something great is about to be born. It is part of your divine design.

Do the "write" thing and capture your thoughts and feelings in the written form. We will make great use of it all as the game unfolds.

Today's Great Day Game Planner

It's great to be alive and well! What will make today a fulfilling and satisfying day? Do the "write" thing, and jot down whatever action steps you'd like to take.

....

....

....

....

....

....

....

Highlight three priority actions. These priority actions will take precedence over all others. Then, time permitting, select others from the planner.

TODAY'S GAME PLAY CHECKLIST

Place a checkmark next to each completed game play:

☐   Today's principle card selected and engaged

☐   Fuel-up activities selected from your lightness and energy menu

☐   Game plan actions entered

☐   Abundant Mind mind game played

Days 20 and 21—Free Day Reminder

WEEK 4

Further Refining Intent

Day 22—Refinement Step 2: Rephrase Your Responses in a Present-Moment Context

As an early game player succinctly put it ...

Meaningful intentions provide the bridge between living for right now, while still shaping, refining and improving the future.

—Rachel Hiller, 90-Day Game player

Nicely said, Rachel. That is exactly what it's all about.

In some instances, visualization techniques and affirmations are expressed in a future-oriented context. For example, the statement, "I am living with the love of my life in our luxurious beach house," is welcomed in a meaningful intention statement if, in fact, that is currently true. However, if you are renting and just making ends meet, and have just experienced the dissolution of an intimate relationship, these future-oriented visions do not reflect the present reality. What may be true is that you are taking steps toward owning your own beach house or seeking the love of your life. Expressed this way, it is process-oriented and is an example of how an intention statement is properly articulated.

Therefore, your statement is a reflection of what you fully believe and invest in because it is a statement of what truly is and what you are acting on. In real time, you will revise the statement regularly with your progress and several other ingredients going forward. These ingredients are designed to promote harmonious alignment of your SEMB states—clear intent, joyful emotion, and mental confidence—drawing you to take practical action.

Future-oriented statements that do not reflect the current reality invite bully-like self-talk, such as, "Who are you kidding?" This dialogue can leave one with sad and sour feelings; a reminder of what they want and do not have. This conflicting internal static is counterproductive to our work here, increases conjanglement, and slows down, if not halts, forward movement altogether.

Since your meaningful intention statement is a reflection of what you are creating presently in the objective external world of action, future-oriented affirmations are not appropriate here. Future-oriented imagery, however, will play an important role as a communication tool with the subconscious mind with significantly favorable impact. You will experience this in a few days when we begin to play more mind games. For now, let's get into the finer points of Refinement Step 2.

"I Ams" and "-ings"

The game incorporates many shifts. One is the progression from:

I want → I can → I will → I am

I Ams

Like the baby's cry, reaching out for a piece of candy, wanting anything is an awareness of what you don't have; something that is missing in your life. This is where all desires begin. Until that desire of wanting is transformed into an intention, we are left with a sense of longing and yearning. When we recognize that we can and are in the process of fulfilling this need or desire, and declare our worthiness to receive it, intention becomes a powerful force.

Gratefully, for most of us, a desire like thirst is filled by getting a drink of water—a simple desire to fulfill. With such a simple desire, the movement from "I want" to "I can" to "I will" to "I am" goes relatively unnoticed. With other desires, more conscious attention is needed. Beliefs may need to be expanded, and greater awareness, appreciation, and acknowledgment of our talents, strengths, and resourcefulness may need to be fortified to proclaim the great "I AM!"

Within your jumpstart question responses, you've stated what you want and directed attention to your capabilities; you can use these talents and strengths to create what you want. Now you will declare and celebrate that you have made the conscious choice to create! You will evoke the profound power of these two little words: "I am!"

The "I am" proclamation generates energy and movement, and affirms that, "I am in the process of creating."

-ings

Quite naturally, you will find "I am" and "–ing" words within your statement as you rephrase your responses in a present-moment context.

Let's visit our friend Carl's work. He's carried forward his upgraded responses from Refinement Step 1, where he rephrased his "don't wants" into "wants." Directly below these, we'll see Carl's Step 2 refinements, now expressing his responses in a present-moment, process-oriented context with lots of "I ams" and "–ings."

1. **What do I want to create?**

Wants: I want to start my days happy, calm, and confident. I want to be profitable and finally have some financial stability. I want to work for myself and make this business a success.

Refinement: I am starting my days happy, calm, and confident. I am taking steps to increase profitability and build financial stability. I am working for myself and making this business a success.

2. **What is motivating me to create this?**

Wants: I want to feel satisfied and energized. I want to build a financial reserve. I want to enjoy working for myself and growing my business.

Refinement: I am feeling satisfied and energized. I am building a financial reserve. I am enjoying working for myself and growing my business.

3. **What talents and strengths do I have that align with my intention?**

Wants: I'm good at client relationships. I enjoy providing them with solutions to their business challenges. I am trustworthy and honest and have a strong knowledge base.

Refinement: (No changes needed.)

4. **Why is creating this valuable to me?**

Wants: I know that if I can just get things organized and set up a few systems, I can really make this business work. I want to make it work.

Refinement: I am getting things organized and setting up systems. I am really making this business work.

5. **How will I and others benefit from my creation?**

Wants: I always wanted to work for myself. It would be satisfying to see my efforts turn into profits. I'd have money to reinvest in my business, hire an assistant, and be out in the field more. My wife would believe in me again and be less stressed. We would be able to provide the things both of us want for our kids.

Refinement: I am working for myself. It is very satisfying to see my efforts turn into profits. I am reinvesting in my business, attracting an assistant, and being out in the field more. My wife believes in me again and is more relaxed. We are beginning to provide the things both of us want for our kids.

Write What is True!

Let's take another look at Carl's work on his response to Jumpstart Question 1.

1. **What do I want to create?**

From: I want to start my days happy, calm, and confident. I want to be profitable and finally have some financial stability. I want to work for myself and make this business a success.

To: I am starting my days happy, calm, and confident. I am taking steps to increase profitability and build financial stability. I am working for myself and making this business a success.

Carl did something important here. He kept it real. He did not write, "I am profitable," because that simply isn't true. He did write, "I am taking steps to …" This reflects the present condition he truly believes.

Going a step further, if Carl didn't fully believe that he "is taking steps to …," he could say, "I am learning to …" The important factor here is that your intention statement is to reflect what is true and what you can completely believe and invest in. Without this level of belief, your logical left-brain will revolt and stunt your progress.

Techniques will be offered to expand your beliefs as we move along in the game. As you and Carl continue to make progress, your growth and expanded beliefs will be reflected within your statements. Ultimately, Carl's statement will include, "I am profitable." In the end, intention statements become gratitude statements. Time permitting, proceed and apply Refinement Step 2; if not, roll it over to tomorrow. We have budgeted two days for this.

Today's Great Day Game Planner

It's great to be alive and well! What will make today a fulfilling and satisfying day? Do the "write" thing, and jot down whatever action steps you'd like to take.

....

....

....

....

....

....

....

Highlight three priority actions. These priority actions will take precedence over all others. Then, time permitting, select others from the planner.

TODAY'S GAME PLAY CHECKLIST

Place a checkmark next to each completed game play:

☐ Today's principle card selected and engaged

☐ Fuel-up activities selected from your lightness and energy menu

☐ Game plan actions entered

☐ Abundant Mind mind game played

Day 23—Refinement Step 2 Exercise: From Future to Present

Refinement Step 2 Exercise: From Future to Present
Refine your responses to the jumpstart questions, changing any "future-oriented" statements into a present moment "process-oriented" context—in the "now" with plenty of "I ams" and "–ings."
1. What do I want to create?
2. What is motivating me to create this?
3. What talents and strengths do I have that align with my intention?

Refinement Step 2 Exercise: From Future to Present

4. Why is creating this valuable to me?

....

....

....

....

5. How will I and others benefit from my creation?

....

....

....

....

Today's Great Day Game Planner

It's great to be alive and well! What will make today a fulfilling and satisfying day? Do the "write" thing, and jot down whatever action steps you'd like to take.

....

....

....

....

....

....

....

Highlight three priority actions. These priority actions will take precedence over all others. Then, time permitting, select others from the planner.

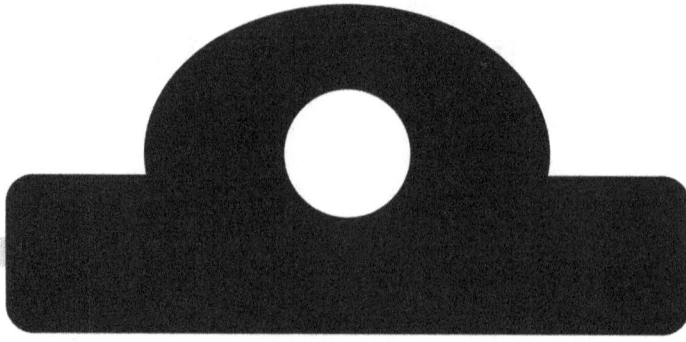

TODAY'S GAME PLAY CHECKLIST

Place a checkmark next to each completed game play:

☐ Today's principle card selected and engaged

☐ Fuel-up activities selected from your lightness and energy menu

☐ Intention statement—Refinement Step 2 completed

☐ Game plan actions entered

☐ Abundant Mind mind game played

Day 24—Refinement Step 3: Complete Your First Draft

This third refinement step is a simple matter of dropping away the questions and streaming your responses together into one flowing statement. Here are Carl's "refined" responses to the jumpstart questions:

I am starting my days happy, calm, and confident. I am taking steps to increase profitability and build financial stability. I am working for myself and making this business a success.

I am feeling satisfied and energized. I am building a financial reserve. I am enjoying working for myself and growing my business.

I'm good at client relationships. I enjoy providing them with solutions to their business challenges. I am trustworthy and honest and have a strong knowledge base.

I am getting things organized and setting up systems. I am really making this business work.

I am working for myself. It is very satisfying to see my efforts turn into profits. I am reinvesting in my business, attracting an assistant, and being out in the field more. My wife believes in me again and is more relaxed. We are beginning to provide the things both of us want for our kids.

As Carl read his responses, he wasn't pleased with the feel or flow. He tweaked the responses a bit further:

I am grateful to be working for myself and for the opportunity to make this business a success. I am starting my days earlier and am feeling happier and calmer. Taking steps to become profitable is increasing my confidence that I am, in fact, on my way to building financial stability.

I am feeling more satisfied and energized. I am building a financial reserve. I enjoy working for myself and growing my business.

Building strong client relationships is one of my greatest strengths. They know I am trustworthy, honest, and knowledgeable in my field. I truly enjoy providing them with solutions to their business challenges.

I am getting things organized and setting up systems. I really am making this business work.

It is satisfying to see my efforts turning into profits. I am reinvesting in my business, attracting an assistant, and being out in the field more. My wife believes in me again and is more relaxed. We are providing the things both of us want for our kids.

Carl likes what he's come up with. He will read it and refine it daily. It will be an ongoing conversation with his soul, doing his part to fulfill its intention.

Using Carl's work as an example, create a first draft of your meaningful intention statement, using the form below. Keep in mind that forms like these are available online.

Refinement Step 3: Complete Your First Draft

Stream your jumpstart responses together into one flowing statement.

....

....

....

....

....

....

....

....

....

....

....

....

....

....

....

....

....

....

Today's Great Day Game Planner

It's great to be alive and well! What will make today a fulfilling and satisfying day? Do the "write" thing, and jot down whatever action steps you'd like to take.

....

....

....

....

....

....

....

Highlight three priority actions. These priority actions will take precedence over all others. Then, time permitting, select others from the planner.

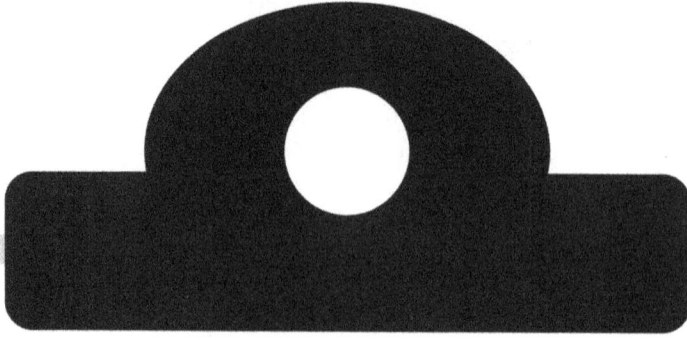

TODAY'S GAME PLAY CHECKLIST

Place a checkmark next to each completed game play:

☐ Today's principle card selected and engaged

☐ Fuel-up activities selected from your lightness and energy menu

☐ Intention statement—Refinement Step 3 completed

☐ Game plan actions entered

☐ Abundant Mind mind game played

Day 25—Choose Success: Your Passions, Talents, and Values

What does success mean to you? Beyond the social hypnosis—defined as "the one with the most toys at the end of the game of life wins"—those of us who have pondered thoughtfully on our own sense of purpose know that defining success is a personal matter.

Donald Trump, Mother Teresa, Derek Jeter, Nelson Mandela, Rush Limbaugh, Steve Jobs, and Mahatma Gandhi are all successes in their own unique ways. Although distinctly different individuals, they, like all other "successful" people, share the following common attributes: They all live their passions and their values, have a clearly defined understanding of their talents and strengths, and have no need to be all things to all people.

Take a moment and think about the people in your world who you would consider successful. Run through the checklist:

- Are they living their passion?
- Do they honor their values?
- Are they keenly aware of their talents and strengths?
- Are they concerned with how others view them or more likely free of that concern with no need to be all things to all people?

There is something beautiful about doing what you do best and aligning with others who have complementary talents. Like a mosaic, quilt, or tapestry, you weave together the brilliant colors of your unique abilities and collaboratively create together. All those individuals mentioned above aligned with others to create their vision.

Each and every one of us has the capacity to be successful now by simply embracing our own unique greatness. Why not choose success now? Get to know your own success formula by directing your attention on your passions, talents, and values, and you will attract everyone and everything you need to create what you want while enjoying the process. Today, you'll begin to compile lists of your passions, talents, and values. Jot down what comes to mind, and add to your inventory as more of them come into your awareness.

Below, you'll find forms to enter your passions, talents, and values. An alternative to writing lists is mind mapping. This approach capitalizes on the brain's natural inclination for mapping thoughts through free association. For example, "I think I'll go to the store to get milk. Hmm ... since I'm going out, I should check to see if Mom's prescription needs to be refilled. I'm so glad she's feeling better. I wonder how Uncle Al is feeling. I should call him. I'll give him a ring when I get back." Somehow, getting milk led to checking in with Uncle Al, and this is from everyday free association.

Mind mapping begins with a central theme positioned at the center of a piece of paper, usually oriented in a horizontal manner, like a movie screen or the print option called "landscape" on your computer. From the central topic point, a line is drawn for each thought with related thoughts connecting to each other.

Details on mind mapping go beyond the scope of our purpose here. If you'd like to know more about this, search for "mind mapping" on Google and, when you click on "Images for mind mapping," you will see an amazing number of examples. There is also a large volume of mind-mapping software for those who enjoy tapping the keys over pen and paper.

What Are You Passionate About?

Take a reflective moment and recall a time when you were filled with passion. What were the qualities? For me, I immediately think of when I first met my wife-to-be, when the idea of learning to fly first came to mind, and when I chose to pursue my new career. For me and many others whom I have interviewed, the experience was filled with:

- Great energy
- A sense of invincibility at some level
- A feeling that anything was possible
- A driving and focused force
- Heightened emotion
- A deep connectedness to a purpose and the value it was going to provide for all involved

Passion creates an expansive energy that draws you to act and is therefore an essential ingredient to incorporate within your meaningful intention statement.

Other passions, like mine of playing guitar, although more subtle, stimulate energy, imagination, creativity, and action as well. These states can contribute directly or indirectly to manifesting meaningful intentions.

For example, John at first did not understand why he should incorporate unrelated passions, like his love for baseball, when he was far more interested in directing his attention to a more profitable sales career. However, shortly after brainstorming on his passions, it dawned on him to buy Yankee tickets. He brought his clients, prospects, and centers of influence to the stadium. Applying his enthusiasm and passion for the sport attracted other like-minded clients to him. They didn't focus on business at the games; instead, they developed relationships and, in turn, this attracted clients who shared the same passion. In the end, this incorporation of seemingly unrelated passions increased sales and referrals, far exceeding the cost of the tickets, not to mention being a whole lot of fun!

As another example, Ron connected with his passion for animals and, some months later, found himself quite unexpectedly transitioning from his financial services career into a far more satisfying one as a dog trainer. This being a natural fit for Ron, he filled his practice quickly, and then refined his specialty of working with service dogs to help draw out emotional connection for autistic children.

Cultivate your passions, and you will be delightfully drawn into action. Passion engages you in the process of conscious creation and, when passion is present, you are fully present as well.

List Your Passions

As you do the "write" thing today, don't limit your lists or mind maps to your current intention. Instead, list everything you are passionate about:

Ask yourself:

- *What draws up strong emotion within me?*
- *What am I most enthusiastic about?*
- *What did I naturally gravitate toward as a child, well before some adult told me that I shouldn't or couldn't?*
- *What stimulates me now?*
- *What passion(s) drew me to playing this game?*

Your Passions List

....

....

....

....

....

....

....

....

Add to the list as other passions come to mind.

List Your Talents and Strengths

Bringing your talents and strengths to mind will support your actions and sense of confidence in the pursuit of your intentions.

Our greatest strengths often elude us. Perhaps it is because they are so deeply assimilated that we do not notice them. On the other hand, you may have been raised with the notion that it is inappropriate to focus on yourself; that you should be directing your attention toward others. Here, you draw on your strengths—not to "puff" yourself up but to strengthen your ability to contribute at a higher level for the benefit of all, and "all" does include you. It's all part of opening up to worthiness and the circle of generosity.

By appreciating your talents and strengths, you embrace a healthy sense of self, are more likely to apply them, and create more value for others as well as yourself.

Here are four interview questions you can ask people in your world in order to jumpstart awareness of your talents and strengths that may currently elude you:

1. What is the first thing you think of when you think of me?
2. What is the most interesting thing about me?
3. What do you see as my greatest accomplishment?
4. What do you see as my greatest strength?

My first coach—the wonderfully talented Meryl Moritz—offered these four questions, which originated from Lynda Falkenstein, who is known as "The Niche Doctor." Meryl said that she learned a lot about the way she comes across to people through these interviews. Meryl discovered that she had strengths that she had taken for granted and that were perceived as quite unique. This has been my experience as well. Why not elect to do five or more of these interviews in the next two weeks and heighten your awareness of your unique abilities?

Your natural talents and strengths are abilities you were born with, whereas skills are strengths that you have developed during your lifetime. For example, you may have been born with a natural ability to play a musical instrument by ear, whereas your ability to become reasonably deft at using a computer may have developed after some training and practice. Jot down your skills too, and direct particular attention toward your natural talents and strengths. They are most accessible and enjoyable and the easiest to employ, reflecting the perfection of your divine design.

My own personal belief, which I do not impose on anyone, is that our Creator designed each of us with unique abilities to facilitate our purpose for being here. So celebrate and appreciate them in gratitude, and make use of them for the benefit of all.

List Your Talents, Strengths, and Skills
Bringing conscious awareness to your competencies builds confidence. Like opening up a toolbox, you will select the appropriate tools to advance your intention.
Ask yourself: ● *What natural aptitudes and actions come easily to me?* ● *What qualities do I possess that enable me to accomplish things effectively?* ● *What skills have I developed over the years?*

Your Talents, Strengths, and Skills
....
....
....
....
....
....
....
....
....
Add to the list as others competencies come to mind.

List Your Values

Values pertain to character, ethics, morals, principles, and standards, such as, integrity, trustworthiness, respect, beauty, independence, community, reliability, and balance.

I'm talking about your moral and ethical code by which you live and the code you intuitively trust—not the values of parents, teachers, peers, or society. This departure from being overly reliant on the opinions of others is liberating. Trust and embrace your personal code, and reinforce your ability to make sound, ethical choices. By living in integrity with your values and being consciously responsible for your actions, you develop inner strength, conviction, and self-confidence.

Susan Corso, wordsmith and author of *God's Dictionary*,[6] points out that our values are a measuring stick for our choices. "When we choose to honor our own values, it is easy to persist in the actions that support our choices." [7] Reflect on some of your previous successes. You will notice that you persisted when your intentions aligned with what you most deeply valued. They are valuable to you. Live those intentions that you value most, and let go of those you do not value enough or at all.

With these ingredients in the forefront of your awareness, your focused energy will attract you into action. You will be consciously competent and confident and in integrity with what matters most to you.

As you engage in the process of your meaningful intention, which speaks directly to your natural talents and passions, expect to experience heightened energy and enthusiasm, building momentum and more consistent action. You will be supremely in the present. Your spontaneous thoughts and behaviors will be seasoned with the richness of where you are directing your attention, which consequently yields outcomes and results in alignment with your thoughts, behavior, and intent.

When you choose to live your passions, talents, strengths, and values without the need to be all things to all people, you have chosen success. When you find yourself struggling to take action outside of these preferences, it's time to come together with those who take pleasure in such activities. Bring their greatness together with yours, and revel in the process with grace and ease.

List Your Values
Live by your values, and you will persist in the actions that support your intentions.
Ask yourself: • *What is most valuable to me?* • *What are the values I choose to honor?*

Your Values List

....

....

....

....

....

....

....

....

....

Add to the list as other values come to mind.

Today's Great Day Game Planner

It's great to be alive and well! What will make today a fulfilling and satisfying day? Do the "write" thing, and jot down whatever action steps you'd like to take.

....

....

....

....

....

....

Highlight three priority actions. These priority actions will take precedence over all others. Then, time permitting, select others from the planner.

TODAY'S GAME PLAY CHECKLIST

Place a checkmark next to each completed game play:

☐ Today's principle card selected and engaged

☐ Fuel-up activities selected from your lightness and energy menu

☐ Intention statement—engaged and refined

☐ Passions, talents, and values list created

☐ Game plan actions entered

☐ Abundant Mind mind game played

Day 26—Reminders and Tips of the Week

Warning!

When you think you've got your intention statement just right, you have gone off course! When you think it's perfect, you've stalled. Keep it dynamic. It is always a draft and, although you see it as fine, it is essential that you continue to re-fine it.

Passions, Talents, and Values Lists

Now that you have directed attention to your passions, talents and values, consider peppering your intention statement with them. Passion stimulates motivation. Awareness of your talents promotes conscious competency and confidence. Values strengthen your commitment and recognition of what matters most to you.

Revisit and grow your passions, talents and values lists regularly.

Are You Keeping Your Great Day Game Plays Going?

If you've skipped a few of the great day game plays in favor of getting into the meaningful intention practice, start off your "free" days with them. Remember: If you do this four to five times weekly, you'll enjoy a thriving, receptive, and engaged state of being.

Need a Hand?

Want to get some feedback on your intention statement? Assistance is just a click away. One-to-one and email coaching are available. We can also help you find a buddy player. Check in with your faciliplayer or write to us at Team@90DayGame.com. We are here to help!

Today's Great Day Game Planner

It's great to be alive and well! What will make today a fulfilling and satisfying day? Do the "write" thing, and jot down whatever action steps you'd like to take.

....

....

....

....

....

....

....

Highlight three priority actions. These priority actions will take precedence over all others. Then, time permitting, select others from the planner.

TODAY'S GAME PLAY CHECKLIST

Place a checkmark next to each completed game play:

☐ Today's principle card selected and engaged

☐ Fuel-up activities selected from your lightness and energy menu

☐ Intention statement—engaged and refined

☐ Game plan actions entered

☐ Abundant Mind mind game played

Days 27 and 28—Free Day Reminder

PART IV

The Power of
Directed Attention

Directing Your Attention on Your Intention

Day 29—Captain's Emotions and Self-Talk Logs

Are you listening? That is, are you really listening? Are you aware of that inner dialogue that accompanies any conversation?

Have you noticed that, when you are in a conversation and while listening, a part of you is hearing your own inner voice? You are not only digesting what the other person/persons are saying, you are also having emotional responses to what's being said. These include thoughts of agreement and/or disagreement, and preparing yourself for what you are about to say in response even though the other party is still talking.

Deep listening is an art form and an invaluable skill worth developing. It enriches relationships and is essential for many occupations. It can be quite challenging to tame our reactions and fully listen. Interestingly, one way of developing the art of deep listening is by becoming increasingly aware of those emotional responses and that inner voice, which is commonly referred to as "self-talk."

In the 90-Day Game, we are particularly interested in tuning in to how we are feeling and what we are saying to ourselves while we are in those conversations with our soul.

"Am I Going Crazy?"

One day, a client of mine said, "My situation is pretty much the same, but I feel totally different about it. I feel as though I have multiple personalities. There are two different voices inside of me, speaking to each other." When clients show up with these kinds of insights, I know that they are not going crazy; they are just waking up. When this fundamental awareness becomes conscious, a fabulous and fresh view of life is soon to emerge.

The great day game plays stimulate greater awareness of your overall state. You feel more in command. You may still be teeter-tottering back and forth, yet you are becoming increasingly confident as you continue to build tomorrow with the tools you are gathering today.

As you listen closely, you will begin to notice these voices within you:

- One that judges you and the other that is lovingly accepting and affirming
- One that is hypnotized by the beliefs of what is socially popular and people-pleasing and the other that intuitively knows what is best for you
- One that asks, "How am I doing?" and the other that asks, "How can I help?"
- One that is a prisoner of past conditioning and the other that revels in the freedom of choice
- One that frantically tries to figure out what's wrong and the other that observes perfection within the perceived imperfection
- One that sees what's missing and the other that sees what's present
- One that carries the weight of a limiting grasp, clutching to the known, and the other that is uplifted by wonder, curiosity, and expansive possibilities
- One that feels disconnected and alone and the other that feels connected and unified
- One that never has enough and the other that is infinitely abundant
- One that reacts to circumstances and the other that knows you are the creator of your circumstances

We all have these voices within us. At times, the prevalent voice of the social hypnosis can draw us off course, making us believe that we are powerless; at other times, the voice of the soul affirms that we are in command and brilliantly awake. At times, we find our strength in how we are viewed by others, and medicate ourselves with the things we buy and ingest, giving us the illusion of comfort and peace; at other times, we are centered within ourselves with great confidence and strength. Our work together will build resilience and strengthen your resolve to be in command of your life.

As you are having this conversation with your soul, you will have emotional reactions and responses; thoughts of agreement and disagreement. At times, you'll feel hardy; at other times, weak; confident one day and intimidated the next. As these emotions come up, do the "write" thing and jot them down. When there are thoughts of agreement, disagreement, or conflicting ambivalence, make a note of them. Capture them using the captain's logs provided in today's material.

There are logs for capturing both emotional responses and self-talk, as we will have two distinct game practices for engaging each of them a little further down the road in Part V, "Navigating Your Great Adventure." Meanwhile, embellish your intention statement with affirming feelings and thoughts that align with your intention.

There are two significant benefits you will gain from capturing these states: objectivity and valuable information.

1. **Objectivity**

I say "capture" these states because, as you bring your attention to them, you become more in command of them. Disturbing emotions can easily have you sliding down a slippery slope that intensifies fears, doubts, and worries. Conflicting thoughts that show up in your inner dialogue can cause you to develop intricate storytelling, which affirms beliefs that conflict with your intention. When you capture them in the written form, you are engaging a part of your brain that enables you to retain your objectivity. You will develop this resilient skill and become quite an adept witness to these inner states. Rather than being captured by them, you will be in command of them.

One might ask, "Why pay attention to them at all? Why not simply shift my attention away from them?" That strategy provides only temporary relief at best, can actually make them stronger, and at worst invites repression, which can be causative of disease. It is far better to learn how to gain command of them.

2. **Valuable information**

The second benefit is that these states, although they appear to be "negative," are not a design flaw by God or Mother Nature. On the one hand, these states protect you from potential danger and keep you alert and away from complacency; on the other hand, this heightened awareness provides the raw material needed to get your deepest needs met and fortify empowering beliefs aligned with your intention. We have game practices to transform so-called "negative" emotions and self-talk. Celebrate it all, and enjoy the process, knowing that it is all valuable guidance information! Just capture it for now on the logs, and we'll work with this valuable information soon.

Captain's Emotions Log	

Read your intention statement.

Ask yourself:
- *How do I feel about what I am creating?*

Rather than describing the emotion, label it with one-word adjectives:

Date	Light Emotions (e.g., engaged, enthusiastic, satisfied)

Date	Deep Emotions (e.g., anxious, tired, frustrated)

Direct your attention to the entries above and ask yourself:
- *What needs are being met, or not being met?*
- *What values are being honored, or dishonored?*

Make a note of any valuable information:

Captain's Self-Talk Log

Read your intention statement.

Ask yourself:

- *What am I saying to myself about what I am creating?*

Write down your self-talk:

Date	**Self-Talk and Beliefs in Alignment with Intent** (e.g., "I'm making great strides," "I can see that my plans are coming together," "I'm living my dream!")
Date	**Self-Talk and Beliefs Incongruent with Intent** (e.g., "I can't do this," "This will never work out," "Why bother?")

Direct your attention to the entries above and ask yourself:

- *What beliefs are being affirmed, strengthened, or fortified?*

Make a note of any valuable information:

Today's Great Day Game Planner

It's great to be alive and well! What will make today a fulfilling and satisfying day? Do the "write" thing, and jot down whatever action steps you'd like to take.

....

....

....

....

....

....

....

Highlight three priority actions. These priority actions will take precedence over all others. Then, time permitting, select others from the planner.

TODAY'S GAME PLAY CHECKLIST

Place a checkmark next to each completed game play:

☐ Today's principle card selected and engaged

☐ Fuel-up activities selected from your lightness and energy menu

☐ Intention statement—engaged and refined

☐ Feelings and self-talk entered in captain's logs

☐ Game plan actions entered

☐ Abundant Mind mind game played

Day 30—That Single Essential Ingredient and the Blue Chevy Theory

All the flight planning, navigation logs, charts, state-of-the-art Global Positioning System (GPS) guidance equipment, and horsepower in the world will not get a pilot to desirable destinations unless he employs one crucial skill. All of the preparation and planning, enthusiasm, and massive action in the world will not get you to accomplish your goals, aspirations, and dreams without utilizing this essential faculty. Having intentions and intentional outcomes are fundamental. Yet, unless you add this ingredient to your formula for success, you are going nowhere.

I have seen countless mission and vision statements in business and reality statements and affirmations in personal development. Although diligently developed, all too often they have proven weak or completely ineffective. They have remained hidden in drawers, deserted in piles of paper, and now collect dust on shelves.

Much time and energy can be invested in hours of massive action as well, without commensurate return. Like a hamster on a circular treadmill, running feverishly along, remaining just where he started, we are left with the sour taste of frustration and disappointment.

No plans are ever implemented and effective actions ever taken without applying this single most important ingredient: the power of directed attention.

To paraphrase Dr. Norman Vincent Peale, if you want to know what your future will be, you don't need tea leaves or have your palm read; all you need to do is pay attention to what you're thinking.

Buddha is quoted as saying, "All that we are is the result of what we have thought. The mind is everything. What we think we become."

Your present reality is nothing else but the results of your previous thoughts and beliefs about yourself and the world around you. By the same token, your future reality will be drawn from your present thoughts and beliefs. It is therefore extremely important to direct your attention on the richness of the present, desirable possibilities and opportunities stimulating your consciousness with thoughts of a wonderfully beautiful and fulfilling life.

Harnessing the power of directed attention restores focus and reins in scattered actions. Why are our thoughts diffused and our actions scattered? Billions of bits of data bombard our senses, continuously vying for our attention. Thankfully, our brains are equipped with a highly complex attention system, involving numerous areas of our brains, some of which regulate the volume of sensory input that comes into our awareness. Without this, we would go mad. This attention system, however, is not responsible for the specific content of data that enters our awareness. What comes in and what we notice are a function of where our attention is at any given moment.

Think of your attention system as your brain's radar screen. An air traffic controller's radar screen displays the movement of aircraft. It is up to the controller to select the range of view and the traffic he chooses to monitor.

Your attention system displays the movement of information in the field of your environment, and it is up to you to command what information you choose to display. Unless you exercise your ability to selectively choose what goes onto your radar screen, your scope will be flooded with conflicting information and, in turn, your thoughts will be diffused and your actions scattered. Information overload! Like the alarms and flashing lights on a controller's radar screen, which alert him of a potential traffic conflict, this state triggers alarms of emotional anxiety, psychological tension, and flashing lights of potential danger.

Where your attention lies influences what you notice, and the meaning that you assign to what you notice largely determines how you feel about things and the action you will or will not take.

Consciously or not, when fears, doubts, and worries are left unattended, they come onto the scope. Your radar will be on alert—seeking, noticing, and attracting all available information in alignment with them to protect you. You will build a rational case, which will strengthen your belief and validate a personal reality that you have much to fear, with sound reasons to doubt yourself and your plans, and feel increasingly unsettled about your present and future conditions. Consciously or not, you will act in alignment with this personal reality because your behavior always follows the beliefs you are attending.

Consciously or not, when the love, faith, and gratitude you have for your life comes onto the scope, your radar will be alert—seeking, noticing, and attracting all available information in alignment with the love, faith, and appreciative zest you have for your life. You will build a rational case, which will strengthen your belief and validate a personal reality that there is much to love about your life, with sound reasons to have faith and confidence in yourself, in your plans, and in divine guidance. When you carry such beliefs, you will attract more for which to be grateful. Consciously or not, you will act in alignment with this personal reality because your behavior always follows the beliefs you are attending.

It is important to note that the relationship we have with fears, doubts, and worries is yet another hypnotic conditioning. One of the greatest benefits that game players gain is the shift in their relationship with them. Our fears, doubts, and worries are not a design flaw by God or Mother Nature; rather, they are a divine call for attention. When appropriately attended, you appraise your fears, doubts, and worries as valuable guidance information. Rather than fighting them or fleeing from them, you will engage them and make great use of them; you will realign with your purpose and intent, further enhancing self-communication. This will be fully addressed in the days to come, and your ability to make this shift requires that essential ingredient: the power of directed attention.

When exercising your power of directed attention, you are able to selectively choose what dominantly goes onto your radar screen. In turn, your thoughts are more focused rather than diffused, and your actions are more purposeful rather than scattered, thus yielding emotional lightness, psychological confidence, and ease.

Blue Chevy Theory

Consider what goes on when shopping for a major purchase, like a home or a car. As you go through the process, considering your options, you are directing lots of attention. As you narrow down the field to, let's say, a colonial-style home or a blue Chevrolet, your senses become quite alert to colonial-style homes or blue Chevys. You see them everywhere: as you are driving along in your car, on the Internet, in magazines, on television, in the background of movies, overhearing conversations, at work, and on the radio. Your field of attention is acute, and your senses are on alert.

Do you see the connection between your meaningful intention and the power of directed attention? Does this help you understand the importance of directing and redirecting your attention toward it?

Developing the Power of Directed Attention

So how do we develop the power of directed attention? Virtually every game play and practice within this game is designed to empower the player with heightened focus and self-communication. At this stage of the game, your attention is being pulled back daily to soulful principles, meaningful intent, rejuvenating activities, and appreciation for the riches present in your life, your accomplishments, and practical actions aligned with the passion, purpose, love, and benefits of your intent. This pulling back, over and over again, continuously tips the scale from our propensity to notice what's missing to the fullness of what is present in our lives. This propensity for noticing what's missing is rooted in that self-protective survival mechanism introduced early on. In the days to come, you will gain an appreciation for the honorable role this mechanism plays, be freed from its limitations, and enroll it as your ally. For now, let's stick with the power of directed attention.

Whatever is on our radar screen impacts what we notice, how we think and feel, and what we act upon.

The great day game plays are developing your power of directed attention through repetition and conscious awareness. We will now direct attention to increasing subconscious awareness and have your subconscious mind team up more profoundly with your conscious mind.

Jose Silva, founder of the renowned Silva Method, developed an approach for establishing communication with the subconscious mind. He recognized the relationship that brain frequencies had with states of consciousness and, through his method, gave millions of Silva Method practitioners worldwide a simple yet profound way to enter deeper levels of consciousness with controlled awareness previously believed to be impossible. The core technique is known as "dynamic meditation."

We will utilize the foundational principles of Silva's approach to further develop the power of directed attention. Anyone who has any interest in gaining greater command of their consciousness and their lives would benefit greatly by taking Silva's courses.

Mind games are mental exercises provided within this game and are based on Silva's discoveries. They are designed to support you in developing access, communication, and command of your inner states of consciousness. Taking my lead from Silva, going forward I will refer to the subconscious mind as the "inner conscious mind" because "sub" suggests that these states are inaccessible or beneath our conscious awareness. Inner conscious states have the potential to become increasingly accessible and, when brought into harmony with outer-conscious states, have a profound impact on what shows up on your mental radar.

Players Are Lucky and Expect Meaningful Coincidences

Carl Jung, the Swiss psychiatrist and psychotherapist who founded analytical psychology, coined the term "synchronicity" in the late 1920s and stated that synchronicity reveals "an intimate connection between the internal image and the external world." When you complement the objective external clarity and focus of your intention statement with the subjective internal images in mind games, you have a powerful force enabling you to gain command of your consciousness.

Although unverified, Lucius Annaeus Seneca, the Roman Stoic philosopher, has been widely attributed as saying in the turn of the first century, "Luck is where the crossroads of opportunity and preparation meet."

Meaningful coincidences are occurring all the time, and they are most evident to the prepared mind. As a game player, you most emphatically have a prepared mind, so expect meaningful coincidences. You will increase their occurrence, be sensitive to and notice opportunities, and enhance your intuitive ability; you'll make practical use of this information, and have a lot of fun with them too. So let's go forward, apply the Blue Chevy theory, get lucky, create what you want, benefit others, and have a lot of fun! How's that for living a fabulous life?

You've been playing one mind game since Day 11—the Abundant Mind mind game. Tomorrow, we'll break down this four-minute exercise to further enhance your understanding of the method and the many benefits you are gaining from this and all the mind games to follow.

Today's Great Day Game Planner

It's great to be alive and well! What will make today a fulfilling and satisfying day? Do the "write" thing, and jot down whatever action steps you'd like to take.

....

....

....

....

....

....

....

Highlight three priority actions. These priority actions will take precedence over all others. Then, time permitting, select others from the planner.

TODAY'S GAME PLAY CHECKLIST

Place a checkmark next to each completed game play:

☐ Today's principle card selected and engaged

☐ Fuel-up activities selected from your lightness and energy menu

☐ Intention statement—engaged and refined

☐ Feelings and self-talk entered in captain's logs

☐ Game plan actions entered

☐ Abundant Mind mind game played

Day 31—Directing Attention through Mind Games

But whatever the dictates of fashion, it seems that those who take the trouble to gain mastery over what happens in consciousness do live a happier life.

—Mihaly Csikzentmihalyi[8]

We may not have complete control over the external events in our lives, but we do have the capacity to direct our attention. Where your attention lies influences your interpretation of reality, largely determines attitude, perspective, and perception, and impacts your choices and behavior.

As the Csikzentmihalyi quote suggests, directing consciousness has grand benefits worthy of our pursuit.

The aim of our mind games is to paint your mental radar screen with emotionally stimulating images that orient your consciousness toward actualizing your meaningful intention. Be it reveling in the process of creating or in the rich and delicious outcomes of your intention, when you direct your attention using dynamic mind games, you trigger a storm of cellular activity. It alters blood chemistry, enhances your emotional state, amplifies your focus, and enrolls your inner conscious mind harmoniously with your conscious mind. With this congruent alignment, you'll be drawn to take practical action with confidence.

Mind games provide your brain's attention system with clarity, stimulating creativity and idea generation, enhancing intuitive sensing, and fostering a greater ease and flow to your practical actions.

In a study published by ScienceDirect.com on April 21, 2011, in the journal *Brain Research Bulletin*, the researchers found that people trained to meditate over an eight-week period were better able to control specific type of brain waves called "alpha rhythms." If I've got the math right, 90 days covers that period—and then some. "These activity patterns are thought to minimize distractions, to diminish the likelihood stimuli will grab your attention," says Christopher Moore of the McGovern Institute for Brain Research at MIT and senior author of the paper. "Our data indicate that meditation training makes you better at focusing, in part by allowing you to better regulate how things that arise will impact you."[9]

As you can see, mind games are a perfect fit for our aims in the game. The game intentionally cycles between objective physical action steps and a variety of playful yet powerful subjective exercises, some of which are these mind games. You've been doing this ever since you began playing the Abundant Mind mind game exercise. Let's break it down now so you can enjoy the benefits from mind games all the more.

Relax

To enter deeper states of consciousness, you'll want to quiet down all of your systems. So the first step in the Abundant Mind mind game—and in all mind games to follow—will be to find a comfortable position. This will minimize physical distractions.

Then you close your eyes. Eighty percent of what you perceive is visual information. The simple act of closing your eyes reduces this sensory input, screening billions of bits of data from entering your visual field.

We're getting quieter! Now your brain frequencies begin to move from the alert beta brain frequency toward an alpha rhythm. Alpha waves help suppress irrelevant or distracting sensory information.

Go to Vagus

Whoever heard that going to Vegas is relaxing? Actually, it's spelled "vagus," and it is stimulating! In fact, we intentionally stimulate the vagus nerve when taking deep breaths,

As David Rakel, MD, from the University of Wisconsin points out,

> "… in the Western life, we're constantly over activating the sympathetic nervous system. It's kind of like being on the starting line of a race and you're all pumped and ready for the gun to go off, but the gun never goes off and that process continues. And that can have a negative influence on our health because our immune system actually works better when we're more relaxed.
>
> So, a simple way to stimulate that relaxation response is just to do some slow, deep breathing. That's, by far, one of the best ways because when you do a deep, abdominal belly breath that stimulates the vagus nerve and the vagus nerve is one of the main stimulators of this relaxation response. Our body does it naturally when we take a deep sigh. It's trying to tell us something. Now, if we can take 10 or 20 deep sighs a day with intention to help relax the body, that's a great way to stimulate the relaxation response."[10]

The good doctor highlights the importance of being intentional. You are in command of your state by virtue of your intention. It is the meaning you are assigning to every game play, practice, and action you take.

My enthusiasm got the best of me! Back to the process …

So breathing—deep belly breathing, that is—stimulates the vagus nerve, the parasympathetic nervous system, and *viola!* The relaxation response.

In the exercise, I suggest that you blow all the air out of your lungs. This helps you establish a belly breath. Most of us don't breathe from the belly but from the chest, and the image of a military man puffing up his chest gives us the idea that this is the way to go. Breathing from the chest occurs because we are stressed.

One class of mortals are the best teachers of belly breathing: babies. Watch a baby while she's sleeping, and you'll see her belly expand like a balloon. Babies are great game players! They are also great at letting go, crying in one moment and giggling the next, while their cheeks are still wet with tears ... but that's another subject.

Focus

Counting down from 10 to 1 provides your mind with a passive target for further quieting and deepening toward the inner state of consciousness. This directs your mind away from scattered, distracting thoughts as you continue to enhance the command of your attention.

Once you reach the count of 1, you have arrived. You are in contact with your sub ... I mean inner conscious mind. Remember: Repetition is the key to changing your brain. Each time you practice, you are reinforcing key words that trigger this state. Words like "relax" and "deeper and deeper," and the focusing on the numbers, make that short-order cook get ready for receptivity. The more you practice, the deeper and more suggestible your state becomes.

Assume that you have arrived and open your creative mind with ...

Appreciation

As most players already know, much has been written about gratitude. I like the word "appreciation" because of its association with increasing value, like antiques, original art, fine wines, and our homes and investment portfolios, if we wait long enough. When you direct attention to the things you appreciate in your life, like your health, relationships, vocations, and avocations, the attention you give celebrating them increases your perception of their value and, because your awareness is present there, you will notice and attract more of the same: more blue Chevys, more meaningful coincidences, and more luck!

Self-Appreciation

Self-appreciation helps you love yourself, recognize your own value, and embrace a willingness to see your own greatness. You may have bought into the belief that it is selfish to direct attention on yourself—another one of those old-school conditioning things. Many of us stumble along, trying to do good things for others from a position of weakness. By directing attention to yourself first, you fill your own cup and give freely from the overflow. If appreciating your own greatness is difficult for you, know that your family, friends, and the world deserve a healthy, confident, and contributing you.

So in the next step of this mind game, you'll direct attention on your successes. Acknowledging your successes is uplifting and tunes you into the success channel, reinforcing that "I can, I have, I will, and I am" shift of growing confidence.

What qualifies as a success?

- Is quitting smoking a success?
- Is landing a new job a success?
- When a salesman makes a sale, is that a success?
- How about a salesman who invests time in making calls? Would you consider taking that action a success, even if he didn't make any appointments?
- What about the salesman who does not make a sale but invests time to learn from his experience. Is that a success?
- How about exercising a little more patience?
- Is approaching the day with a spirit of enthusiasm a success?
- Is the choice to play this game a success?

Successes come in a wide range of sizes from large to small. Don't think that only monumental achievements are successes. Any action you intentionally choose to take and subsequently act on is considered to be a success, regardless of the outcome.

These are the simple steps that set the stage for stimulating inner conscious conversations, which is the essence of mind games. The benefits of meditation and, in this instance, dynamic mental exercises like mind games, are numerous.

Physiological Benefits of Meditation and Dynamic Mental Exercises

- Reduces stress
- Increases relaxation
- Lowers heart rate
- Reduces blood pressure
- Lowers cortisol and lactate levels, favoring ease and weight reduction
- Reduces free radicals, which cause tissue damage and many diseases and are a major factor in aging
- Increases energy and stamina
- Strengthens your immune system

Mental and Emotional Benefits of Meditation and Dynamic Mental Exercises

- Minimizes distraction
- Enhances mental clarity and focus

- Replaces overwhelm with a sense of well-grounded capability
- Increases patience and understanding
- Expands creativity
- Awakens and develops intuitive ability

Experiential Benefits of Meditation and Dynamic Mental Exercises

- Reduces reactiveness
- Enhances purposefulness
- Enhances relationships
- Increases personal and professional performance and achievement
- Fosters more efficient and effective use of time
- Bolsters confidence
- Results in greater flow and ease in taking action

As with all mental, emotional, and soulful game plays and practices, the principle of grace and ease applies. When you begin, you may find that your mind wanders. Avoid getting upset about this and instead celebrate it! You are increasing your awareness of a state, which is normal. When this occurs, smile and understand that this is part of the process. You are developing the power of directed attention, greater command of your consciousness, and your life. Be light about it, and simply direct your attention back on course. Over time, you will be amazed at your capacity to be the powerful director of your attention and, in turn, your fabulous life!

Today's Great Day Game Planner

It's great to be alive and well! What will make today a fulfilling and satisfying day? Do the "write" thing, and jot down whatever action steps you'd like to take.

....

....

....

....

....

....

....

Highlight three priority actions. These priority actions will take precedence over all others. Then, time permitting, select others from the planner.

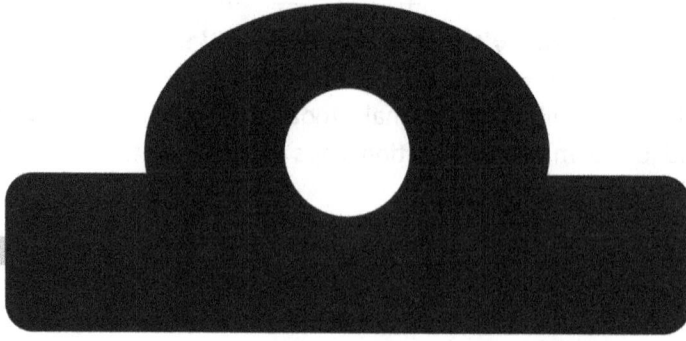

TODAY'S GAME PLAY CHECKLIST

Place a checkmark next to each completed game play:

- ☐ Today's principle card selected and engaged

- ☐ Fuel-up activities selected from your lightness and energy menu

- ☐ Intention statement—engaged and refined

- ☐ Feelings and self-talk entered in captain's logs

- ☐ Game plan actions entered

- ☐ Abundant Mind mind game played

Day 32—Captain's Appreciation Log: Gratitude and Successes

Getting Riches and Progress Firmly on Your Radar

By now you have become familiar with the allure of the social hypnosis and how our survival instinct is continually bringing concerns on our radar screen. Without the captain's intervention, this will be what is dominant on our radar, slowing progress and dampening our spirits. We thank the survival mechanism for protecting us from potential hazards, yet we need to provide a counterbalance to remain buoyant and in the creation game.

Attention on the passion, purpose, and benefits of our intention and the lightness and energy activities support this aim. Many of our mind games reflect upon the riches present in our lives and our accomplishments for this very purpose as well. To make them more objectively concrete, the captain—that's you—will once again do the "write" thing and build an appreciation log.

The things we appreciate grow in value. As we direct attention to them, we discover more of the same. The two categories of appreciation therefore are "gratitude" and "successes."

Anything we are appreciating in the moment is entered into the gratitude column. Any actions taken that contribute toward our meaningful intention are entered as successes. Be certain to acknowledge all actions. Simple and easy ones count and have a cumulative effect when noted.

Invest time reflecting on your list. Notice the needs you are meeting and the values you are honoring. This will connect the dots between what your soul desires and the actualization of your intention.

Update this log regularly, and you'll tip the scale in your favor.

| | | Captain's Appreciation Log | |

Appreciate the riches present within your fabulous life, and acknowledge yourself and your progress.

Date	Gratitude (whatever you are appreciating in the moment)	Successes (actions taken that are contributing toward your meaningful intention)

Direct your attention to the entries above and ask yourself:

- *What needs are being met?*
- *What values are being honored?*

Make a note of any valuable information:

Today's Great Day Game Planner

It's great to be alive and well! What will make today a fulfilling and satisfying day? Do the "write" thing, and jot down whatever action steps you'd like to take.

....

....

....

....

....

....

....

Highlight three priority actions. These priority actions will take precedence over all others. Then, time permitting, select others from the planner.

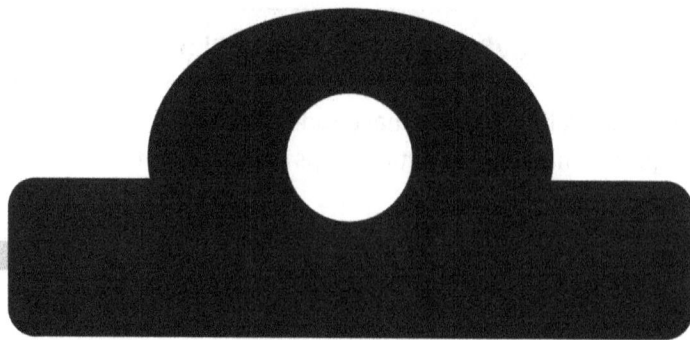

TODAY'S GAME PLAY CHECKLIST

Place a checkmark next to each completed game play:

☐ Today's principle card selected and engaged

☐ Fuel-up activities selected from your lightness and energy menu

☐ Intention statement—engaged and refined

☐ Feelings, self-talk, and appreciation entered in captain's logs

☐ Game plan actions entered

☐ Abundant Mind mind game played

Day 33—Reminders and Tips of the Week

Just a Coincidence

Often, there are obvious coincidences, but our conditioned response is to discount them. We think that it's something that happened by chance. I call them "meaningful coincidences," and they are happening all the time. We simply need to be tuned in to noticing them. Players actively seek to connect the dots between their game play actions and these invigorating events. They are a function of where we direct our attention, influencing the things we notice.

Blue Chevy Parking Lot

We are inviting players to park their blue Chevy experiences in our online parking lot. Having this collection will be fun reading and increase the expectancy for all players to have similar "incidences" or coincidences, as the case may be. Send your contributions to Team@ 90DayGame.com.

Although your blue Chevys are greatly appreciated, we are not in a position to offer you a trade-in deal for a new car. You are, however, welcome to use the game to attract a new one, if you'd like.

Go to Vagus Regularly

Taking deep, intentional belly breaths calms your nervous system, promoting grace and ease. You can go to vagus anytime. Here are a few ways you can turn delays and unwanted interruptions into useful opportunities to go to vagus:

- In your car, at stop lights, and in traffic jams
- Out and about while waiting in line at a store or for your waiter to bring you an order
- In the office when your computer freezes or you are downloading a large file

Anytime you can use a little more patience or want to feel more relaxed, take a brief vacation and head to vagus.

Self-Assessment Check-In

Assessments are not tests. If you're on track, great; if you aren't, steer clear of judgment and just get back on course.

Are you keeping pace?

Remember:

- At too slow a pace, your brain will not experience the rhythm of day-to-day-repetition that forms neural pathways required to make the desired changes and habits you want to assimilate.

- At too fast a pace, you will not be able to internalize the content effectively.

Are you playing four to five times weekly?

If you got busy and skipped a few of the great day game plays, play them on lunch breaks, in the evening, or on free days.

Keep the rhythm going and look out for those blue Chevys. They are there. Are you seeing them?

Need forms? You'll find captain's logs and other forms at 90DayGame.com.

Today's Great Day Game Planner

It's great to be alive and well! What will make today a fulfilling and satisfying day? Do the "write" thing, and jot down whatever action steps you'd like to take.

....

....

....

....

....

....

....

Highlight three priority actions. These priority actions will take precedence over all others. Then, time permitting, select others from the planner.

TODAY'S GAME PLAY CHECKLIST

Place a checkmark next to each completed game play:

- ☐ Today's principle card selected and engaged

- ☐ Fuel-up activities selected from your lightness and energy menu

- ☐ Intention statement—engaged and refined

- ☐ Feelings, self-talk, and appreciation entered in captain's logs

- ☐ Game plan actions entered

- ☐ Abundant Mind mind game played

Days 34 and 35—Free Day Reminder

Mind Games and the Power of Metaphor

Day 36—Mental Rehearsal: The Been There, Done That Mind Game

Would you like to accomplish more with less effort? Of course you would. Who wouldn't? This mind game, like all of them, brings the outer world of action into harmony with the inner world of vision, thought, and emotion where all outcomes are born. The power of mental rehearsal lies in this congruent alignment of all SEMB resources.

Through the effective use of imagination, mental rehearsal gives your brain and mind the sense that you've taken action on something already and, with that familiarity, you are more at ease and sure of yourself when taking action objectively. When confident and at ease, you are more graceful, eloquent, attractive, intuitive, and present. Remember: The brain has a love affair with the familiar and is uneasy with the unfamiliar. Having gone down the path already, your brain knows how to get there.

The applications for mental rehearsal are infinite (e.g., in preparation for tests, business meetings, sales presentations, blind dates, and even a visit from your in-laws). Objective practice builds confidence, and subjective practice amplifies it all the more.

Meet game player John. John advises clients in the areas of insurance, investments, and wealth-creation strategies. After more than four hours of diligent preparation, he is enjoying a high degree of confidence that his proposal will knock the socks off of his client Bill, a successful restaurateur in Westchester County, NY.

He had gathered all the facts and figures, and his detailed proposal included eye-catching visual graphics, charts, an extensive narrative, and a bullet-point summary. The next morning, he awakened with great enthusiasm as he was going to be able to show off his work to his client Bill, who will most certainly appreciate the brilliance of his plan. In his mind, his sale was assured.

As a seasoned 90-Day Game player, John was going to start his day with a mind game. He selected the obvious one from the menu: Been There, Done That. John entered the calming suggestible state and proceeded to run through his mental rehearsal, starting with the following SEMB checklist as presented in the audio:

- **Soul:** What is my intention? Is it filled with passion, purpose, love, and benefits for all?

- **Emotion:** How do I feel about the action I am preparing to take?

- **Mind:** Do I believe in what I am about to do?

- **Behavior:** Am I ready to take practical action?

After running through the checklist, John imagined himself in Bill's office, greeting him with a warm smile, a hearty handshake, and some casual rapport-building conversation. He imagined himself sharing his enthusiasm with Bill, eagerly showing him what he diligently prepared, and sensing how impressed Bill was at the obvious investment of time and dedicated effort John invested on Bill's behalf.

In his mind, John went through the presentation, mindfully pausing for feedback from Bill, to be certain that he understood the reasoning behind the plan and the many benefits it affords. He highlighted the protection for Bill and his family, the sparkling retirement income he can look forward to, and the deep and emotional satisfaction he will have from the legacy he'll leave for his children and grandchildren many years down the road.

Eager to enjoy the fruits of his conscientious preparation, John headed out to see Bill with an air of grace, ease, and confidence.

Upon arrival, John was calm, cool, and collected as anticipated. The warm, welcoming connection followed as planned, and John and Bill began to get down to business. Little conversation took place before John found himself pausing for Bill's feedback sooner than expected. Although Bill said little, John had a surprising change of heart and kept his briefcase closed. It dawned on him that what Bill needed more than anything right now was peace of mind. They had a brief exchange, centered on the immediate need for protection and how that was what mattered most. Bill shared that he had been hesitant up until now: "I don't know exactly why, but a light bulb just went off for me. I know this is what I want and need to do."

After the required disclosure documents were discussed and a few forms were signed, both Bill and John felt good that the most urgent need was addressed. Before John left, he complimented Bill for taking action. Bill expressed his appreciation to John, how deeply he trusts him, and how he looks forward to further conversations.

John told me he was very happy that he left with the sale in hand, but he shared that he took away something even more valuable. He recognized that his earlier attention was mistakenly more on himself than on his client. He was focused on impressing Bill and looking good in his eyes, overshadowing Bill's needs. He believed that the value he received from 10 minutes of mental preparation far exceeded what he gained from four hours of proposal preparation. It was that short exercise in mindfulness that got him clear on his purpose.

I assured John that it takes both forms of preparation to maximize performance. His dutiful thoroughness gave him insights into what Bill needed now and going forward, and mental rehearsal gave him the confidence to be present and in tune with Bill. Both enabled him to better sense what his client wanted.

Again, the power is in the congruent alignment of all SEMB resources. Mental and physical preparation are equally valuable, complement one another, and produce a multiplying effect of value.

This point is illustrated in the research done on mental rehearsal. In 1943, a study led by psychologist R. A. Vandell set out to determine the effects of mental rehearsal on sports performance. Three groups of basketball players were studied over a period of twenty days. The performance to be measured was in free throw shooting. One group physically practiced and collectively improved their performance by 24%. A second group mentally rehearsed the same activity without physical practice and improved their performance by 23 percent. A third group did neither physical nor mental practice and experienced no improvement. This landmark study, and the research that followed, indicates that combinations of physical and mental practice has been shown to be more efficient than either form of practice alone, with the effect of mental practice being greater when physical practice is added, even in small amounts.[11]

The effectiveness of mental rehearsal has also been tested by healthcare professionals with satisfying results. During my radio interview with Dr. Bernie Siegel MD—an internationally recognized expert in the field of cancer treatment and complementary, holistic medicine and a mind-body connection pioneer—Bernie, as he prefers to be called, stated that he would have patients mentally rehearse the positive outcome of their surgery three times a day, for one week prior to the event. In this way, the brain experienced 21 successful procedures. His patients reported less postoperative pain and bleeding and a more rapid recovery.[12]

Numerous studies on guided imagery substantiate Dr. Bernie's findings. One such controlled study conducted by the Department of Psychology, at University College London, UK, was to test the effects of using mental imagery to "increase patients' feelings of being able to cope with surgical stress."[13] The test involved 26 abdominal surgery patients engaged in mental rehearsal compared with 25 others.

Quoting directly from the abstract, "imagery patients experienced less postoperative pain than did the controls, were less distressed by it, felt that they coped with it better and requested less analgesia."[14]

As you can see, the Been There, Done That mind game supports our aim to build the confidence and resilience needed to stay in the game, create what you want, and enjoy the ride to the greatest degree possible.

Let me emphasize one important point here. A player should make no attempt to duplicate exactly what goes on in the mental exercise. Instead, take that confidence with you and let it free you to be fully present with whomever you are with and whatever you are doing.

Many of my clients speak and perform before groups. They know the importance of both objective practice and mental rehearsal. The practice and preparation can be intense, but when it is time to perform, the most important thing is to be present with your audience. Whether you are performing before an audience of hundreds, thousands, one individual or just you, being fully in the moment is the gift.

John was present, allowing his intuition to guide him. He made the sale because he was well prepared and was present with his client. His proposal remained in the bag. He put his client ahead of his ego. With the circle of generosity principle in mind, he carried the spirit of giving and receiving, provided a valuable service, and in turn both Bill and John benefited in a variety of invaluable ways.

What did John's experience have in common with these athletes, performers, speakers and patients who practice mental rehearsal? In all instances, physical and mental preparation built their confidence, enhanced the richness of their experiences and produced better outcomes.

How to Play with Mental Rehearsal

Mental rehearsal can be played in two ways:

1. By visualizing yourself from your own perspective; or

2. As an observer, as though you were watching a scene in a movie.

With either approach, you will run through the SEMB checklist first, and then feel yourself going through each step of a process. Bring visual images, sounds, feelings, and all objective senses into the imagery to the extent they come easily to you. Don't concern yourself with details when playing mind games; that simply engages the rational mind. We are interested in engaging the imaginative, intuitive mind. Simply relax and enjoy the process.

Since you most often partake in great day game plays first thing in the morning, it is a perfect fit to mentally rehearse your day right after you've laid out your great day game plan. Walking through the anticipated events of the day takes the edge off a busy schedule or enhances a lighter one.

Here's a tip: if you complete your great day game planner the evening before, you can mentally rehearse it then and again in the morning; the more repetitions the better.

With practice, you will flow through your days and accomplish your aims with increased confidence, grace and ease. You will be present and your intuition will guide you.

Today's Great Day Game Planner

It's great to be alive and well! What will make today a fulfilling and satisfying day? Do the "write" thing, and jot down whatever action steps you'd like to take.

....

....

....

....

....

....

....

Highlight three priority actions. These priority actions will take precedence over all others. Then, time permitting, select others from the planner.

TODAY'S GAME PLAY CHECKLIST

Place a checkmark next to each completed game play:

☐ Today's principle card selected and engaged

☐ Fuel-up activities selected from your lightness and energy menu

☐ Intention statement—engaged and refined

☐ Feelings, self-talk, and appreciation entered in captain's logs

☐ Game plan actions entered

☐ Been There, Done That mind game

Day 37—Envision the Outcome: Freeing Your David

Today, you will use the power of your directed attention toward your meaningful intention with a new mind game—Freeing Your David.

> *Rather than thinking about carving a statue out of stone, I picture in my imagination the completed work, in all of its exquisite detail. I then project the picture from my mind into the stone, where it becomes entombed, imprisoned within the stone. My job as the artist is not to carve an image into the stone but to free it from the stone. And this I do with passion because I know the image is already there, alive and breathing. The process is quite simple. That which I desire, I must first imagine. That which I can imagine, I create.*
>
> —Michelangelo

The Wright brothers, although ridiculed at the time, first needed to imagine a flying machine in order to create the convenience of flight that we all enjoy today. Einstein changed our entire view of the universe by imagining he was riding on a beam of light. Michelangelo said that his job as the artist is not to carve anything into the stone but to free it from the stone. He first imagined the infamous David complete in all of its exquisite detail stating, "That which I desire, I must first imagine. That which I can imagine, I create."

In order to bring your intentions into material reality you must first imagine the desired outcome. When composing your meaningful intention statement, you tapped into your soul's yearnings and identified needs. Although, at first, they came from an awareness of what was missing, you shifted that awareness into a strategic framework to meet those needs. This required you to imagine the desired outcome, and understand its value and how you and others will benefit.

In the game, you use your imagination each day when you ask yourself, *What will make today a fulfilling and satisfying day?* The tone and tenor of this question influences your line of thought and where you will direct your attention on any given day. That which you desire, you first imagine and that which you imagine you create. By acting in alignment with that vision, you are bringing it to life.

The fact is, consciously or unconsciously, you have been doing this already. Be it the clothes you chose to wear today or the decision about where you'll buy your lunch tomorrow, you must first imagine it at some level before you can act on it. The game simply brings this natural process to conscious awareness so you can use it dynamically to create what you truly want.

The dynamic principle of fantasy is play, a characteristic also of the child, and as such it appears inconsistent with the principle of serious work. But, without this playing with fantasy no creative work has ever yet come to birth. The debt we owe to the play of imagination is incalculable.

—Carl Jung[15]

We are a gifted species given this creative faculty of imagination and the majority of us don't make use of it consciously. What a waste! We were led to believe that this profound ability was to be left behind with kindergarten childishness as we entered the "real" world of logic and intellect. As Einstein put it, we have created a society that honors the servant (the rational mind) and has forgotten the gift (the intuitive mind). Like my vivid childhood recollection shared earlier of "incorrectly" drawing a snowman in first grade and for those of you who were instructed not to color outside the lines by well-meaning adults, we complied. For many of us, that is when the cramping of our conscious use of the creative imagination began.

We have learned to shut down the intentional use of this natural, God-given resource; however, this sacred gift of conscious creative imagination can be and will be reawakened, developed, and stimulated. Moreover, we can assimilate the use of this natural faculty into our daily lives.

Clearly, conscious imagination was as essential to Michelangelo as his clay and paints. He was not alone with this insight. Carl Jung had a profound appreciation for the imagination and understood its vital role in creative work. Stephen Covey, American educator, author, businessman, and keynote speaker, understood this as well when he said in his landmark work, *The 7 Habits of Highly Effective People*, "We must begin with the end in mind."[16]

Is It Real or Just Your Imagination?

As far as your brain is concerned, there is no distinction between a "real" and an "imagined" event. For example, did you ever have a dream where you were being chased or involved in some other threatening scenario? Did you wake up sweating? Was your heart pounding? Were you still trembling, not certain that you wanted to go back to sleep, or couldn't get back to sleep?

Have you ever awoken from a sweet dream so intoxicating that, when you opened your eyes, you wished you were still there and the glow of the experience remained with you?

They were just dreams, yet they cause physiological responses because the brain does not know the difference between a real and a vividly imagined event.

As you direct attention to freeing your David, that is, seeing your intentional outcomes in all of their exquisite detail, you stimulate your creative mind at a brain frequency close to sleep. The brain will interpret this as a "real" event and like a good short-order cook; it will seek information to actualize this outcome.

The Freeing Your David mind game utilizes another natural faculty that will be elaborated on in a few days: your brain's ability to incubate on an image and illuminate with fresh insights. New ideas may dawn on you right away, or you may have one or more illuminations some time later. This often opens up streams of thought, giving birth to strategies, behaviors, and actions that may not have occurred in the absence of such mindful directing.

Once again, no hard labor. Play this mind game lightly and easily with the audio provided. That is all it takes. Allow yourself the freedom to play with what may feel like childish fantasy; we will give the rational mind its due later within this process. All the insights and epiphanies in the world are of little value unless they are organized and implemented. This cannot be accomplished without the faithful servant's rational talents.

Today's Great Day Game Planner

It's great to be alive and well! What will make today a fulfilling and satisfying day? Do the "write" thing, and jot down whatever action steps you'd like to take.

....

....

....

....

....

....

....

Highlight three priority actions. These priority actions will take precedence over all others. Then, time permitting, select others from the planner.

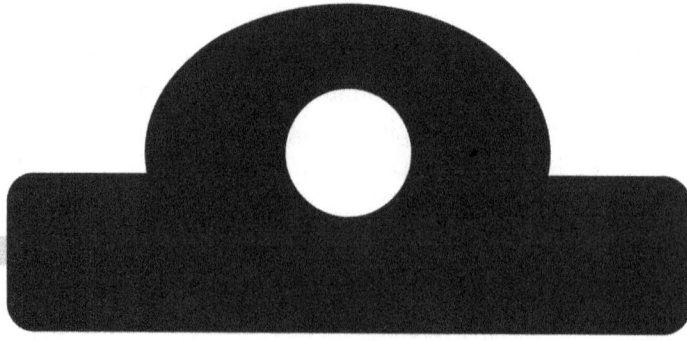

TODAY'S GAME PLAY CHECKLIST

Place a checkmark next to each completed game play:

☐ Today's principle card selected and engaged

☐ Fuel-up activities selected from your lightness and energy menu

☐ Intention statement—engaged and refined

☐ Feelings, self-talk, and appreciation entered in captain's logs

☐ Game plan actions entered

☐ Freeing Your David mind game played

Day 38—Images and the Power of Metaphor

You've learned how your brain translates all thoughts into images and, like a good short-order cook, it attracts and gathers information, and fills your order based on wherever your attention is and the meaning you are assigning to the object of your attention.

For example, you can look out the window on a rainy day with your attention on the weather. In this case, the weather is the object of your attention. The meaning you assign to a rainy day may be that it is dreary and depressing, or mellow and refreshing. You may be grateful for the rain because it has been dry and your lawn and garden thirst for water, or it is interrupting your plans for an outdoor event. The meaning you assign to the rainy day creates an image and, through association, triggers emotion and other related thoughts and will impact your attitude, perspective, and behavior.

On Day 18, you revised your intention statement by rephrasing the language you used to inform your "cook" of what you want from the menu of possibilities rather than what you don't want. The examples were related to health, career, finance, and relationships. Rather than focusing on losing weight, ridding yourself of a dreadful job, getting out of debt, and combating loneliness, I recommended focusing on health and wellness, a satisfying career, financial ease, and rich relationships. Although the objects of attention are the same, based on the meanings assigned, different images are generated, and different emotions are triggered along with different associated thoughts—all of which impact your attitude, perspective, and behavior.

As subtle as all of this may seem, a shift in perspective and attitude literally changes your life. We have all heard, understand, and most likely agree that an attitude of gratitude makes sense. The tricky piece is putting it into practice, and this can only be done through practice.

That's why it's a 90-Day Game! Any musician will tell you that practice is essential to gain mastery of an instrument, so repetition is the key. True, the musician requires a level of discipline to pick up the instrument, but the instrument, being a physical object, makes it easy to engage once the choice is made. The abstract nature of things, like perspective and attitude, makes it more challenging to practice. It is the attitudes you hold in the present moment that shape your future. Gratefully, the game is in essence your instrument for this mastery.

Like taking a train uptown or downtown, the meanings you assign to the objects of your attention put you on the track either toward or away from where you choose to go.

Today, we develop this further by focusing on how images stimulate emotions and impact how you feel. With this understanding, you will offer your short-order cook a more refined recipe from which your chef will select the finest ingredients suited to your own unique taste.

Illusions of Mind That Attract and Gather Energy

Whether it is the external environment that captures your attention or the command you've developed to direct it, mental images are a product of where your attention lies. How you think and feel about the object of your attention and the language you use to describe it shape your perspective and attitude, and, in turn, the mental images sent to your short-order cook. Once the order has been placed, the brain seeks and sorts information in alignment with those images aiming to actualize it into material reality.

In the IMAGE acronym (Illusions of Mind That Attract and Gather Energy), images are illusions in the sense that, although they appear to be "real," they can be quite deceiving. They are a reflection of the meanings we are assigning to them at any given moment and therefore only one of many possible perceived realities.

As we explore emotion and thought more deeply in the days to come, you will discover how flexible your perception of reality is, and how the power of directed attention and the generation of emotionally stimulating images influence what you create.

Like the synchronicity and meaningful coincidences experienced when in the process of shopping for a new home or car (the Blue Chevy Theory), it is the emotional stimulation that has the most profound impression and impact. Any good car salesman knows that the feel of the wheel and the smell of the leather will stimulate your urge to buy.

Since the brain does not know the difference between an actual experience and a vividly imagined one, generating emotionally stimulating images intentionally, at a highly suggestible state, place them front and center on your mental radar. Metaphor is a particularly powerful form of imagery as it bypasses analytic thought and significantly impacts emotion.

Garden Mind Games

It is time to introduce you to a series of playful, pleasurable, and potent mind games, applying the power of metaphor, each of which is designed to flood your mental radar with rich imagery rife with elevating emotion at a deeper level of consciousness.

The first of three garden mind games is called Planting the Seed; the other two, Weed and Feed and Reaping the Harvest, will soon follow. You will be guided through each garden mind game with the audio provided. Like all mind games—simple yet profound—the less effort, the more effective.

Persephone's Story

Persephone is a game player who made great use of the garden mind games and, with her own creative style, enjoyed both the process and fulfilling results. Persephone writes:

> "My garden is a real garden that actually exists in a nature preserve near where I live. It's a butterfly garden that overlooks the Hudson River with paths that run through it and a really nice bench that looks out to the Palisades. Working with John, we came up with the idea of my using the garden in daily meditations for planting a seed of intention around getting a better job.

"I would sit in my home office on the couch and, in my mind's eye, I would stroll through the paths and take in the beautiful flowers and butterflies until I came to a patch of the garden that was overgrown and not yet planted. I imagined myself clearing it and planting a seed to grow more gratifying work—a job that fit my interests, skills, and passions better than the one I was in. In daily meditations, I would go back to this part of the garden and water the seed. I would put some fertilizer into the earth in the form of envisioning what culture I work well in, what skills I like using, what pay I wanted to make, and what type of boss I worked well with. I'd keep going back, sometimes sitting on the bench, and every day my vision of what I was looking for would expand.

"It took a month or so of doing these garden meditations, until one day I was with a colleague and she mentioned a new, exciting project she was starting that sounded quite interesting to me. I asked if we could meet and talk about it and, as she described the project, I pinched myself because it was made just for me. I got hired easily as the project coordinator, and it was the best work I've ever had.

"I know that I manifested it in the butterfly garden in my mind … It's such a powerful tool, but I had to nourish my intention with my heart's desires, believe that I deserved to have them, and then my own imagination and childlike delight manifested the wonderful work."

Like Persephone, let go of your old-school conditioning to do it just right. This is not a test, and no grades will be issued. There is no wrong way. Let go of the idea that you need to see vivid, mental pictures for this to be effective. Simply enter the experience.

We all have brain preferences—some visual, some auditory, and others more "feeling" oriented. Although you will experience all of them to some degree, most will naturally lean toward one or two of these more dominantly. Therefore, some players will form strong mental pictures, others will focus on a crisp soundtrack, and others will be deeply moved by the experience. With continued practice and play, you will amplify all of them to greater and greater degrees.

Your Perfect Blueprint

Rather than struggling to become all you can be, our aim is for you to uncover the perfect blueprint you already are. Your soul has that blueprint. Unlike our mortal experiences in the physical world, your soul remains unblemished and free from early childhood influences and societal expectations. Let it guide you back home. Like seeds within nature, your seed of intention is naturally coded with your soul's blueprint and all that's required to bloom into its innate splendor.

With this in mind, engage the exercise with your focus on the symbolic image of this seed rather than on your literal intention. Activate the sacred gift of your imagination—the gift that was shut down as childish folly. Bring back its power and freedom, its lightness and amusement, as you plant this symbolic seed into the fresh fertile soil of your inner conscious mind.

Know that you will revisit this incredible garden to nurture it with loving care. You will water and fertilize it with your attention and revel in all stages of its growth: the initial sprouts, the blossoms, and the magnificence of its strength as it becomes a vibrant tree, bearing delicious, sweet, ripe fruit.

Beyond this exercise, allow yourself to be open and receptive to insights as they dawn on you; then, by all means, take practical action. No struggling is required. Like your soul's innate wisdom, you also came equipped with the natural talents and strengths needed to fulfill your purpose.

Considering that the Planting the Seed mind game takes roughly 18 minutes, you will play with it tomorrow. Or, time permitting, you can go there now. It's your choice!

Today's Great Day Game Planner

It's great to be alive and well! What will make today a fulfilling and satisfying day? Do the "write" thing, and jot down whatever action steps you'd like to take.

....

....

....

....

....

....

....

Highlight three priority actions. These priority actions will take precedence over all others. Then, time permitting, select others from the planner.

TODAY'S GAME PLAY CHECKLIST

Place a checkmark next to each completed game play:

☐   Today's principle card selected and engaged

☐   Fuel-up activities selected from your lightness and energy menu

☐   Intention statement—engaged and refined

☐   Feelings, self-talk, and appreciation entered in captain's logs

☐   Game plan actions entered

☐   Select and play a mind game today:

     ○   Abundant Mind

     ○   Been There, Done That

     ○   Freeing Your David

Day 39—Planting the Seed Mind Game

Today, you will be guided through an enjoyably relaxing and uplifting metaphoric mind game. Planting the Seed mind game takes just under 18 minutes.

This mind game will begin with entering a quiet, suggestible state by closing your eyes, taking a few deep breaths, and counting down from 10 to 1. You will then project yourself mentally to the center of your living room. If you have a favorite room that you enjoy being in, such as a family room or game room, feel free to begin there. From the center of this room, you will face the largest wall, create a door on that wall, open, and enter it.

You will proceed down a spiral staircase and through a hallway. At the end of this hallway, you will remove your shoes and enter another room, which is marked with a sign labeled "Your Inner Conscious Mind." As you enter this brightly illuminated room, you'll be warmly greeted and handed a staff, which you will graciously accept, and then move further into the room.

This room has a number of tables covered with white linen. You will select one. On the table before you, there will be a number of items resting on it. These will be used in the next garden mind game entitled the Weed and Feed mind game.

Further in front of you, there is a little stage, similar to a puppet show stage. It has a white screen that soon will have the image of a beautiful garden. You will step into the scene and find yourself within this exquisite garden. You'll enjoy the delicious aroma of countless flowers, a comfortable breeze, a warm caress of the sun, and much more. It is here where you will plant your seed of intention deep within your inner conscious mind.

Now run the audio, open up your imagination, and enjoy!

Today's Great Day Game Planner

It's great to be alive and well! What will make today a fulfilling and satisfying day? Do the "write" thing, and jot down whatever action steps you'd like to take.

....

....

....

....

....

....

....

Highlight three priority actions. These priority actions will take precedence over all others. Then, time permitting, select others from the planner.

TODAY'S GAME PLAY CHECKLIST

Place a checkmark next to each completed game play:

☐ Today's principle card selected and engaged

☐ Fuel-up activities selected from your lightness and energy menu

☐ Intention statement—engaged and refined

☐ Feelings, self-talk, and appreciation entered in captain's logs

☐ Game plan actions entered

☐ Planting The Seed mind game played

Day 40—Reminders and Tips of the Week

Make It Personal

> *The soul never thinks without a picture.*
>
> —Aristotle[17]

The design of mind games is intentionally simple, and you can easily begin to invent your own. As a budding expert at alert witnessing, you'll begin noticing metaphors within your self-talk. They are reflections of your beliefs. For example:

- *This is an uphill battle.*
- *I'm hitting a wall.*
- *I'm feeling weighed down.*

Metaphors are filled with meaning. Once an image is mentally created, you can reshape it, expand it, and play with it. Remember: Images are not necessarily "pictures." Images described as you speak, within your internal dialogue and through feelings, are all valid forms of imaging.

When noticed, enter a mind-game state and reshape the image:

- *I am reaching the top of the hill* or *I am flowing downhill* versus *This is an uphill battle.*
- *I am going around, over, or breaking through the wall* versus *I'm hitting a wall.*
- *I am dumping the excess baggage from my hot-air balloon, sailing up above the clouds, and feeling light* versus *I'm feeling weighed down.*

At times, you'll notice joy-filled metaphors. When you do, immerse your mind with those images, such as:

- *I feel like I'm floating on air.*
- *The fog has lifted.*
- *I'm on top of the world.*

Images influence attitude and perspective, and impact beliefs and behavior. Use your metaphoric blocks to build an expansive stairway to a higher view and way of thinking. Expect mood shifts and insights to follow.

Mental Mentors

How would you like to get advice from the people you admire and respect the most, whenever you want it? People don't pray to clay statues; the statue is a focal point mentally created to communicate their prayers to a higher power. In Napoleon Hill's most famous work, *Think and Grow Rich* (1937), he had his cabinet members, Silva Method graduates have their counselors, and I have a bust of Einstein in my office. Statues, cabinet members, counselors, and my Einstein bust are all mental representations born of the imagination. They are illusions of mind that attract and gather energy, and we use that energy to access information.

I imagine asking my buddy Al (as I affectionately refer to Albert Einstein, meaning no disrespect) questions, seeking his guidance. Am I channeling Einstein? I don't think so. Hmm … what would Al say? One thing's for sure: It does help me think differently. The sacred gift of imagination enables you to create this dynamic. It's fun and quite effective.

Half-Time Check-In

As we approach the midpoint of the game, it is a great time for a self-assessment—not self-judgment but an objective assessment for bringing your game to an optimally satisfying level. So ask yourself:

- *Are you keeping the principle cards in a handy place, making time to enjoy life, and taking breaks?* If not, you may be carrying a belief that you have too much to do and no time to do it. If so, revisit your lightness and energy menu, refresh yourself, and you'll see how the time invested returns to you in the form of greater efficiency. If you don't allow yourself to enjoy life now, when will you?

- *Have you been highlighting three priority actions? Are they getting done consistently?* If not, they may need to be broken down into smaller steps. Position yourself to succeed. Also, be certain to have reasonable expectations. Chances are that you are getting things done, so acknowledge your progress.

- *Are you keeping your intention statement dynamic?* Add recent successes from your appreciation log or pop in a meaningful metaphor.

- *Speaking of logs, are you making entries often?* They will be most useful in the second half of the game.

Feedback Please

Help us continue our quest to make this process increasingly effective:

- How is your game experience going?
- Are you making progress?
- Are you having greater clarity, confidence, and enthusiasm about your plans?
- Have you already created what you came to the game for?
- Have you shifted to a deeper or different intention altogether?

Report successes, challenges, satisfactions, and frustrations. We see them all as valuable information! Send your comments to Team@90DayGame.com.

Today's Great Day Game Planner
It's great to be alive and well! What will make today a fulfilling and satisfying day? Do the "write" thing, and jot down whatever action steps you'd like to take. .... Highlight three priority actions. These priority actions will take precedence over all others. Then, time permitting, select others from the planner.

TODAY'S GAME PLAY CHECKLIST

Place a checkmark next to each completed game play:

☐ Today's principle card selected and engaged

☐ Fuel-up activities selected from your lightness and energy menu

☐ Intention statement—engaged and refined

☐ Feelings, self-talk, and appreciation entered in captain's logs

☐ Game plan actions entered

☐ Select and play a mind game today:

○ Abundant Mind

○ Been There, Done That

○ Freeing Your David

Days 41 and 42—Free Day Reminder

PART V

Navigating Your Great Adventure

Navigate Your Intention with a Cool Head and a Warm Heart

Day 43—Get Your OARs in the Water

Did you ever go on the water with a friend in a cabin cruiser or a motorboat? Did your friend ever offer you the opportunity to steer it? Perhaps you agreed, but with some reservation as you really were quite unfamiliar with it. At times, the boat may have seemed to have a mind of its own and, even as you turned the wheel, it did not respond as you expected. There were instruments near the wheel, but you had no idea how to read them. The buoys designed to keep you on course and clear of obstacles felt more like obstacles themselves, which you desperately wanted to avoid hitting.

Your friend, however, is quite familiar with the boat's equipment, knows how to read the onboard instruments and the guidance information the buoys provide, and he understands how the little ship responds to the control inputs of the wheel. His familiarity makes the journey rather effortless, yet even the ship's captain must remain alert to unexpected weather and obstacles while reveling along the journey.

Your friend comes prepared for the trip, knowing his chosen destination. He has his charts, has plotted his course, and got a full weather briefing. He directs his attention out to and beyond the buoys, and scans his charts and onboard instruments.

You come prepared for your trip too. You know what you have chosen to create, and you are directing you attention toward desirable, intentional outcomes. You brief yourself with the great day game plays and remain on course with your great day game planner. The quality of the ride will have a lot to do with how skillfully you navigate. Like the buoys, your emotions and self-talk can be viewed as obstacles or as valuable guidance information.

Today, we'll hop into a paddle boat and get a little training to buoy (sorry—couldn't help myself) your confidence and skillfully navigate your intentions with a cool head and a warm heart.

Imagine yourself in a lake or flowing down a stream. You can enjoy the gentle swaying in the lake and simply relax, or you may want to paddle across to gain a different view. In the case of the stream, you can allow the currents to guide you, but you can also use your oars to direct your course to avoid certain obstacles or steer toward a preferred path.

In the game, you will use a different set of oars to guide your course and leverage your challenges in ways that keep you and your intention buoyant.

OAR

OAR is an acronym for a three-step process: (1) observe; (2) appraise; and (3) respond. Like the sailor or the pilot who has gone adrift, the sooner he responds, the easier it is to recapture his course. He first needs to *observe* that he has drifted, *appraise* the situation to regain his orientation, and then employ the best means to *respond* with an efficient course correction.

Today, we will focus our attention on the O—observe—and the others will follow in a few days.

The "O" in OAR—Observe: Becoming the Alert Witness

The qualities of alert witnessing include attentiveness and compassionate self-observation of our moods and self-talk.

The word "alert" emphasizes prompt attentiveness of your state. This self-observation is a loving act, free of judgment. Entertain your moods with a sense of amusement, with an "Oh, isn't that interesting?" attitude, and welcome an occasional chuckle when conjangled. It will lighten things up!

Witness your state as though you are a third party who is observing with a loving, supportive, and light attitude, the way you would with a friend or loved one. The practice of alert witnessing helps us recognize the ever-changing nature of our moods and how we react and respond to them.

It is imperative that we do not overinvest in any mood but rather take stock in the valuable information that all moods, emotions, and thoughts offer. All moods, when observed with prompt, compassionate amusement, will lead you to uncover needs—some of which you'll gratefully acknowledge as being met, and others that will be met through the valuable guidance information alert witnessing provides.

Good versus Bad

As you continue to direct your attention toward your intention mostly every day, and engage it mindfully, you will certainly experience a variety of emotional reactions and responses, which will be accompanied by a stream of inner dialogue. Depending on your mood, the emotions that are stimulated will either be aligned or misaligned with your intention.

Naturally, we want emotions and thoughts to favor our intention and, when they do, we are conditioned to judge them as "good." When our emotional reactions and thoughts appear to be misaligned, we are quick to judge them as "bad." This inclination to stamp labels on moods can cause us to miss valuable guidance information and cues, which can serve our intention or possibly something even better.

These either/or, good/bad, happy/sad judgments are conditioned reflexes and quite normal for mere mortals. It is how most of the world navigates life. Our aim is to be joyfully abnormal. We want to break this either/or type of thinking and view things from a higher vista in order to set an environment where we can appraise rather than judge our emotional state. This is at the heart of our work in alert witnessing.

Our aim is to cultivate an ability to notice our reactions and, as the old Coke commercials said, take a pause that refreshes. Then we are positioned to mindfully respond in a way that serves our intention. This pause refreshes our mental screen. We take the witness position, detach from it, and are amused by it with the aim to see it all as valuable guidance information. It is all grist for our creative, intentional mill. When we do this, we can utilize our emotions rather than be used by them.

Game players often come to the game with an idea of what they want and, as they learn to engage and build confidence in their emotional guidance system, they often exchange their game objective for a more meaningful one.

Karen came to the game to enjoy growing her network marketing business. As she gave herself permission to engage her emotions, she exchanged her intention for a deeper one: to become a mom. She remained receptive to her emotional signals and soon recognized that this was not the time, as the relationship with her husband was on a fast track to dissolution. As she continued to remain open and receptive to her emotional signals, Karen once again exchanged her intention to recreate her relationship with her husband. They have been enjoying their lives together for years now and, as of this writing, Karen and her husband are expecting their first child.

Deeper emotions may be uncomfortable as they resonate with needs that are not yet met. It is the engagement of these emotions that will lead us to discover significant needs that may be conscious, or currently unconscious, and offer us the opportunity to get those needs met.

Like the ship's captain who is confidently familiar with his onboard guidance systems, tomorrow you will become familiar with your own internal guidance resources.

Today's Great Day Game Planner

It's great to be alive and well! What will make today a fulfilling and satisfying day? Do the "write" thing, and jot down whatever action steps you'd like to take.

....

....

....

....

....

....

....

Highlight three priority actions. These priority actions will take precedence over all others. Then, time permitting, select others from the planner.

TODAY'S GAME PLAY CHECKLIST

Place a checkmark next to each completed game play:

☐ Today's principle card selected and engaged

☐ Fuel-up activities selected from your lightness and energy menu

☐ Intention statement—engaged and refined

☐ Feelings, self-talk, and appreciation entered in captain's logs

☐ Game plan actions entered

☐ Select and play a mind game today:

    ○ Abundant Mind

    ○ Been There, Done That

    ○ Freeing Your David

Day 44—Meet the Crew

Libby, Amy, and Tex

Both a ship's captain and an aircraft pilot need to be familiar with their onboard guidance systems, and a lack of familiarity with them is risky business. Misinterpretations can lead them astray and increase tension, compromising safety. You have a rather sophisticated set of guidance equipment as well. Your familiarity with it, and your ability to interpret its signals accurately, will impact your great adventure. By refining your navigation skills, you will realize your intentions and enjoy the trip along the way.

Captains and pilots have something you don't have: manuals and operating handbooks. So let's give you one, free of intricacy and very practical. Your guidance system is made up of emotions and thoughts. Since these are rather abstract, we are going to give these traits personalities, making them easy to understand. Carrying forward the journey metaphor, they will be your crew members who will support you along your voyage.

Like all of us, our cast of characters has unique abilities and, like any good team, they bring their strengths together to support each other. Please note that their names are derived from various parts of the brain, and no gender implications are intended whatsoever.

Meet Libby, who represents the emotional center—an area of the brain referred to as the "limbic system." Her role in the game is to remain receptive to the vast volume of valuable guidance information your wide range of emotions offers. It is this emotional guidance information that will make it possible for you to identify and meet your soul's yearnings, personal needs, and increase awareness of your values.

Next is Amy, who represents the amygdala and serves a vitally essential and honorable role to protect us from danger. She is, however, quite capable of overreacting and can sometimes pull the fire alarm when someone just strikes a stick match. Amy's overly reactive nature can be spurred on by tension, stress, fear, doubt, worry, and confusion, to name just a few of her common triggers. These triggers often cause us to overidentify with perceived threats.

Libby and Amy have a dear friend, Tex. He is the storyteller. His name is derived from the neocortex. Like Spock from *Star Trek*, Tex is logical and responds rationally. Tex plays the role of that short-order cook we've been referring to. He makes no judgments or assessments as he builds his rational cases. Tex simply fills the order for what we want and, just as skillfully, will serve up what we don't want based on whatever information is presented to him. In order to function in a way that serves our best interests, Libby, Amy, and Tex need to hold hands and remain connected.

Their harmonious relationship is critical for integrating thought and emotions. Agitated emotions cause static and disrupt neural connections, and therefore we cannot "think straight" when we are emotionally upset. When someone says that they can't think straight, it's not just an expression for how they feel; it is literally the result of neural disconnections within the brain when highly stressed. Left in an emotional quagmire, Libby and Amy's connection with Tex is interrupted. It is as though Tex, sensing imminent danger, has headed for the hills but, of course, Tex is unemotional. He is in fact present, but Amy's and Libby's overwhelming emotional fog makes it appear to them that he has disappeared. Until that fog clears, Tex is nowhere to be found.

This state of confusion can lead to false assumptions and judgments and cause us to believe that we are incompetent, incapable, and, at times, may cause concern that something is seriously wrong with us.

Through alert witnessing, we respond promptly and compassionately. We soothe Amy before she sees the need to pull the emergency cord. Taking action promptly will promote the relaxation and ease needed to integrate neural circuitry, maintain connection with Tex (or reconnection, as the case may be), and regain healthy functioning roles of all crew members. Like friends joining hands, sustained neural circuitry leads to comfort, possibility thinking, and practical action. We remain confident, engage our strengths, and move forward on our meaningful intentions for the benefits of all.

The game plays have been preparing you for this new and invaluable life skill. The soulful tones of the principles, incorporating enjoyable activities into our day, relaxation techniques, uplifting messages of grateful appreciation, successes from the mind games, and the confidence of the great day game plans all serve to build emotional resilience, which aids you in developing the invaluable skill of alert, compassionate, and amused witnessing.

Who's the Captain?

As you navigate your great adventure, you will have an increasing appreciation for your natural, inborn guidance system. You'll be pleased to have Libby on board, reporting on the status of needs—some which are being met and some which are yet to be met. You'll be grateful for Amy's guidance, alerting the team of potential danger, and keeping the crew from becoming complacent. Tex will bolster your confidence with rational stories, which will translate into a powerful belief structure.

It's time to select your captain. Who will it be?

How about Libby? She is sensitive to stimuli from both the environment around us and within us. She has the capacity for a wide range of emotional input, yet we recognize that the emotions she senses come up spontaneously. She alone does not have the capacity to assign them useful meanings.

Although we appreciate Amy's commitment and contribution to protecting us from danger, her inclination to occasionally overreact and push the panic button may not make her the best candidate to lead the team.

Okay, perhaps Tex is the one. Like Spock from *Star Trek*, he is rational. After all, he does not react emotionally, and his ability to take in data and organize it for implementation is outstanding. But, in the absence of meaning, he'll build a rational case for whatever is presented to him. Tex is that short-order cook we talk about. He's a good order taker, but he'll build a rational case for just about any side of any story. Do we really want our leader to go invisible when times are tough? We know, through no fault of his own, that Tex is nowhere to be found in the midst of Libby's and Amy's agitated fog. Our leader needs to be visible and present in the most challenging of times.

Although these team players have their own valuable skills, and we honor their unique abilities, they—like everyone—cannot be all things to all people. They are a talented team, but they need to be guided to work together efficiently.

That is where you come in:

- You are the director of this cast of characters.
- You are the choice maker.
- You are the one who will ultimately assign meanings to Libby's emotions.
- You are the one who will present the data Tex will use to organize and plan.
- You will be the one who chooses to take action or not.

So how will you, as captain, lead your team? There is one more crew member needed aboard. As a matter of fact, you've been receiving its guidance throughout this game. It is your soul. Together, your ongoing conversation has created a dynamically evolving intention statement. You are continually refining and aligning it with your sense of purpose.

Your intention is filled with the ultimate ingredient that gives meaning to Libby's spontaneous emotions and useful data for Tex's thoughts. It is invisible, but we all know of its presence. It is a pre-sense. We know it before thinking and feeling. We'll never see it under a microscope, but we sense it at all levels. It is the only true emotion, and you know intuitively and objectively what that is. Meaningful intentions are filled with it. It is the source of our passion and purpose, and what inspires us to consider others in our plans as well as ourselves. Yes, you know: It is love.

Although Tex only intellectually understands it, he is able to build a rational case for its validity within the context of creating. Although at times it can escape her awareness, Libby intuitively senses it. Your intention is that conversation with your soul, and only you have the power to direct your attention toward it. The choice to do so is solely in your command.

- You are the one who will leverage each team player's strengths.
- You are the captain of the crew.
- You are the one who assigns meanings to your emotions in ways that serve your soul's urges.
- You are the one who assigns meaning to your thoughts that serve your intention.

What Is This Thing We Call "Soul"?

We've explained who Libby, Amy, and Tex are. Then what is—or who is—this soul you are in conversation with and receiving guidance from? Here's another acronym for your consideration: SOUL—the Source of Unconditional Love. This is the meaning I chose to assign to soul. For me, the state of unconditional love is the most powerful resource we have. To me, my soul is like a cord to the mainframe, to the source of creation itself; the source of all knowledge, the only resource that can inform me of my purpose here and how I am divinely designed to live it; the force that animates my entire being. I am intimately connected with it.

For some, their soul is their connection to God, with the Creator of all that is; for others, it is their link with the universe or their bond with Mother Nature or their higher self. What meaning do you choose to assign to "it"? That is all that matters.

In the absence of a focal point of attention, you are all over the map, and your ability to assign meanings to your emotions and thoughts is equally scattered. This is where the power of intent shines, and it is the light of love that illuminates it. It is your choice if you choose to exercise this power or not.

Mood Elevators

This is not a discussion in pharmacology but more playful language to set up the next refinement to your great day game planner. Like elevators, our moods go up and down. When experiencing deeper moods, such as fears, doubts, and worries, it "feels" as though life will be like that forever. With far less intensity, lighter moods are enjoyed but don't carry the drama of the deeper moods and, like many enjoyable things, it is easy to take pleasant states for granted. Therefore, between Amy's protective nature of being on alert to danger and the feeling that this state is going to last forever, these deeper moods get far more attention than the lighter ones.

With daily observation, most players discover that they have lighter, more empowering, and more energetic days than they ever realized before.

Today, we add a simple mood tracker to the great day game planner to increase awareness of your state of being. It's a graphic with columns, which resembles elevator shafts, where you will objectively observe and assess three states: emotion, self-talk, and energy. Our only interest right now is to be an alert witness and begin noticing patterns with curiosity and amusement. As you observe your state, keep in mind that it is all valuable guidance information, which you will use to meet your needs, upgrade your beliefs, energize your life, and create what you truly want.

As we go forward, we will engage emotion and self-talk in empowering ways that serve your intention and enhance the quality of your life.

Today's Great Day Game Planner

It's great to be alive and well! What will make today a fulfilling and satisfying day? Do the "write" thing, and jot down whatever action steps you'd like to take.

....

....

....

....

....

....

....

Highlight three priority actions. These priority actions will take precedence over all others. Then, time permitting, select others from the planner.

Mood Elevators

Draw a line or shade in each of the mood elevators to reflect your state of being in the moment.

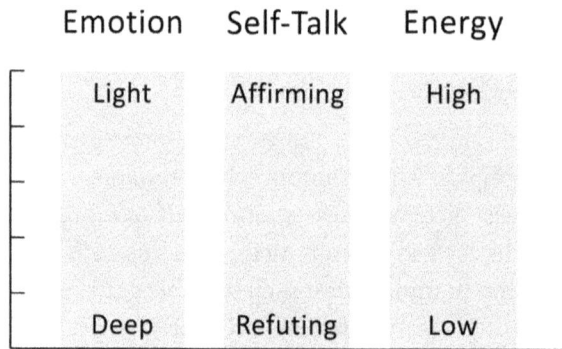

Emotion	Self-Talk	Energy
Light	Affirming	High
Deep	Refuting	Low

TODAY'S GAME PLAY CHECKLIST

Place a checkmark next to each completed game play :

☐ Today's principle card selected and engaged

☐ Fuel-up activities selected from your lightness and energy menu

☐ Intention statement—engaged and refined

☐ Feelings, self-talk, and appreciation entered in captain's logs

☐ Game plan actions entered

☐ Your state of being on the mood elevators assessed

☐ Select and play a mind game today:

　○ Abundant Mind

　○ Been There, Done That

　○ Freeing Your David

Day 45—Paddling to Rumi's Guest House

The "A" in OAR—Appraise: Welcoming Emotion as Valuable Guidance Information

When you touch a hot stove, the nerves in your hand signal pain. You might judge the discomfort as "bad" but, in reflection, you may be grateful for that pain as it protected you and your hand from further damage. You observed the pain, appraised it as a call for attention, and responded by taking your hand off the stove.

Inner states of mind protect us in a similar way. We often label some of our thoughts and emotions as "negative" but, when understood, like the discomfort when touching the stove, we will observe them and appraise them as a divine call for attention. We will learn to respond to that valuable guidance information in ways that support us in realizing our intentions, and enjoy the ride along the way all the more.

Just as the body signals with pain to alert us to an ailment that needs attending, the soul is relentless. You can try to ignore, fight, or flee its messages, but the soul will persist because it has needs that only, when met, will allow you to be who you were designed to be.

These messages come first in a whisper, then a scream, then a shove on the shoulder, and ultimately a whack with a frying pan. Know that the soul will make its presence known. Better to yield, listen, and understand its yearnings. It is how you will get your deepest needs met.

You are now tracking your emotions, self-talk, and energy on the mood elevators and making entries in the captain's logs. The aim is to develop the art of alert witnessing by dispassionately observing your states with a spirit of curiosity and amusement, free of judgment, knowing that all you observe is valuable guidance information—more grist for your creation mill.

We will now take the second step in the continuum of Observe, Appraise and Respond.

Appraise

Although Libby (the limbic brain) and Tex (the neocortex) are intimately interconnected, we will respect their unique personalities and communicate with them accordingly, with Libby on an emotional level and with Tex on an intellectual level.

We will begin with our friend Libby through another engaging metaphor, *The Guest House,* by Jalāl ad-Dīn Muhammad Rūmī, popularly known as Rumi, a 13th-century Persian poet, theologian, and Sufi mystic. This poem has been translated into English by Coleman Barks:

The Guest House

This being human is a guest house.
Every morning a new arrival.
A joy, a depression, a meanness,
some momentary awareness comes
as an unexpected visitor.
Welcome and entertain them all!
Even if they are a crowd of sorrows,
who violently sweep your house
empty of its furniture,
still, treat each guest honorably.
He may be clearing you out
for some new delight.
The dark thought, the shame, the malice.
meet them at the door laughing and invite them in.
Be grateful for whatever comes.
because each has been sent
as a guide from beyond.[18]

The Rumi Welcome

In our conditioned view of emotion, we use labels, categorizing some as good (positive) and others as bad (negative). In our work together, we drop these labels as our game player Karen did, and instead welcome and honor all of our emotions and appreciate them as valuable guidance information.

… treat each guest honorably.
He may be clearing you out
for some new delight.

Emotions are not a design flaw by God or Mother Nature but a divine guidance system to be honored and appreciated. This is how your soul communicates its guidance to you with the primary intention of identifying and meeting your deepest needs.

Emotions are spontaneous; we do not control them. As Rumi put it,

A joy, a depression, a meanness,
some momentary awareness comes
as an unexpected visitor.

Yes, they come up quite unexpectedly.

Our aim is to first observe them—not judge, label, fight, or flee from them. Then, we appraise them, seeking their value, and respond to them in productive and highly beneficial ways.

Because of the spontaneous nature of emotions, they are not within your control, but you do have command over how you interpret, appraise, value, and make use of them. Emotions are the raw, spontaneous reactions to stimuli, and feelings are the meaning we assign to those emotions.

Emotions are not to be feared nor fought, but welcomed and embraced with a flavor of amusement, lightness, and rich opportunity.

The dark thought, the shame, the malice.
meet them at the door laughing and invite them in.

Honor emotions as a divine call for attention, and appreciate them as valuable guidance information. They will lead you to getting your deepest needs met. Within every emotion lies great opportunity.

When you choose this perspective, an astounding shift in psychology occurs. With each new "visitor," rather than slamming the door or attacking the invader out of fear, you honor and welcome your emotions intuitively, knowing that they serve a meaningful purpose.

Welcome and entertain them all!
... each has been sent
as a guide from beyond.

When we cease our overidentification with emotions, and instead see them as helpful guides, an amazing thing happens. Fear collapses into honor, appreciation, and gratitude.

Be grateful for whatever comes.

A Fresh Perspective

This approach is not one supported by the social hypnosis. Society is accustomed to the blame-and-shame game and, like a frightened tribe, we come together and commiserate with our miseries. As subtle as the daily complaints of it being too cold, too hot, too rainy, or too dry are, and as attractive as the sympathetic attention we may get from a friend or family member for our sadness or unfortunate circumstances, this is not a formula for growth, manifestation, or a joyful life.

The game player has a new perspective outside of this hypnosis, accepts and acknowledges that there are peaks and valleys within the game of life, and uses the peaks to see the broad vista of opportunity present and the valleys to see the next opportunity perched on the peak before them.

Although this perspective makes perfect sense to our rational friend Tex, and as attractive as it is to Libby, it takes dedication to wake up from our conditioned reactiveness. Yes, it is challenging, and all great games have challenges. Your dedication to reconditioning your automatic reactions into conscious responses offers you a lifetime of ongoing rewards. All of the great day game plays and practices have been and will continue to prepare you for having this grand new command of your life.

Preparing for Our Guest House Visit

> *Rather than trying to stop your reactions, why not let them play out? Then, use them to get to know yourself a lot better.*
>
> —Thomas J. Leonard, founder of Coach University[19]

Let's review what we have so far from our OAR framework:

- **Observe:** Your alert witnessing is prompt, attentive, and compassionate and holds a flavor of curiosity and amusement. When you are reactive, you may initially feel that you have failed at this game objective, and nothing is further from the truth. You are not a machine with an automatic cutoff switch from your emotional reactions. You will have them. As Thomas Leonard suggests, let them play out and learn from them by engaging them in reflection. In so doing, you process the emotion, disarm it by learning from it, discover how to respond to similar situations down the road, and are freed from the trigger of repetitive reactiveness.

- **Appraise:** In reflection, you will replay Amy's alarming reaction together with Libby and Tex. You and your crew members will reflect on the emotion and appraise its value. We call this practice "Rumi-nating." Distinct from ruminating, where one compulsively focuses on the symptoms of their distress, Rumi-nating celebrates our divine design. We take Rumi's perspective and attitude, welcome and engage our emotions, and let them inform and guide us to meet our deepest needs and honor our most cherished values.

You will ask:

- What is weighing down Libby's spirits?
- Is Amy feeling threatened? If so, what is the perceived danger triggering Amy's protectiveness?
- What is the feeling (that is, the meaning that the crew is assigning to this emotion)?
- What need is not being met and/or what value is being violated?
- What valuable guidance information can the team gather from this emotion?
- How will you make use of this valuable guidance information in a way that meets your needs, honors your values, and serves your meaningful intention?
- How has this emotional reaction become a gift to the team?

- Having Rumi-nated, what emotion is now present, and what is the feeling/meaning you choose to assign to it?

- What few words can I jot down to express appreciation for this mood's arrival?

In the end, you and your team celebrate the value of both the emotion and the fresh appraisals derived from Rumi-nating.

Tomorrow, we will revisit with Carl. He has something to Rumi-nate on, and his Rumi-nating will be instructive for your personal use of this core practice.

Today's Great Day Game Planner

It's great to be alive and well! What will make today a fulfilling and satisfying day? Do the "write" thing, and jot down whatever action steps you'd like to take.

....

....

....

....

....

....

....

Highlight three priority actions. These priority actions will take precedence over all others. Then, time permitting, select others from the planner.

Mood Elevators

Draw a line or shade in each of the mood elevators to reflect your state of being in the moment.

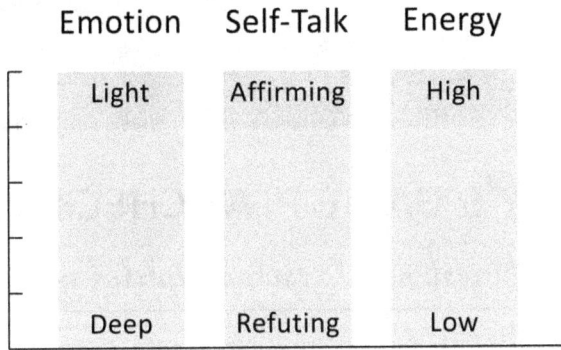

Emotion	Self-Talk	Energy
Light	Affirming	High
Deep	Refuting	Low

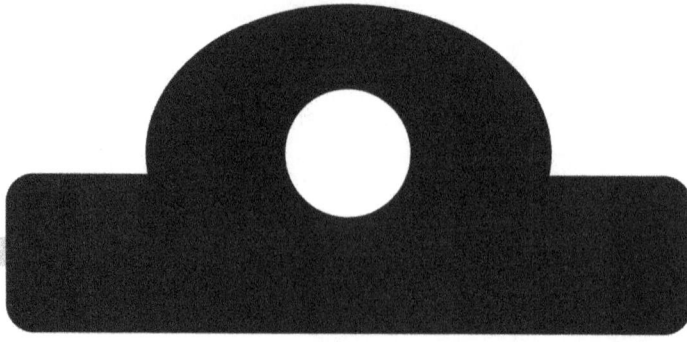

TODAY'S GAME PLAY CHECKLIST

Place a checkmark next to each completed game play:

☐ Today's principle card selected and engaged

☐ Fuel-up activities selected from your lightness and energy menu

☐ Intention statement—engaged and refined

☐ Feelings, self-talk, and appreciation entered in captain's logs

☐ Game plan actions entered

☐ Your state of being on the mood elevators assessed

☐ Select and play a mind game today:

    ○ Abundant Mind

    ○ Been There, Done That

    ○ Freeing Your David

Day 46—Carl's Rumi-nation

Discovering Needs and Values

Emotions come up spontaneously and influence our thinking and behavior. Whether you are thrilled or repulsed by your emotional state, it is an opportunity to benefit from Rumi-nating. Rumi-nating is a great way to process emotion, deepen awareness of your emotional nature, and discover the wealth of valuable information that is available from your inborn guidance system.

At times, we experience emotions and have no clue as to why. You may wake up enthused or with the blues, unaware of the source of this state. We have a game play designed specifically for those situations, which we'll play in a few days. For now, we will focus on the emotions we are aware of, utilize our ability to reflect, and benefit from the insights our emotional experiences offer.

Carl Visits the Guest House

Let's revisit with Carl. He is playing along with us, his commitment to realize his intention is clearly evident, and he does want to enjoy the ride along the way. His enthusiasm is building, and he is becoming quite adept at alert witnessing.

Carl has been doing the "write" thing by jotting down his observations, knowing that it is all valuable guidance information. He also gets that capturing it in the written form empowers him to play with it in various game strategies where he will reorder the disorder and align his emotions and thoughts with his intention.

Carl went to bed with a busy mind, overstimulated by the day's activities. He finally fell asleep at 3:30 a.m. and got up at 7:30 a.m., feeling quite exhausted from a short and restless sleep with less-than-pleasant feelings about himself. He mused that these emotions may simply be a product of being tired and that may be all there is to it. Being a game player, rather than writing it off, he saw it as an opportunity to write it down, exercise this game practice, and Rumi-nate.

"After all," Carl thought, "I may uncover some valuable information."

He writes …

> "My busy mind churned until 3:30 a.m., and I sure would have liked to have slept later, but I was too restless to sleep. Since I have no client commitments today, I can gift myself this day in any way I choose. Rather than celebrating my positive movement, my mind went to what is missing. It can best be described as disappointment in me and in the various roles I play.
>
> "I gave up a lot to start my own business—particularly income, which not only impacts me but my family too. I feel I could have/was capable of giving

more—not only money but time in supporting my kids. They often seem to be struggling, and I feel inadequate and helpless and question myself. If I were there for them more, maybe they would be struggling less.

"So, I think it is best to invest my time now in this Rumi-nating process. In the end, it seems as though I make it about me—a lot of should have/could have stuff, like I could have given my wife and kids a better life financially and maybe they would be less concerned. I could have stayed with my old company and continued to build on what I had if I didn't focus on 'my' dream. So exactly what am I feeling now? How can I use these emotions to enhance my family's conditions?"

Carl asked himself a powerful question here, and it is at the heart of navigating both emotions and thoughts: "How can I use these emotions to enhance conditions?" With that in mind, Carl is quite well prepared to engage his emotions and Rumi-nate. He takes out the appropriate Rumi-nating questionnaire and proceeds.

Rumi-nating on a Deep Mood

- What is weighing down Libby's spirits?

I am feeling disappointed in myself.

- Is Amy feeling threatened? If so, what is the perceived danger triggering Amy's protectiveness?

I feel that I have failed at my role as a provider, and my family may experience financial risk.

- What is the feeling (that is, the meaning that the crew is assigning to this emotion)?

Failure, inadequacy, selfishness

- What need is not being met and/or what value is being violated?

Provider

- What valuable guidance information can the team gather from this emotion?

I want to be a better provider.

- How will you make use of this valuable guidance information in a way that meets your needs, honors your values, and serves your meaningful intention?

I will remain on course with my intention. I will allow it to meet my needs and the needs of my family going forward.

- How has this emotional reaction become a gift to the team?

It has made me realize how much I really love my family and want to provide for them to the best of my ability. I think it's more about change and a feeling of uncertainty, which brings this up for me.

- Having Rumi-nated, what emotion is now present and what is the feeling/meaning you choose to assign to it?

The emotion is love. I am a loving family guy. I am going to use the power of my love for them and continue my progress. I can, I will, and I am doing this! I am communicating with my soul, trusting my heart, and following my intuition, and I will continue to do so. I believe that this is my intended purpose; it is what my soul is craving and guiding me to do. Having this business actually gives me far more opportunity to help others and create an even better life for my family.

- What few words can I jot down to express appreciation for this mood's arrival?

I accept myself and am grateful for this valuable guidance information. I recognize my love of family. I will actively seek ways to provide more for them while traveling along on my great adventure.

Carl was surprised to see how much lighter he felt and how much better he felt about himself. He observed his spontaneous emotions and appraised himself as a loving man. With a renewed sense of mission and purpose, he will redirect his energy back on course with his intention.

It is interesting to notice that, when ease begins to restore, new insights arrive. For Carl, it dawned on him that, as he put it, "… it's more about change and a feeling of uncertainty, which brings this up for me." From out of the fog of upset, his judgmental feelings of failure, inadequacy, and selfishness faded, and his love of family and self-compassion came to light.

As convinced as he is that this revelation will remain with him, and as certain as he is that he will remain on course, it is important to recognize that insights can be as fleeting as any mood or emotion. In order for Carl to truly retain this valuable shift, he must capture it and fortify it. This is where the "R" in OAR comes into play, which we will cover on Day 51. First, however, it will be your turn to Rumi-nate.

Today's Great Day Game Planner

It's great to be alive and well! What will make today a fulfilling and satisfying day? Do the "write" thing, and jot down whatever action steps you'd like to take.

....

....

....

....

....

....

....

Highlight three priority actions. These priority actions will take precedence over all others. Then, time permitting, select others from the planner.

TODAY'S GAME PLAY CHECKLIST

Place a checkmark next to each completed game play:

☐ Today's principle card selected and engaged

☐ Fuel-up activities selected from your lightness and energy menu

☐ Intention statement—engaged and refined

☐ Feelings, self-talk, and appreciation entered in captain's logs

☐ Game plan actions entered

☐ Your state of being on the mood elevators assessed

☐ Select and play a mind game today:

  ○ Abundant Mind

  ○ Been There, Done That

  ○ Freeing Your David

Day 47—Reminders and Tips of the Week

Go With the Flow

Next stop is the guest house, where you will practice Rumi-nating. Between now and then, be an alert witness to your emotions, do the "write" thing, and let them flow. If you are inviting a deep and challenging emotion, give Amy the permission slip to express the anger, frustration, fear, or whatever it is, fully and freely. If you are reveling with joyous emotions, let Libby express them fully and freely as well. Then, bring your notes into the guest house.

If you are uncertain, engage your intention statement and notice what emotions come up for you. Alternatively, review your captain's log and find an emotion to play with and practice Rumi-nating.

Be Present

Having a busy, racing mind can make it challenging to be present. When the alert witness in you notices this and wants to quiet things down, grab a pen and paper, and carry it with you. A small, pocket-sized pad or index cards work best, but a folded-up piece of paper is fine too.

With each thought, jot down a key word. This will help you let go of the thought, knowing that you can return to it later. If more thoughts come up, note them in like manner. You will begin to notice that things are quieting down. Later, dedicate some "present moment" time to look at the key words. Which of them deserves more thoughtful attention? Attend to them, and dump the rest. Chances are that you are having these thoughts for good reason! As captain, welcome them and gain value from addressing them.

If needed, do this for another day. Distraction will be significantly reduced, and you'll enjoy a quieter, more peaceful mind.

Lap, Don't Nap

Napping is fine and can be quite rejuvenating. When you are playing mind games, you'll prefer to be more alert. Drowsy or not, try playing mind games with a pad on your lap. With practice, you will find yourself to be increasingly alert during mind games, and you'll be able to focus dynamically on one train of thought more than you've ever been able to before. With this increased level of concentration, you'll benefit from insights that may not have dawned on you in the absence of such contemplation. Make no assumption that you'll remember! Write down these insights, and you'll be glad you did.

In the spirit of "no shoulds allowed," if you do choose to nap, limit it to 20 to 30 minutes. Beyond that, you'll wake up groggy, defeating the purpose of the nap, and it may throw off your sleep pattern as well.

Today's Great Day Game Planner

It's great to be alive and well! What will make today a fulfilling and satisfying day? Do the "write" thing, and jot down whatever action steps you'd like to take.

....

....

....

....

....

....

....

Highlight three priority actions. These priority actions will take precedence over all others. Then, time permitting, select others from the planner.

Mood Elevators

Draw a line or shade in each of the mood elevators to reflect your state of being in the moment.

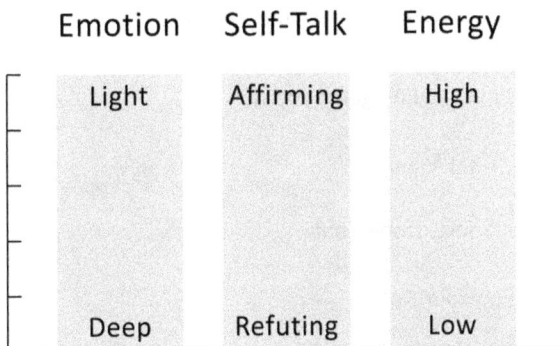

Emotion	Self-Talk	Energy
Light	Affirming	High
Deep	Refuting	Low

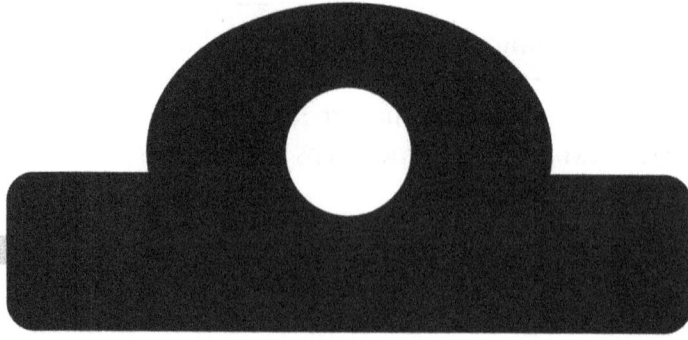

TODAY'S GAME PLAY CHECKLIST

Place a checkmark next to each completed game play:

☐ Today's principle card selected and engaged

☐ Fuel-up activities selected from your lightness and energy menu

☐ Intention statement—engaged and refined

☐ Feelings, self-talk, and appreciation entered in captain's logs

☐ Game plan actions entered

☐ Your state of being on the mood elevators assessed

☐ Select and play a mind game today:

  ○ Abundant Mind

  ○ Been There, Done That

  ○ Freeing Your David

Days 48 and 49—Free Day Reminder

PART VI

Exploring the Oceans of Your Emotions

WEEK 8

Rumi-nating and Inviting Insights to Dawn on You

Day 50—Your Turn to Rumi-nate

Rumi-nating on Deep and Light Moods

Now it's your turn to unlock the valuable guidance information your emotions hold for you. Does an emotion comes to mind that you feel you'd be well served to explore more deeply? If, in the moment, no relevant emotion comes to mind, engage your meaningful intention statement. While reading it, pay particular attention to the emotions your intention stirs.

Alternatively, check your captain's emotions log. Are any of your entries currently relevant? If so, bring them into the guest house, and welcome them in. As you come together with Amy, Libby, and Tex, do the "write" thing and complete one of the brief and valuable questionnaires provided. There are questionnaires for both deep moods and light moods. Choose whichever is appropriate.

If you are uncertain how to respond to any of the questions, you will find it helpful to refer back to Carl's work and review how he responded to them.

Rumi-nating on Deep Moods

What is weighing down Libby's spirits?

....

....

Is Amy feeling threatened? If so what is the perceived danger triggering Amy's protectiveness?

....

....

What is the feeling (that is, the meaning that the crew is assigning to this emotion)?

....

....

What need is not being met and/or what value is being violated?

....

....

What valuable guidance information can the team gather from this emotion?

....

....

How will you make use of this valuable guidance information in a way that meets your needs, honors your values, and serves your meaningful intention?

....

....

How has this emotional reaction become a gift to the team?

....

....

Rumi-nating on Deep Moods

Having Rumi-nated, what emotion is now present, and what is the feeling/meaning you choose to assign to it?

....

....

Jot down a few words of appreciation for this mood's arrival:

....

....

Rumi-nating on Light Moods

What is lifting Libby's spirits?

....

....

What is the feeling (that is, the meaning that the crew is assigning to this emotion)?

....

....

What need is being met and/or what value is being honored?

....

....

What valuable guidance information can the team gather from this emotion?

....

....

Rumi-nating on Light Moods

How will you make use of this valuable guidance information in a way that meets your needs, honors your values, and serves your meaningful intention?

....

....

What is the meaning you choose to assign to this emotion?

....

....

How is this emotional response a gift to the team?

....

....

Having Rumi-nated, what emotion is now present and what is the feeling/meaning you choose to assign to it?

....

....

Jot down a few words of appreciation for this mood's arrival:

....

....

Today's Great Day Game Planner

It's great to be alive and well! What will make today a fulfilling and satisfying day? Do the "write" thing, and jot down whatever action steps you'd like to take.

....

....

....

....

....

....

....

Highlight three priority actions. These priority actions will take precedence over all others. Then, time permitting, select others from the planner.

Mood Elevators

Draw a line or shade in each of the mood elevators to reflect your state of being in the moment.

Emotion	Self-Talk	Energy
Light	Affirming	High
Deep	Refuting	Low

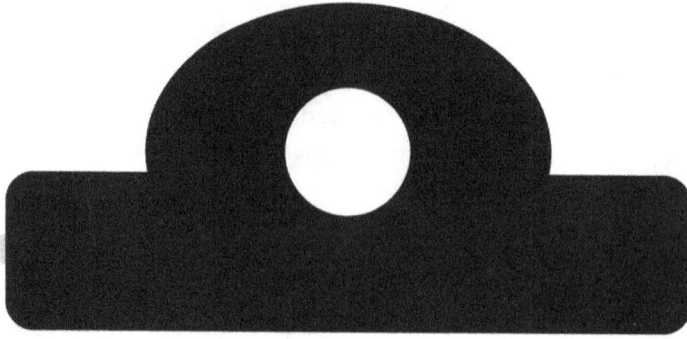

TODAY'S GAME PLAY CHECKLIST

Place a checkmark next to each completed game play:

☐   Today's principle card selected and engaged

☐   Fuel-up activities selected from your lightness and energy menu

☐   Rumi-nated on a deep or light emotion

☐   Intention statement—engaged and refined

☐   Game plan actions entered

☐   Your state of being on the mood elevators assessed

☐   Select and play a mind game today:

     ○   Abundant Mind

     ○   Been There, Done That

     ○   Freeing Your David

Day 51—Refining Intent: Valuable Guidance Information from Rumi-nating

The "R" in OAR—Respond

After Carl Rumi-nated on his deep emotions, he reveled in his revelations, convinced that his powerful insights and brisk return back on course would remain with him permanently. As with any fresh feelings, however, they can vanish just as quickly as they arrive. Many of our emotional reactions and resulting feelings are deeply rooted from years of repetition. When a similar thought or event presents itself, that old feeling is triggered. For example, an old family photo can trigger joy or sorrow, comfort or resentment, or a myriad of other feelings based on the meaning we have assigned to that image for many years.

When we have a fresh insight, the associated feeling is not well established in memory, making it easy to forget the insight or that we ever had an insight at all.

This is where the "R" in OAR comes into play. You first observed your emotions, then assigned them meanings by appraising them in ways that served your intention. Now you'll respond by taking practical action in alignment with your intention.

The most practical action you can take, and the one that will assure that your insight will be retained, is done through repetition. It is repetition of the new feeling that overrides old, habitual, emotional reaction.

"Petition" is defined as a request made for something desired. You re-petition (that is, you request again and again) to reinforce this fresh feeling, so it becomes firm and strong and ultimately your automatic response.

Incorporating this is simple because the structure for this repetition has already been set. Simply update your meaningful intention with this fresh insight, continue engaging it four to five times weekly, and, through the wonder of nature, your magnificently malleable brain will build a neural connection strengthened by every recurring read.

Carl Responds

Carl took the insights he jotted down from Rumi-nating and refined his intention statement with the following:

I am profoundly aware of how much I love my family, how much I want for them, and the strong value I hold to provide them with financial ease and emotional support.

Staying on course with my intention enables me to meet my needs and the needs of my family now and going forward.

I am reveling in the dynamism of this change with great certainty, knowing that I have all it takes and am on the path that my soul is guiding me to take.

I am directing the power of love I have for my family by living my intention. Having this business is giving me far more opportunity to help others and create an even better life for us all.

From the insights you've gained by observing your emotions and appraising them with a Rumi-nating questionnaire, it is time to do the "write" thing and refine your intention statement with this new valuable guidance information. Articulate the needs that you are now committed to meet and/or the personal values that you are committed to live into your statement.

The Success Response and the Resiliency Gap

The success response is a state of increasing responsiveness and decreasing reactiveness to emotions, thoughts, and events.

The resiliency gap is the span of time between an emotional disturbance or sadness and your return to a joyful understanding and ease. Each person has a different gap. Some may be upset for days, if not weeks; for others, it's hours, minutes, or even seconds. Paradoxically, the gap closes more quickly when you give yourself the permission to engage disturbances and sadness.

Rumi-nating empowers you to:

1. Process the emotion.

2. Disarm it by learning from it.

3. Discover how to respond to similar situations as they arise.

4. Free yourself from the trigger of repetitive reactiveness, moving you progressively closer to developing Rumi's responsiveness (that is, being "grateful for whatever comes").

This is your success response in play. Watch your resiliency gap close and your success response build as you Rumi-nate and practice paddling with your OARs. As your resiliency strengthens, watch for these sensations:

- A sense of inner calm and acceptance

- A knowing that everything will be and actually is okay

- A sense of being lighter and more joyful

- Occasional bursts of exhilaration and bliss for no apparent reason

- An overwhelming sense of gratitude

- An ease and effortlessness

- Letting go of the need to control outcomes

As one player put it, "I am aware of a subtle calmness. Things now seem to flow with relative ease. I have an awareness of what needs to be done, and it doesn't seem intimidating or forced."

Consciousness, now being freed from fearful reactions, begins to align with a strengthened responsive command to inner and outer stimuli. The noticing of synchronicity and meaningful coincidences occur more frequently and become a new normal way of being.

Remember: Amy is part of your survival mechanism. Her responsibility is to protect you from danger. There is no counterpersonality to Amy. There is no urgent survival need for a joy alert. Therefore, moods that resonate with danger are far more noticeable and the emotional residue far more profound than joyful moods.

So attend to your lighter emotions, and welcome those into your guest house as well. Appreciate their value, and you will become more aware of needs that are being met and values that are being honored. By directing the light of your attention on these joyful emotions, their presence will illuminate more brightly on your mental radar, and you will notice and attract more of like kind.

Here's a quick recap for you:

- **O:** Observe by being a prompt and compassionate alert witness, and do the "write" thing.

- **A:** Appraise your mood using the Rumi-nating questionnaire.

- **R:** Respond by incorporating your insights into your meaningful intention statement, and seek opportunities to act in alignment with this newfound understanding.

Today's Great Day Game Planner

It's great to be alive and well! What will make today a fulfilling and satisfying day? Do the "write" thing, and jot down whatever action steps you'd like to take.

....

....

....

....

....

....

....

Highlight three priority actions. These priority actions will take precedence over all others. Then, time permitting, select others from the planner.

Mood Elevators

Draw a line or shade in each of the mood elevators to reflect your state of being in the moment.

Emotion	Self-Talk	Energy
Light	Affirming	High
Deep	Refuting	Low

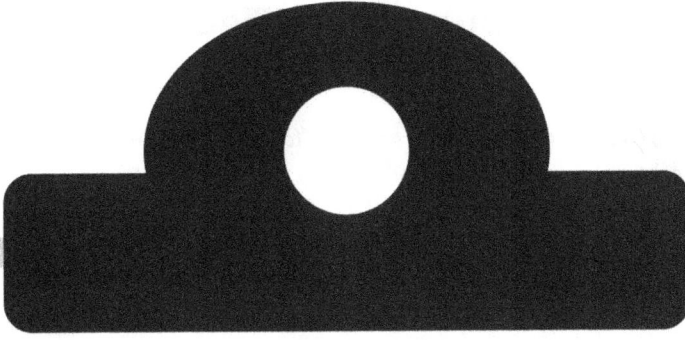

TODAY'S GAME PLAY CHECKLIST

Place a checkmark next to each completed game play:

☐ Today's principle card selected and engaged

☐ Fuel-up activities selected from your lightness and energy menu

☐ Intention refined with fresh rumi-nating insights

☐ Game plan actions entered

☐ Your state of being on the mood elevators assessed

☐ Select and play a mind game today:

  ○ Abundant Mind

  ○ Been There, Done That

  ○ Freeing Your David

Day 52—When in Doubt, Don't Figure It Out

*The intellect has little to do on the road to discovery: There comes a leap
in consciousness, call it intuition or what you will and the solution comes
to you and you don't know why. All great discoveries are made this way*

—Albert Einstein[20]

Let's suppose that you've Rumi-nated on some uncomfortable emotions and were unable to ascertain any useful insights. What to do? Well, I say, "When in doubt, don't figure it out"; instead, give your rational mind a break, and let the creative mind bring it to you.

Research has shown that, when one expends too much effort, a level of tension blocks access to information. Most of us have had the experience of forgetting someone's name or the title of a book. The more effort we put toward recollecting the information, the more tension we experience along with a reduced likelihood of retrieving the information. Once one disengages from the effort and redirects attention to something else—*voilà*—the information jumps out of the files of memory.

There are instances, other than moods, where we try to "figure it out" but, try as we may, we can't figure it out because the information we need is not in our conscious awareness. How do we access it?

While attending Coach University, I had a buddy coach named Patrick. We would support each other in our course work and in each other's lives. One day, I was playing the role of coach, and he was my coachee. Patrick told me of a challenge he was facing in his work. I don't recall specifically what the challenge was, but I do know that he was determined to find a solution. He told me that he was going to chain himself to his desk until he figured it out. I told him I would not have any part of his self-abuse and recommended that he step away. After some discussion, he reluctantly agreed.

His young son was off from school that day. It was autumn in the Northeast, and he knew that his son loved to catch the falling leaves. His son welcomed the opportunity to go out and play with his dad. Within 10 minutes or so, my office phone rang, and his name appeared on my caller ID. I was prepared to lovingly scold him for not letting go, but there was no need for this. He was eager to report that the insight he was looking for had dawned on him in his backyard. *Eureka!* The illumination arrived.

Have you had such an experience? You've been fueling up with your lightness and energy menu, I trust. If not, why not? This is a perfect example of what happens when we trade struggling for grace and ease.

This is the value of engagement and disengagement that makes creating what you want easier and more fun. Let's look at this more closely, and go back to an interesting discovery made quite some time ago. This will make clear why my coaching buddy had his illumination and how you will have them as well.

The Wallas Stage Model of Creativity

Back in 1926, Graham Wallas—social psychologist, educationalist, and cofounder of the London School of Economics—developed a model for the creative process. Wallas became curious by the findings of several prominent scientists of his day. Accounts of what they referred to as the "creative process" were being studied by Hermann von Helmholtz, a German physician and physicist, and Jules Henri Poincaré, a French mathematician, physicist, and engineer. Both Helmholtz and Poincaré were considered to be philosophers of science who were attempting to explain illumination and insight experiences in both scientific and other creative work.

The Wallas model involves four stages:

1. Preparation
2. Incubation
3. Illumination
4. Verification

Let's walk through my Coach University buddy's experience to make these stages come alive.

Preparation

Patrick was well prepared. He had clear intent, had done the practical research, and had gathered all the relevant data he could find. He was thoroughly engaged.

Incubation

When Patrick released himself from the chains of his desk, he shifted his attention away from the perceived problem and reveled in play with his son. It was this disengagement that created air in his consciousness.

The research suggests that disengagement, which is the incubation phase, enables the "forgetting" of misleading clues that persist as long as we insist on struggling for solutions. The problem solver becomes fixated on inappropriate strategies remaining attached to the problem.[21]

Illumination

The phrases "it dawned on me" and "it came to me" are expressions that we instinctively say when we experience an illumination or insight. This is the *Aha!* or *Eureka!* that follows incubation. For Patrick, the solution dawned on him during disengagement. By directing his attention away from active problem solving toward the freedom of play, the insight arrived.

Perhaps you are now beginning to have a deeper appreciation for these two quotations cited earlier on Day 11:

From R. Buckminster Fuller: "You never change things by fighting the existing reality. To change something, build a new model that makes the existing model obsolete."[22]

From Einstein: "We can't solve problems by using the same kind of thinking we used when we created them."[23]

Verification

In this final phase, you test the *Aha!* to see if it, in fact, does provide the solution. So when you find yourself stumped, challenge yourself to step away. Try on a little grace and ease, visit your lightness and energy menu, indulge in a favorite activity, and let your creative mind handle the details.

We will now combine our understanding of Wallas's brilliant model and the power of your inner conscious mind with a brand new mind game.

Take a BMW Ride

So you've taken a break, slept on it, and Rumi-nated, and you're still stuck? The solution hasn't yet dawned on you. What to do?

Or maybe something just seems off. You woke up in an uncomfortable emotional state and, even after Rumi-nating you're still unable to figure out what's up. You think that maybe it's just something you ate, and your body is trying to digest it, or maybe it's a gut feeling, an intuitive signal trying to communicate with you. In all of these cases, you are lacking information, and that is where our next mind game comes into play.

Our beloved objective senses, at times, obscure the power of our subjective senses. We tend to try and "figure it all out" with our rational brains. Admittedly, that is the best place to begin, but when you've done all you can with your intellect and are still stumped, it is time to tap into the sacred gift and open up to receiving information intuitively.

When you've done everything you can think of, stop thinking and go for a BMW ride. No, it's not a car ride. Just read on. Here's The Wallas model once again but, this time, we will relate it to brain states before and during mind games.

Relax. I'll keep it simple.

The Wallas Model

1. Preparation
2. Incubation
3. Illumination
4. Verification

Preparation

When preparing, like Patrick did by researching and gathering information, his brain was in an alert state. This wide-awake state is referred to as "beta brain activity."

Incubation

When playing in the backyard or when you're in a calm meditative state, relaxing with your eyes closed and playing a mind game, you enter an alpha state. That is the state of incubation. Guess what? It means that you have been incubating every time you've played a mind game! It also means that you have been setting the environment for illuminations. Have you had any lately? Maybe now you know why.

Illumination

Theta is an open, free-flowing, and highly suggestible state. There is an absence of active logical thinking. Chances are that you are bumping into a theta state when you are playing with metaphoric imagery in the garden exercise.

In the BMW mind game, you are going to let go of your need to figure it out. Instead, you will use your body's innate wisdom as an intuitive antenna. You will direct your attention to your body. If you identify tension in any particular part of your body, place your attention there.

You'll then ask your body open-ended questions (that is, you'll ask questions which cannot be answered with a yes or a no). You won't even make any attempt to seek an answer. Instead, simply ask these questions and wait for the insights to dawn on you. They may come to you shortly after the exercise, in the shower the next morning, or in a few days.

The key here is to let go and allow. Just play along. If you find this challenging, go back to the spirit of alert witnessing and be amused without making yourself wrong or making up a big story. Just assume that you are doing it right since there is no way of doing it wrong.

Once again, mind games require no effort. Go light and easy, and you'll get the best results. If you happen to doze off during this exercise, don't be surprised. This mind game is designed to bring you to the edge of sleep (that is, a theta brain state). Know that, although you may be lightly sleeping, you are still conscious and, chances are, you will regain conscious awareness when the exercise ends.

Another common comment that people make when they are tired of struggling to "figure it out" is, "I think I'll sleep on it." This too is an effective strategy for all the reasons mentioned above.

Verification

The last step is to try on the insights and see how they work for you.

BMW stands for Body-Mind Wisdom. Let your inner conscious mind and your body partner up, expect illuminations, and enjoy. When in doubt, don't figure it out; instead, take a BMW ride, and you are bound to see a few more of those blue Chevy's coming your way.

Whether you are stumped now or not, experience the BMW mind game. It's a great idea generator. In keeping with our 15- to 20-minute-per-day time frame, the ride is set for tomorrow; however, if time permits, feel free to hop in now.

Today's Great Day Game Planner

It's great to be alive and well! What will make today a fulfilling and satisfying day? Do the "write" thing, and jot down whatever action steps you'd like to take.

....

....

....

....

....

....

....

Highlight three priority actions. These priority actions will take precedence over all others. Then, time permitting, select others from the planner.

Mood Elevators

Draw a line or shade in each of the mood elevators to reflect your state of being in the moment.

Emotion	Self-Talk	Energy
Light	Affirming	High
Deep	Refuting	Low

TODAY'S GAME PLAY CHECKLIST

Place a checkmark next to each completed game play:

☐ Today's principle card selected and engaged

☐ Fuel-up activities selected from your lightness and energy menu

☐ Intention statement—engaged and refined

☐ Feelings, self-talk, and appreciation entered in captain's logs

☐ Game plan actions entered

☐ Your state of being on the mood elevators assessed

☐ Select and play a mind game today:

    ○ Abundant Mind

    ○ Been There, Done That

    ○ Freeing Your David

Day 53—The BMW Mind Game

Let Go and Allow Fresh Insights In

Stumped? Not certain what to do? In a funk and don't know why? Or maybe you'd simply love to have some new, creative insights dawn on you. In all cases, when you want to retrieve or attract fresh information into your consciousness, go ahead and hop in for a BMW ride.

The BMW mind game audio will be your metaphoric GPS. Let go, allow, and enjoy the ride!

Today's Great Day Game Planner

It's great to be alive and well! What will make today a fulfilling and satisfying day? Do the "write" thing, and jot down whatever action steps you'd like to take.

....

....

....

....

....

....

....

Highlight three priority actions. These priority actions will take precedence over all others. Then, time permitting, select others from the planner.

Mood Elevators

Draw a line or shade in each of the mood elevators to reflect your state of being in the moment.

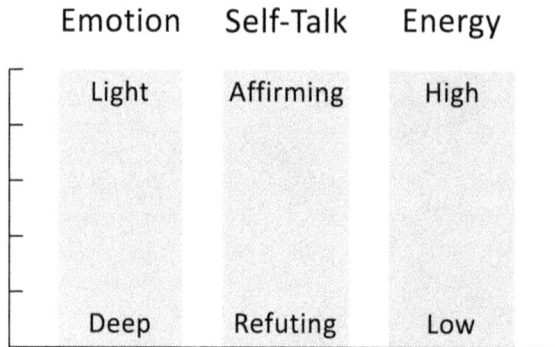

Emotion	Self-Talk	Energy
Light	Affirming	High
Deep	Refuting	Low

TODAY'S GAME PLAY CHECKLIST

Place a checkmark next to each completed game play:

☐ Today's principle card selected and engaged

☐ Fuel-up activities selected from your lightness and energy menu

☐ Intention statement—engaged and refined

☐ Feelings, self-talk, and appreciation entered in captain's logs

☐ BMW mind game played

☐ Game plan actions entered

☐ Your state of being on the mood elevators assessed

Day 54—Reminders and Tips of the Week

The Long and Short of It

Boy, after Rumi-nating, that Carl sure added a rather lengthy revision into his intention statement. New players often ask me, "How long should an intention statement be?" Keeping to our "no shoulds allowed" policy, when it comes to length, there are no hard-and-fast rules. It is always best to write what is most potent for you in the moment.

With frequent revisions, players tend to edit things down. In Carl's case, his Rumi-nating entry went from over 100 words to this:

I am reveling in this dynamic career change and using the power of love to build a thriving business. It provides financial peace and emotional ease for my family, job satisfaction for me, and better lives for us all.

In short, express freely and revise regularly.

A Wallas for All Seasons

Whether you are stumped, in doubt, or simply seeking fresh insights to make things even better, it pays to play with your creative mind.

Be it lightness and energy breaks or BMW rides, or electing to simply sleep on it, they are all strategies that choose grace and ease over struggle. They promote Wallas's four stages of preparation, incubation, illumination, and verification through a cycle of engagement, disengagement, and reengagement.

Before you take that break, play that mind game, or snooze, first bring to mind your objective. What is the outcome, solution, or insight you are looking for? This is the preparation piece. Then let go and allow the illumination to dawn on you. The clearer the desired outcome is, the better the results. Once the insight dawns on you, verify it and, if it strikes you right, act upon it right away.

Lift the Fog

Emotionally charged circumstances require a degree of objectivity that can be challenging. Observing and appraising with Rumi's welcoming attitude, rife with the expectation, most often does the trick to lift the fog, uncovering insights, epiphanies, and valuable guidance information. Additionally, doing the "write" thing and responding to the questions within this strategy engage more of your brain's resources, effectively reuniting Amy, Libby, and Tex. And now you have BMW rides to allow insights to dawn on you. If your Amy and Libby are still lost in the fog of emotional agitation, and are desperately seeking Tex, consider connecting with a buddy or a coach, or join a telegame. Visit 90DayGame.com to find resources that match your personal style.

Today's Great Day Game Planner

It's great to be alive and well! What will make today a fulfilling and satisfying day? Do the "write" thing, and jot down whatever action steps you'd like to take.

....

....

....

....

....

....

....

Highlight three priority actions. These priority actions will take precedence over all others. Then, time permitting, select others from the planner.

Mood Elevators

Draw a line or shade in each of the mood elevators to reflect your state of being in the moment.

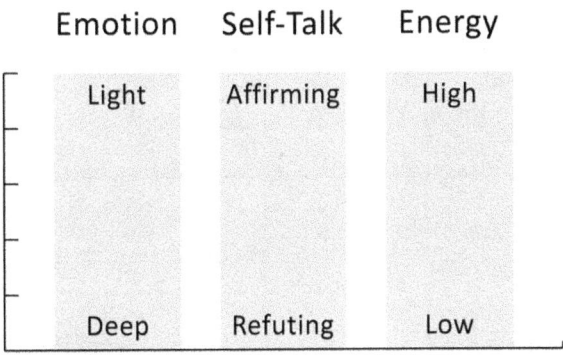

Emotion	Self-Talk	Energy
Light	Affirming	High
Deep	Refuting	Low

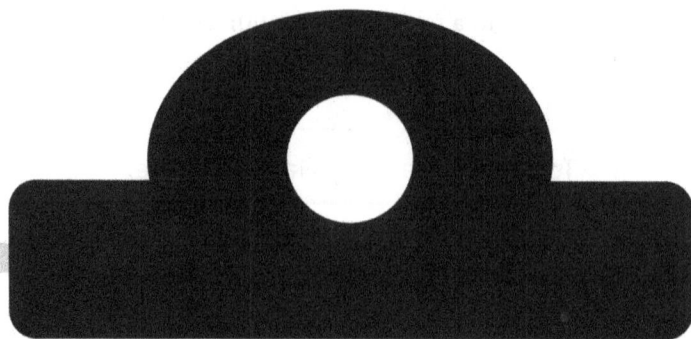

TODAY'S GAME PLAY CHECKLIST

Place a checkmark next to each completed game play:

☐ Today's principle card selected and engaged

☐ Fuel-up activities selected from your lightness and energy menu

☐ Intention statement—engaged and refined

☐ Feelings, self-talk, and appreciation entered in captain's logs

☐ Game plan actions entered

☐ Your state of being on the mood elevators assessed

☐ Select and play a mind game today:

    ○ Abundant Mind   ○ Freeing Your David

    ○ Been There, Done That   ○ BMW

Days 55 and 56—Free Day Reminder

PART VII

Navigating the Waters of Self-Talk

WEEK 9

Self-Talk—The Self-Fulfilling Prophecy

Day 57—Battle or Befriend

With Libby in mind, you applied Rumi's wisdom, welcomed all moods and emotions into your guest house, and treated them honorably. You put preconceived judgments aside, knowing that each was a guide from beyond; a divine call for attention. As you Rumi-nated, you discovered needs, some joyfully being met and others that cry out to be met, and values that are being honored and those that are to be honored. In the guest house, you resolved your commitment to get your needs met.

Through the simple yet effective process of Rumi-nating, you compassionately observed your emotions with a light and amused heart, appraised them as valuable guidance information, and responded by refining your intention statement with the needs and/or values you uncovered, unifying your crew back on course with your intentions.

Whether You Think You Can or You Can't, You're Right

Now we turn to your inner dialogue: that ongoing voice (or perhaps more accurately put, those ongoing voices) vying for your attention. Unlike emotions, self-talk involves other regions of the brain, and therefore needs to be communicated with differently. You will, however, continue to paddle with the OARs (Observing, Appraising, and Responding) in ways that serve your creation.

195

This quotation may be new to you, or you may have heard it a thousand times; either way, it remains true. Henry Ford said, "Whether you think you can or can't, you're right." In this way, self-talk is a self-fulfilling prophecy.

Much of what has been written on self-talk is focused on so-called "negative" self-talk, framed with images of attacking demons, gremlins to slay, inner brats to punish, and egos to be dethroned. Under the assault of such images, it is no wonder that we fight, freeze, or flee from this battle and, in doing so, lose the opportunity to engage our self-talk in ways that can empower us. Over the course of the next few days, you will learn a simple yet effective means of accessing this power, fortifying the beliefs needed to realize your intentions.

Since most of the social hypnosis is focused on fixing problems rather than intentionally creating, it is no wonder that the preponderance of material on this topic is about therapeutic fixing stuff, with little on how our understanding of self-talk can be used in creative, productive, and empowering ways—ways that often circumvent many problems from arising.

Early on in the game, you began and continue to apply what could be considered "positive" self-talk. After all, what is your meaningful intention statement but an affirming conversation with yourself and your soul to create what you truly want while enjoying the process? In order to be freed from the root of this hypnotic labeling trap of positive versus negative, and good versus bad, we need to return to our main premise: All of it is valuable guidance information. As skillful game players, we will utilize it all!

Are these images of demons, gremlins, and brats accurate representations of what is going on? Does it make sense for us to go to battle with ourselves over images of our own making? Or, are these images simply costumes masking something deeper?

Reflecting on Day 38, you were introduced to an acronym for *image* (Illusions of Mind That Attract and Gather Energy). They are illusions in the sense that, although these dastardly images appear to be accurate representations of what is true, they are merely reflections of meanings that we're assigning to thoughts, emotions, or events at any given disturbing moment. Therefore, they reflect only one of many possible meanings that we can be assigning.

These images influence our perception of what is "real," impacting the choices we make and the actions we take. With this level of influence, it is imperative for us to examine the meanings we assign, the interpretations we make, and the assumptions that, by default, we live by.

Unmasking the Demons

> *Oz never did give nothing to the tin man that he didn't already have.*
>
> —Dewey Bunnell[24]

When Toto pulled back the curtain in *The Wizard of Oz*, the illusion Oz created was revealed, disempowered, and then powerfully transformed. It was not the wizard, but the image that the wizard created, complete with flashing lights and echoing sound effects, which had them trembling in fear.

When the demons, gremlins, and brats of self-talk are unmasked, we discover sadness, unsettled thoughts, uncomfortable feelings, a lack of confidence, and an unnecessary belief of insecurity and incompetence. There is no "real" threat other than the one we're imagining.

Once the wizard was unmasked, his sense of inadequacy was uncovered. He projected an image of what he believed a great and powerful Oz "should be" but, once uncovered, and after some obvious embarrassment, his true greatness was revealed and demonstrated by his loving kindness. His divine, authentic, adequate self was present. Dorothy and the gang not only befriended him, they enlisted his support, and, in doing so, reawakened their authentic natures of courage, heart, and wisdom and the path back home.

In much the same way, by observing and listening to our self-talk, we can engage it, embrace it, befriend it, and enlist it as an ally. We are then in a position to exchange these images for more accurate ones—or, at the very least, more useful ones—to cease the war within and embrace our fears, doubts, and worries with understanding, compassion, and love.

New Masks, New Images—From Scared to Sacred

Let us honor the sacred gift of imagination by exchanging the repelling images for more attractive ones that serve our intentions. I offer you two: a frightened puppy and an overly protective parent. Both move us toward compassion. You wouldn't run from or kick a trembling puppy, would you? Instead, you would cuddle it and reassure the pooch that he is indeed safe. As bothersome as an overly protective parent may be to a child, underneath this fearful demeanor, there is a loving intent to save their child from harm's way. I believe these are more accurate and productive images to entertain.

Just like the Wizard of Oz, Toto's active engagement uncovered the illusion—the valuable information needed to shift from the unsettling unknown to the stability of the known.

> *… the only thing we have to fear is fear itself—nameless, unreasoning, unjustified terror which paralyzes needed efforts to convert retreat into advance.*
>
> —Franklin Delano Roosevelt[25]

Our aim in navigating these waters is to maintain emotional buoyancy and open up new channels for further self-discovery. With our rich framework of game plays, meaningful intent, mind games, and Rumi-nating, players are less hindered by challenges and instead revel in exploring them. As resilience grows, the crew is less threatened by the images produced from fears, doubts, and worries, and instead develops a success response of loving compassion, affirming faith, and growing confidence in themselves and their plans. They cultivate an attitude of gratitude because, like emotions, self-talk provides valuable guidance information. The player then shifts beyond intellectually understanding to knowing that there really is nothing to fear! It is this freedom that we are after, and it is available to all of us.

When you find yourself at war with your fears, doubts, and worries, cultivate an image of a trembling little puppy, pet it, cuddle it, and reassure it that it is safe. Alternatively, you can bring up the image of an overly protective parent whose loving intention is to keep their child safe from perceived harm, and ease his concern by providing him the information needed to feel safe.

The next game practice will go well beyond comforting and reassuring your inner pooch and parent. It will give you the tools to build great confidence in yourself and the certainty that the essence of your intentions will be realized.

Rather than fighting, freezing, or fleeing from the bad neighborhood of demons, gremlins, and brats, you will unmask the illusions and unproductive interpretations of so-called "negative" self-talk, reveal the valuable information found beneath the disguise, and strengthen your meaningful intention statement with empowering affirmations.

Tomorrow, we'll revisit Carl. He'll share his current, historic, and sometime hysteric self-talk with us.

Today's Great Day Game Planner

It's great to be alive and well! What will make today a fulfilling and satisfying day? Do the "write" thing, and jot down whatever action steps you'd like to take.

....

....

....

....

....

....

....

Highlight three priority actions. These priority actions will take precedence over all others. Then, time permitting, select others from the planner.

Mood Elevators

Draw a line or shade in each of the mood elevators to reflect your state of being in the moment.

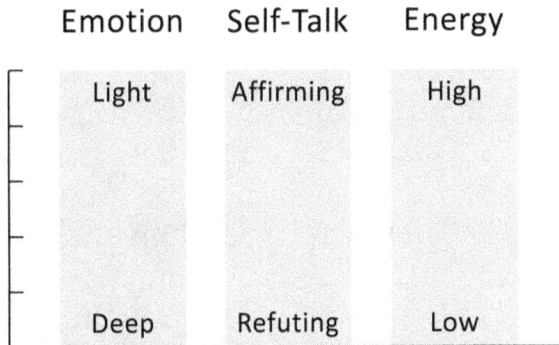

Emotion	Self-Talk	Energy
Light	Affirming	High
Deep	Refuting	Low

TODAY'S GAME PLAY CHECKLIST

Place a checkmark next to each completed game play:

☐ Today's principle card selected and engaged

☐ Fuel-up activities selected from your lightness and energy menu

☐ Intention statement—engaged and refined

☐ Feelings, self-talk, and appreciation entered in captain's logs

☐ Game plan actions entered

☐ Your state of being on the mood elevators assessed

☐ Select and play a mind game today:

    ⭕ Abundant Mind   ⭕ Freeing Your David

    ⭕ Been There, Done That   ⭕ BMW

Day 58—Carl Is Heading to Court

The Opportunity to Regain Freedom

> *Well I know it wasn't you who held me down*
> *Heaven knows it wasn't you who set me free*
> *So often times it happens that we live our lives in chains*
> *And we never even know we have the key*
>
> —Robb Strandlund and Jack Tempchin[26]

Carl has a court day coming up. Carl has not been arrested; he is already in jail but not in the conventional sense. He is in a prison of his own making. As a 90-Day Game player, he is coming to understand this quite well.

Carl's self-imprisonment stems from the voice that only he can hear. It is the voice of his inner dialogue. This particular voice shows up when he is struggling in his career life—at least that is what logic led him to believe. This is a real chicken-and-egg issue.

Is this voice a result of, or the root cause of, his career challenges? Actually, it is both. The voice first develops from the experience of emotional tension; the concern that his dream may not pan out. As doubt firmly steps in, Tex does his thing, building a rational case for why it is logical to doubt himself and his plans. Then repetitive attention becomes a part of his personal reality. The belief is established, and his behavior naturally follows the belief. Remember, our behavior will always follow the beliefs we are attending at any given moment.

So first it is the cause, then it is the result. And this will continue until he makes the choice to challenge the belief. He'll set out to gather additional information—real, experiential evidence for Tex to work with—and fortify the belief that, "I can, I will, and I am."

Carl's aim will be to align the "S" of soulful intent and the "E" of rich emotion with the "M" of mental confident belief, and the "B" of congruent behavior will follow. With harmonious alignment of all four energy resources, he will get back on course and create what he truly wants.

When asked, Carl will tell you that he has been in lockup for many years, and his desire for freedom and achievement are what brought him to play the game.

Carl has been quite the player. He's crafted himself a meaningful intention statement that speaks to these deep desires. He has been having an active conversation with his soul and refines his statement regularly as the process is designed. He's made many shifts in his morning routine and his behavior. Carl is enthusiastic about his possibilities, yet he finds himself all too often having another conversation—one dominated with doubts of himself and his plans, related fears, and worries far more often than he would like.

Over the years, Carl has become an expert at being his own prosecutor. He has a volume of rational evidence for why he is in prison and will most likely remain in prison. His haunting self-talk continues to convince him that he cannot have what he wants. When you look closely at your self-talk, you will discover that it is always revealing what you currently believe.

The good news for Carl is that this court date is an opportunity to be released on probation and, if he succeeds, he will do his best to remain a free man.

Carl will need to identify rational evidence for his defense and release. As you may recall, Carl had some heavy emotions which he Rumi-nated on, and reappraised them into feelings that support his needs. He also discovered a few other needs that he is committed to meeting, and all of this is now reflected in his refined intention statement.

Carl reports that this has loosened up the soil around his seed of intention, and he is more resilient than ever before. When he does drift, he notices, responds, and returns back onto his course far more promptly. This is certainly helping his perspective and attitude and increasing an overall sense of optimism. I love when that happens and, when it does, that means more shifts are soon to follow.

As his own defense attorney, he needs to be a good listener, understand the prosecution's case, and build evidence that counters the opposing position. Most importantly, the defense's case must focus on Carl's motivations for how his release will have a favorable impact on his life and the lives of others. In the end, this will be presented to the judge for a verdict.

In the courtroom, all of the rational evidence to be presented will be of beliefs, some of which refute and some of which uphold his confidence in himself, in his plans, in his talents and strengths, and all of it from his inventory of real-life experiences.

Of course, Carl is the prosecutor, the defense attorney, and the judge. With that in mind, one would think that this would be an easy win, but we know that there is more to it than that, or so-called "negative" self-talk would cease immediately by simply making the choice.

When we take a closer look, we can see there is perfection within the perceived imperfection of a menacing inner dialogue. Although it is easy to judge bothersome self-talk as "negative," when viewed through the prism of alert witnessing and the appraisal principle, self-talk—like deep emotions—is filled with valuable guidance information. Just as Toto pulled back the curtain on the wizard, let's strip that "negative" label off self-talk and see the value hiding behind it.

Your inner dialogue comes up spontaneously and, when you practice alert witnessing, you are grateful for all of it. As emotion guides you to identify and meet unmet needs and honor your values, self-talk guides you to discover the beliefs you are unconsciously investing in and, through that awareness, you discover the beliefs you need to build and fortify in order to realize your intentions.

It is essential for you to understand that your behavior will always follow your beliefs. I'll say it again because it is most important: Your behavior will always follow your beliefs. This is what Henry Ford meant when he said, "Whether you think you can or can't, you're right." Each is a belief, and each will impact your behavior.

When my children were little, we reveled in our nightly reading together. For quite some time, *The Berenstain Bears*[27] books were among our featured favorites. One of the stories was on habits where Sister Bear had developed a habit of biting her nails. Mama Bear brought Sister Bear outside and demonstrated how their wheelbarrow created an impression on the earth, which got deeper and deeper at every pass. She showed Sister Bear how challenging it was to get the wheelbarrow out and how easily it would fall back into the well-established trough.

Self-talk shares these characteristics and, like the deepening ditch, our neural pathways mirror this tendency and become more firmly established. We make things firm through repetition. That is one reason why it is so important to engage your intention statement regularly.

Therefore, so-called "negative" self-talk is a repetitive habit and, left unbridled, leads to self-defeating behavior. Your belief in that storyline will cause you to behave in ways that create more of what you do not want. When skillfully engaged, it will lead you to constructive behavior: first, by allowing you to notice that you have unwittingly built a barricade obstructing your progress, and that you have been adding more bricks and mortar to it every time you repeat those thoughts and self-defeating behavior; then, the solvent of conscious awareness is what dissolves the obstacle, clearing the path for you to pave the road for forward movement.

Like Sister Bear's nail biting, Carl has reinforced a habit of thinking that directs attention on what he does not want. The word "affirmation" means "to make firm" and, by virtue of the same process of inner dialogue and real experience, Carl will make firm a new pathway: the one of his choice.

People who share their so-called "negative" self-talk with me find it effortless to provide a laundry list of reasons why they believe they can't have what they want. It is at the forefront of their awareness and part of their daily thinking. I find it fascinating that when asked to provide evidence of beliefs and experiences that align with what they want to create, that list is available too—and, more often than not, it's a longer list than the self-defeating evidence!

From this we can see that Amy is actively in protective mode, seeking information to keep us safe, highlighting all the things that can go wrong, and holding up her stop sign. It is natural and part of our automatic survival instinct. Utilizing the courtroom technique, you will strengthen your ability to notice when this is occurring. You will interrupt this pattern of behavior by highlighting what can go right. This will calm Amy down, lift Libby's spirits, and provide Tex the information he needs to build a rational case for forward movement.

This does not mean that we are ignoring facts. What it does mean is that we make a good study of what we believe to be facts and determine if there are other factors to be considered. As you will see, the prosecutor will have ample opportunity to present his case.

Just this past week, I met with a coaching client named Matt, whom I had not seen in a good number of months. Matt shared his reality with me. He is an amazing man who was diagnosed with multiple sclerosis roughly nine years ago. He was determined not to let this diagnosis cripple him with fear. He intuitively knew that his outcomes would be greatly influenced by his attitude and, with a rich mindset, he'd take actions that would serve him well.

He partnered with a renowned medical doctor in New York City, who respected and supported Matt's healthy, affirming perspective. Matt is a Silva Method graduate, played the 90-Day Game a few years back, and plays mind games regularly. Matt played college baseball and is eager to get back on the field.

When I asked him if he had been visualizing himself playing baseball, among other things, he said no. He said, "I don't see myself in the imagery." I asked him why he thought that was, and he said, "I don't really know. Maybe I really don't believe it." Matt and I went to court on this right away.

I asked him for evidence, from real experience, that supports the belief he does not want to invest in. He said that he struggles with walking and occasionally trips, and his foot at times drags. He also tires quickly on hot days.

I then asked him for evidence, from real experience, that supports the belief he does not want to invest in. He said that he has been consistently walking better than expected and shared a recent event with me to that effect. His chiropractor told him that his hips are maintaining alignment better than ever, he is lifting more weight at the gym than other men his age and size, his massage therapist said that he is increasing his flexibility and strength, he is advancing faster than most in his yoga class, and his medical doctor has changed his medication because he has and continues to get healthier. He has not had an exacerbation in more than six years. His doctor is convinced that he will be back on the field, and so am I.

Is Amy protecting Matt from disappointment or perhaps concerned that he may injure himself? This may be the case, or maybe there are some other unconscious reasons; however, in the end, it doesn't matter as long as Matt brings that possibility out of the shadows of the inner conscious and into the light of consciousness where he can challenge Amy's assumptions.

Matt recognized that, on balance, he has far more evidence supporting his favorable outcomes than otherwise. To fortify this, he will craft an empowering affirmation—a strategy we will soon cover—and visualize himself back on the field, causing him to have another success to build further rational evidence for his case. He will time himself walking a city block, and target a faster speed to work towards. With every success, he will strengthen and affirm his case, and free himself from perceived limitations.

From Matt's challenge with multiple sclerosis, he has now set out plans for a new intention: to meet with recently diagnosed people and help them to cultivate a healthy perspective, so they too can have the best outcome possible. Matt has reappraised his circumstances in a way that benefits him and others. That is what game players do.

Matt's Insights

A few days later, Matt popped me an email and wrote, "When one gets this diagnosis, the fear factor comes into play. You ask yourself, 'What will happen to me? Will I be a burden on my family?' When you live in fear, you pay attention to the difficulties. When you focus on the vision and take small actions each day, you will see improvements. That shift from noticing the difficulties to noticing the accomplishments changes your life."

Einstein and Fuller would be proud.

He goes on to say, "As much as I have had some issues recently, I continue to look for improvements. I had issues that I dealt with for many years, which I slowly improve on. When I look back, I can see tremendous improvement. I need to remind myself that I had the difficulties for many years. The improvements can take some time as I shift the functioning of my body."

Tomorrow, we'll sit in the courtroom and join Carl at his parole hearing.

Today's Great Day Game Planner

It's great to be alive and well! What will make today a fulfilling and satisfying day? Do the "write" thing, and jot down whatever action steps you'd like to take.

....

....

....

....

....

....

....

Highlight three priority actions. These priority actions will take precedence over all others. Then, time permitting, select others from the planner.

Mood Elevators

Draw a line or shade in each of the mood elevators to reflect your state of being in the moment.

	Emotion	Self-Talk	Energy
	Light	Affirming	High
	Deep	Refuting	Low

TODAY'S GAME PLAY CHECKLIST

Place a checkmark next to each completed game play:

☐ Today's principle card selected and engaged

☐ Fuel-up activities selected from your lightness and energy menu

☐ Intention statement—engaged and refined

☐ Feelings, self-talk, and appreciation entered in captain's logs

☐ Game plan actions entered

☐ Your state of being on the mood elevators assessed

☐ Select and play a mind game today:

    ○ Abundant Mind   ○ Freeing Your David

    ○ Been There, Done That   ○ BMW

Day 59—Carl's Day in Court

The Prosecutor, the Defense Attorney, and the Judge

Be it emotions or self-talk, as a player, reshaping your reality begins with being an alert witness. When you notice emotional heaviness or hear an old, unproductive storyline in your internal dialogue, it's time to take action. The sooner, the better, lest your imagination embellish the story and take you to places you'd prefer not to go.

Rumi showed us that buoyant emotions are always available in the guest house. Now, belief shaping is at hand in the courthouse. The case built by your defense attorney is your ticket to freedom from your own self-made prison.

The Courtroom Exercise

When you notice your inner jukebox playing some old tapes that are not serving you, you could select a different, more upbeat and jolly one; but, when some of these old tapes persistently show up on autoreplay, it's time to take 'em to court and exchange them for what I call "empowering affirmations."

Here's a brief briefing on the basic steps, followed by a visit with Carl and his day in court, which will illustrate the practical application. It's time once again to pick up your OARs. Let's paddle!

- **Observe**
  - o Do the "write" thing and write down your self-talk.
  - o What is the prosecutor's case for why you can't have what you want?
  - o What rational evidence has the prosecutor identified from your direct experience?
  - o What is the belief or beliefs your prosecutor is investing in?
- **Appraise**
  - o What is the defense attorney's case for why you can have what you want?
  - o What rational evidence does the defense attorney have from direct experience that refutes the prosecutor's case as well as substantiates the defense's position?
  - o What belief or beliefs need to be invested in and reinforced to free you from prison?
- **Respond**
  - o What is/are the beliefs you choose to make firm?
  - o Refine your meaningful intention statement with the empowering and affirmative belief or beliefs that you will make firm.

○   What action will you take to cause yourself to have a new, successful experience—one that further affirms movement toward the realization of your intentional outcomes?

Let's run through the courtroom exercise with our friend Carl. First, the "O" in OAR.

Step 1: Observe

Do the "Write" Thing

Carl did the "write" thing and jotted down his disempowering self-talk. This is an important step as it flushes out the conscious and semiconscious residue, demonstrating that Carl is not afraid of his self-talk. Rather than freeze, fight, or flee from it, he engages, explores, and investigates it with the nonjudgmental curiosity characteristic of alert witnessing. In doing so, he becomes aware of the beliefs he is investing in. Armed with this information, the defense attorney is able to build a case that directly refutes these beliefs and, within that process, uncovers what Carl needs to believe to be set free.

Carl writes down all of the self-talk he can recall. This is quite easy because this inner dialogue has been repeated over and over again throughout many years:

There's not enough time to do what I want to do.

There is too much to handle to move my business to the next level.

Will my plans ever work out?

Who am I kidding? What's the use?

The Prosecutor's Case

Now it's the prosecutor's job to build his case with real evidence.

There's not enough time to do what I want to do.

The prosecutor cites occasions when Carl ran out of time, repeatedly missing the mark, and not fulfilling his plans for the day. Carl has gotten up too late, has gotten distracted by emails, and has been late for appointments. Carl lacks discipline and is unorganized.

There is too much to handle to move my business to the next level.

Carl is the chief cook and bottle washer. He is not sufficiently staffed to get things done. He has to do it all by himself. He doesn't have sufficient funding to get the support he needs.

Will my plans ever work out?

Given his behavior, lack of discipline, and understaffed conditions, we believe he will not ever reach his objectives.

The Prosecutor's Summation

Who am I kidding? What's the use?

The prosecution believes that it is time for Carl to face the facts, let go of this pipe dream, and get a real job. Left to this assessment, the judge is likely to agree with the prosecutor. Before the gavel comes down too quickly here, however, it is only fair to hear what the defense attorney has to say about these accusations.

Now we will move to the "A" in OAR.

Step 2: Appraise

- What is the defense attorney's case for why you can have what you want?
- What rational evidence does the defense attorney have from direct experience, which refutes the prosecutor's case as well as substantiates the defense's position?
- What belief or beliefs need to be invested in and reinforced to free you from prison?

The Defense Attorney's Case

"With respect to the following claims, we have additional information that refutes these assumptions, your honor.

"Since Carl began the 90-Day Game, he has been rising earlier than he had in the past, has disciplined himself to get showered and dressed before checking email, and has not been late for a single appointment.

"Carl has also taken steps to enlist interns from the local college and has interviews lined up for next week. He will delegate his administrative duties and online marketing efforts to his interns, thereby freeing himself for increased face-to-face activity with clients and other centers of influence, who will refer more prospective customers.

"Every Wednesday morning, Carl attends a breakfast networking meeting where he obtains fresh leads and develops new relationships. He leaves these meetings and begins his business day by 8:30 a.m., where previously he would have just been getting out of bed.

"We recognize that the business has not yet significantly benefited from these changes; however, we anticipate that these activities will soon show results. It is our position that giving up on the business now would be a huge mistake.

"With Carl's freedom, he will be providing valuable services from his years of experience in the field, and will soon be in a position to provide his interns the opportunity to advance to paid positions."

Step 3: Respond

The Defense Attorney's Summation

"We believe that Carl has demonstrated that he is and will continue to build a viable business. We believe that Carl is well positioned for success, and his success will benefit his family and clients and provide employment for others.

"Should the court stand in Carl's favor, Carl agrees to stay on track with the actions cited above, hire his first intern, and include the following empowering affirmations into his intention statement:

"*Old self-talk:* *There's not enough time to do what I want to do.*

"*Empowering affirmation:* *I recognize that we all have 24/7. I am getting better at selecting priority actions and will maintain realistic expectations of what needs to be accomplished on any given day.*

"*Old self-talk:* *There is too much to handle to move my business to the next level.*

"*Empowering affirmation:* *I simply need to and am taking the next best step to achieve my intentional outcomes.*

"*Old self-talk:* *Will my plans ever work out?*

"*Empowering affirmation:* *I acknowledge the actions I have taken and am taking, and will continue to take action. My plans are working out.*

"*Old self-talk:* *Who am I kidding? What's the use?*

"*Empowering affirmation:* *My confidence in myself and in my plans is growing daily. I owe it to myself, my family, my clients and the opportunities for my soon-to-be hired interns and staff.*"

The defense went on to say that Carl agrees to take the following actions:

"These empowering affirmations will also be stated and repeated whenever Carl observes that his previous self-talk is sliding back due to habit.

"He will welcome his so-called 'negative' self-talk with a grateful spirit, and appraise it as an opportunity to reinforce his intention and fortify his beliefs with empowering affirmations.

"He will respond by interrupting the old, habitual self-talk and replace it with the empowering self-talk, until the inner dialogue becomes the new, habitual self-talk."

The court agreed to Carl's probation, knowing that, as long as he follows the commitments outlined in court, he will continue to be a free man. He will move forward with his intention for the benefit of all, recognizing his need to continue to be an alert witness, and reassure Amy that there is nothing to fear and all is well.

Out of the Darkness and into the Light

A significant objective of our courtroom exercise is to draw out inner conscious beliefs from the shadows of the mind into the light of conscious awareness. Once aware of these beliefs, we are empowered to make significant changes in our feelings, thoughts, and behavior. When you come to understand the nature of self-talk, the idea of beating yourself up for what you have or have not done, or what you are or are not doing, becomes obviously ludicrous. Within the understanding of the perceived "problem" lies the valuable information that will guide you to realizing your most heartfelt desires and intentions.

Carl shared his courtroom experience and empowering affirmations with his friend Lee, who introduced him to the game. In discussing his "case," Carl came to an epiphany: all of his self-talk was rooted in the concern of what may be, rather than what is. Struck by this awareness, it dawned on him that there was one principle card he kept drawing and one that came up with far more frequency than any other: present.

Carl became keenly aware of a significant discovery and found the key to unlocking his cell, setting himself free. That same key opened him up to a new way of being and the beginning of what was quickly becoming something he had always truly wanted: a peaceful mind.

Carl said that if this was all he got from the game, it was worth the price of admission. Being present was a gift he could now give to himself.

Was that card, which was coming up again and again, sent to him by, as Rumi would put it, a guide from beyond, from his inner conscious mind, or was he tapping into his soul's code? In the end, it matters little. Carl is extremely grateful and looks forward to the next day, viewing it as the first day of the rest of his new life.

You can use empowering affirmations in two ways: (1) to upgrade your self-talk when you notice that it is off course with your intention; or (2) to further strengthen supportive beliefs that align with your intention. They too are worthy of attention and reinforcement.

Whenever you feel that you're drifting or hear yourself contradicting, it means that it's time to pick up your OARs and take your beliefs to court.

Tomorrow, you will have your day in court.

Today's Great Day Game Planner

It's great to be alive and well! What will make today a fulfilling and satisfying day? Do the "write" thing, and jot down whatever action steps you'd like to take.

....

....

....

....

....

....

....

Highlight three priority actions. These priority actions will take precedence over all others. Then, time permitting, select others from the planner.

Mood Elevators

Draw a line or shade in each of the mood elevators to reflect your state of being in the moment.

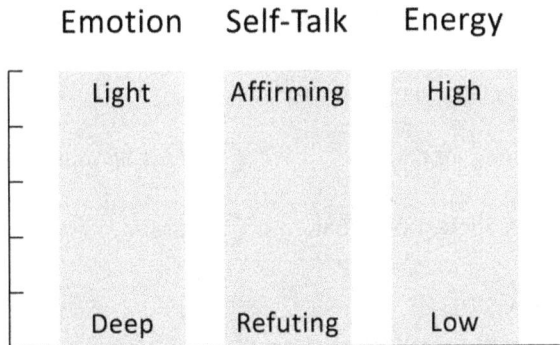

Emotion	Self-Talk	Energy
Light	Affirming	High
Deep	Refuting	Low

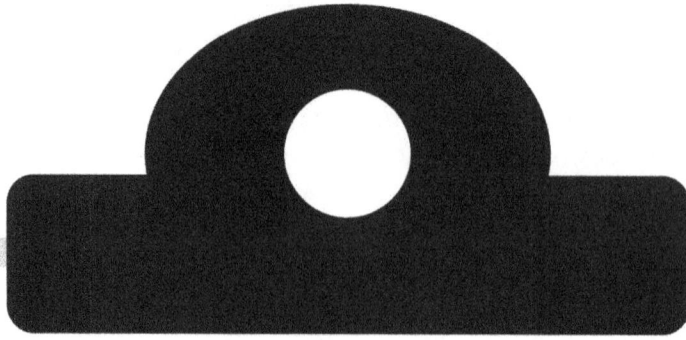

TODAY'S GAME PLAY CHECKLIST

Place a checkmark next to each completed game play:

☐ Today's principle card selected and engaged

☐ Fuel-up activities selected from your lightness and energy menu

☐ Intention statement—engaged and refined

☐ Feelings, self-talk, and appreciation entered in captain's logs

☐ Game plan actions entered

☐ Your state of being on the mood elevators assessed

☐ Select and play a mind game today:

   ⭕ Abundant Mind   ⭕ Freeing Your David

   ⭕ Been There, Done That   ⭕ BMW

Day 60—Your Day in Court

The Courtroom Exercise

Get ready for this next exercise by reading through your meaningful intention statement with particular attention on your inner dialogue. Are you noticing any conflicting self-talk distracting you from your intention? Particularly something that is having you question your belief in your intention? If so, get ready to take it to court. If not, take a look at your captain's self-talk log, and select a belief that you'd like to take into the courtroom.

What's really wonderful about this exercise is that you not only get the benefit of increased awareness and empowering beliefs to fortify, you also walk away with a quieter, kinder mind.

I trust that you'll find this process quite freeing!

The Courtroom Exercise Step 1: Observe
Do the "write" thing and write down your self-talk.

The Courtroom Exercise Step 1: Observe

What is the prosecutor's case for why you can't have what you want?

....

....

....

....

....

....

What rational evidence has the prosecutor identified from your direct experience?

....

....

....

....

....

....

What is the belief or beliefs your prosecutor is investing in?

....

....

....

....

....

....

The Courtroom Exercise Step 2: Appraise

What is the defense attorney's case for why you can have what you want?

....

....

....

....

....

....

What rational evidence does the defense attorney have from direct experience that refutes the prosecutor's case as well as substantiates the defense's position?

....

....

....

....

....

What belief or beliefs need to be invested in and fortified to free you from prison?

....

....

....

....

....

The Courtroom Exercise Step 3: Respond
What is/are the beliefs you choose to make firm? ....
Refine your meaningful intention statement with the empowering and affirmative belief or beliefs that you will make firm. ....
What action will you take to cause yourself to have a new, successful experience—one that further affirms movement toward the realization of your intentional outcomes? ....

Today's Great Day Game Planner

It's great to be alive and well! What will make today a fulfilling and satisfying day? Do the "write" thing, and jot down whatever action steps you'd like to take.

....

....

....

....

....

....

....

Highlight three priority actions. These priority actions will take precedence over all others. Then, time permitting, select others from the planner.

Mood Elevators

Draw a line or shade in each of the mood elevators to reflect your state of being in the moment.

Emotion	Self-Talk	Energy
Light	Affirming	High
Deep	Refuting	Low

TODAY'S GAME PLAY CHECKLIST

Place a checkmark next to each completed game play:

☐ Today's principle card selected and engaged

☐ Fuel-up activities selected from your lightness and energy menu

☐ Intention statement—engaged and refined

☐ Had your day in court

☐ Game plan actions entered

☐ Your state of being on the mood elevators assessed

☐ Select and play a mind game today:

    ◯ Abundant Mind   ◯ Freeing Your David

    ◯ Been There, Done That   ◯ BMW

Day 61—Reminders and Tips of the Week

Catch the Gems

Like the magician's rabbit, epiphanies can go "poof" just as quickly as they arrive. Do the "write" thing and capture those gems before they dissolve into thin air. If your intuition delivers an action step, and it feels right, go for it and act promptly!

Pocket Primers

Whether it's a new insight that "dawned on you" or an empowering affirmation, it is part of the game process to bring those insights into your meaningful intention statement, and reinforce them in your mind game imagery. Pocket primers provide an additional way to internalize these insights and beliefs. These portable trigger tools prompt your attention.

Simply jot down the insight or empowering affirmation, and put it in your pocket. I prefer index cards as they are a heavier weight than ordinary paper, making them easy to locate and notice. When you bump into it, take it out and read it. Just bumping into it will prompt your attention, keeping your consciousness primed and the insight at the forefront of your awareness.

Player's Clinics

Want some coaching on crafting your meaningful intention statement? Want to gain greater objectivity for Rumi-nating? Want to be more skillful in court?

Clinics are offered on these and other topics regularly and are conducted by teleconference. All you need is a telephone. Go to 90DayGame.com and view the Player's Clinic schedule.

Become a Player's Club Member

Player's Club members enjoy discounts to Player's Clinics, one-to-one coaching, telegames, and more. Find out more at 90DayGame.com.

Today's Great Day Game Planner

It's great to be alive and well! What will make today a fulfilling and satisfying day? Do the "write" thing, and jot down whatever action steps you'd like to take.

....

....

....

....

....

....

....

Highlight three priority actions. These priority actions will take precedence over all others. Then, time permitting, select others from the planner.

Mood Elevators

Draw a line or shade in each of the mood elevators to reflect your state of being in the moment.

Emotion	Self-Talk	Energy
Light	Affirming	High
Deep	Refuting	Low

TODAY'S GAME PLAY CHECKLIST

Place a checkmark next to each completed game play:

☐ Today's principle card selected and engaged

☐ Fuel-up activities selected from your lightness and energy menu

☐ Intention statement—engaged and refined

☐ Feelings, self-talk, and appreciation entered in captain's logs

☐ Game plan actions entered

☐ Your state of being on the mood elevators assessed

☐ Select and play a mind game today:

○ Abundant Mind   ○ Freeing Your David

○ Been There, Done That   ○ BMW

Days 62 and 63—Free Day Reminder

PART VIII

Expanding Your Horizons

WEEK 10

Revisiting the Garden
and Advancing Clarity

Day 64—The Weed and Feed Mind Game

From the process of Rumi-nating and your day in court, you have discovered deep needs, values, and beliefs:

- Needs that are being met and needs that are to be met
- Values that are being honored and those that need to be honored
- Beliefs that were misaligned with intent and aligned beliefs that are now being fortified

You've refined your meaningful intention statement with needs, values, and empowering affirmations. Every time you direct your attention on your intention and have that ongoing conversation with your soul, you are deepening neural pathways. You are reshaping your brain, and your conscious thoughts and actions increasingly mirror your soul's code. You are recognizing that these direct experiences are transforming your beliefs into a deep sense of knowing.

Much of these discoveries were identified by objective action: the questions and the responses. As effective as Rumi-nating is at identifying emotional needs and values, and as powerful as the repetition of empowering affirmations are in strengthening neural pathways, the inner conscious mind must also be congruent with soul, emotion, thought, and action. This is the ultimate essential role that mind games play.

Today, you will revisit the garden and have an effective conversation with your inner conscious mind.

You will reengage this imaginative journey in the same fashion as you did when planting the seed beginning in your home, in your selected room, through the door, down the spiral staircase, through the hallway, and into the brightly illuminated room.

You will now make use of the materials on the table, which is covered with white linen, before you revisit the garden.

The ornately designed book with gold-leaf trim is representative of all your beliefs: those that you have had, those that you currently have, and those that you will have. The bridge from the objective discoveries you have made to the fertile soil of the inner conscious mind will be built at the table.

Ceremonies and rituals are powerful mediums for change for most, if not all, cultures. You will bring to awareness the limiting beliefs you have carried by removing those pages from the book, burning them safely with the stick matches on the plate of fine china. You'll watch them dissolve into embers and ash, and wipe the plate clean.

You will then pick up the ornate pen, and write your empowering affirmations into the book. Although vivid, rituals are more emotionally engaged, almost trance-like, and are absent of intellectual detail. Therefore, rather than concerning yourself with precise language, particularly when you are writing in the book, focus on the essence, understanding, and value of this new empowering belief.

From this ceremonial bridge, you will reemerge into the lush garden with all of its brilliant color, aromatic splendor, warmth, and gentle breezes. You'll be fully with the metaphor, amazed at how your seed has grown into a young, vibrant, and healthy fruit tree. You will remove any weeds you may notice with surprising ease, discard them into a wheelbarrow, and nurture your tree's emergent growth, lovingly watering the earth beneath it. While in the garden, take pleasure in some tasty fruit already present within your fabulous garden, knowing that you will return to reap more with the next harvest.

Now allow the audio to guide you, and enjoy the Weed and Feed mind game.

Today's Great Day Game Planner

It's great to be alive and well! What will make today a fulfilling and satisfying day? Do the "write" thing, and jot down whatever action steps you'd like to take.

....

....

....

....

....

....

....

Highlight three priority actions. These priority actions will take precedence over all others. Then, time permitting, select others from the planner.

Mood Elevators

Draw a line or shade in each of the mood elevators to reflect your state of being in the moment.

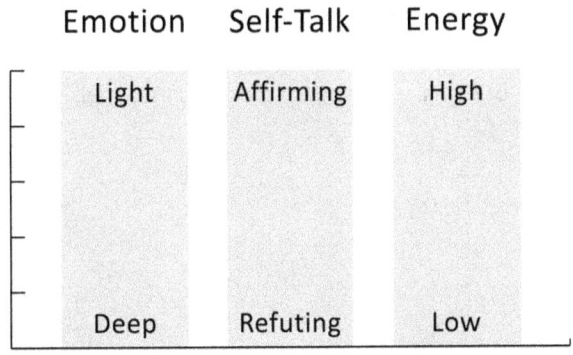

Emotion	Self-Talk	Energy
Light	Affirming	High
Deep	Refuting	Low

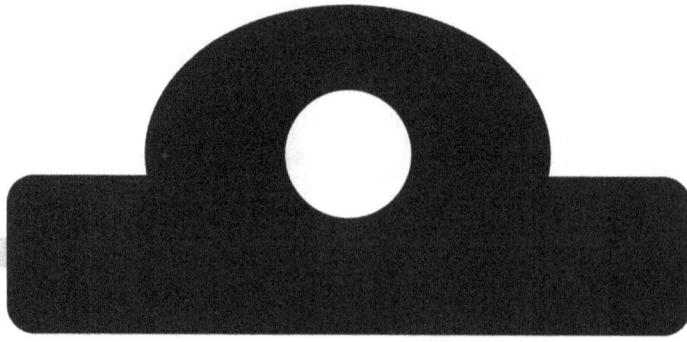

TODAY'S GAME PLAY CHECKLIST

Place a checkmark next to each completed game play:

- ☐ Today's principle card selected and engaged

- ☐ Fuel-up activities selected from your lightness and energy menu

- ☐ Intention statement—engaged and refined

- ☐ Feelings, self-talk, and appreciation entered in captain's logs

- ☐ Weed and Feed mind game played

- ☐ Game plan actions entered

- ☐ Your state of being on the mood elevators assessed

Day 65—The Finite and the Infinite

Remaining Open beyond What You Think Is Possible

When you are clear, the path appears. Increasing clarity of what you truly want heightens your sensitivity to notice and attracts the ingredients you need to create it.

In 1995, I decided to become a certified instructor of the Silva Method. I originally took the course back in 1974 when I was 18 years old. This method is what spurred my interest in the awesome capacity of consciousness. By applying this system, I was able to overcome all of my many allergies, totally eliminate years of chronic back pain from a car accident, cure an erratic heartbeat, and double my income within six months when my wife and I chose for her to stay home to raise our twins.

I took the instructor training with the founder José Silva. Admittedly, my initial reason for taking the instructor training was mainly to further enhance my own personal mastery of the method. It was José Silva, however, who made me see the value of going forward and teaching the course.

After facilitating my first session, I was hooked. So many people reported huge shifts and benefits that I was drawn to go further and conduct these sessions more regularly. Enjoying my career in the financial field, I had no need to generate income from teaching the program, yet I soon found myself more than a little disappointed. Feeling all dressed up with nowhere to go, I was dissatisfied with the number of people I was attracting to take the course. What could possibly be the problem? Soon it became clear that the problem was one of perspective. My apparent inability to fill the classes led me to explore this further, deeply within myself.

Running through the essence questions, which you will respond to tomorrow, I was able to become clear on the essence of my intention. I wanted to have an impact, set an environment for well-being and the rejuvenation of spirit that I now enjoyed, to inspire and be inspired, and to be a catalyst for change and transformation.

One evening, while my wife Joan and I were lying in bed reading, she pointed to a class offered through The Learning Annex in New York City titled "How to Become a 6-Figure Consultant." She showed it to me, thinking that this may lead me in the right direction. I took a look and found another ad alongside it on the same page. It was a course about a new, growing industry called "coaching." It described something that I thought I came up with, as I did offer all of my students a complimentary telephone coaching session once they completed the course. Well, I did attend the session and, minutes into the class, I absolutely knew that I was going to go forward and enroll in the training program at Coach University.

As it turned out, I found myself quite unexpectedly transitioning to a new career! When I looked at the responses to my essence questions, I realized that becoming a coach was a perfect match for the essence of my intent: to have an impact, set an environment for well-being and the rejuvenation of spirit, to inspire and be inspired, and to be a catalyst for change and transformation.

My finite view was to teach the Silva Method; however, the infinite had grander opportunities in mind. Had I filled the classes easily, I may not have this most rewarding career, a coaching company, the radio shows, and more. Oh, by the way, coaching created lots of activity and interest in my work and, every time I presented the Silva Method, the room filled!

This personal story illustrates many key aspects to the meaningful intentions framework. There is more to our soul's desire than meets our conscious eye:

- It is in our best interest to remain open to the possibility that our deepest desires can be met by means that we may have not yet conceived.

- We can allow ourselves to be intuitively guided.

- Meaningful coincidences and synchronicity are available to us all.

- Forcing our idea of what we "think" we really want can preclude us from having even grander opportunities realized.

In his brilliant work, *Care of the Soul: A Guide for Cultivating Depth and Sacredness in Everyday Life*, Thomas Moore states, "It is also our task to find artful means of articulating and structuring that [soul] power, taking full responsibility for it, but trusting too that the soul has intentions and necessities that we may understand only partially."[28] Again, our finite, conscious awareness does not have the full picture. When the jigsaw puzzle comes together, only then do we see the perfection of its wholeness. That's another vote for keeping the conversation with your soul alive.

Detaching From the Finite

Although our rational minds conjure up an image of what we desire, we do ourselves a disservice to become attached to the object of that desire. The image serves as a tuning mechanism that puts us on the right channel, so to speak, with the kind of stuff we desire. When we get caught up in the need to have the object of our desire, however, we cut ourselves off from the unbounded possibilities of things that are much grander. Our finite, conscious mind offers us limited data. When we engage the sacred gift of the intuitive mind, as Einstein recommends, we usher in unbounded opportunities to experience joys beyond our wildest dreams.

Tomorrow you will respond to essence questions, which will set the stage for your creative mind to gain further clarity to meet your soul's deepest needs and desires.

Today's Great Day Game Planner

It's great to be alive and well! What will make today a fulfilling and satisfying day? Do the "write" thing, and jot down whatever action steps you'd like to take.

....

....

....

....

....

....

....

Highlight three priority actions. These priority actions will take precedence over all others. Then, time permitting, select others from the planner.

Mood Elevators

Draw a line or shade in each of the mood elevators to reflect your state of being in the moment.

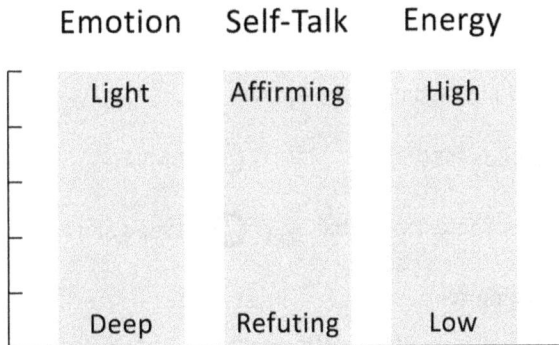

Emotion	Self-Talk	Energy
Light	Affirming	High
Deep	Refuting	Low

TODAY'S GAME PLAY CHECKLIST

Place a checkmark next to each completed game play:

☐ Today's principle card selected and engaged

☐ Fuel-up activities selected from your lightness and energy menu

☐ Intention statement—engaged and refined

☐ Feelings, self-talk, and appreciation entered in captain's logs

☐ Game plan actions entered

☐ Your state of being on the mood elevators assessed

☐ Select and play a mind game today:

    ⚪ Abundant Mind   ⚪ BMW

    ⚪ Been There, Done That   ⚪ Weed and Feed

    ⚪ Freeing Your David

Day 66— Gaining Further Clarity of Intent

The Essence Questions Exercise

Follow these three simple steps:

1. Bring your meaningful intention to mind.

2. Using the sacred gift of your imagination, envision your intentional outcomes as if they were fully realized.

3. Respond to the essence questions below.

Are you ready? Let's play!

The Essence Questions
Now that I have fully realized my intention:
What needs does it satisfy? ....
How does it feel to have this in my life? Express your feelings spontaneously, using single-word descriptors (e.g., exhilarated, uplifted, joyful, grateful, and appreciative). ....
How do I feel about myself now that I have created this in my life? Again, express your feelings spontaneously, using single-word descriptors. ....

The Essence Questions
What benefits am I enjoying?
....
....
....
How are others benefiting from my creation?
....
....
....

What if you were able to satisfy your deepest needs, enhance the quality of your life, and feel about your life and yourself as you described above while you and others enjoy the benefits you wrote about but obtained them through some other means? Would that be just fine with you?

Continue to do the "write" thing, and refine your dynamic meaningful intention statement with whatever insights come to you.

Today's Great Day Game Planner

It's great to be alive and well! What will make today a fulfilling and satisfying day? Do the "write" thing, and jot down whatever action steps you'd like to take.

....

....

....

....

....

....

....

Highlight three priority actions. These priority actions will take precedence over all others. Then, time permitting, select others from the planner.

Mood Elevators

Draw a line or shade in each of the mood elevators to reflect your state of being in the moment.

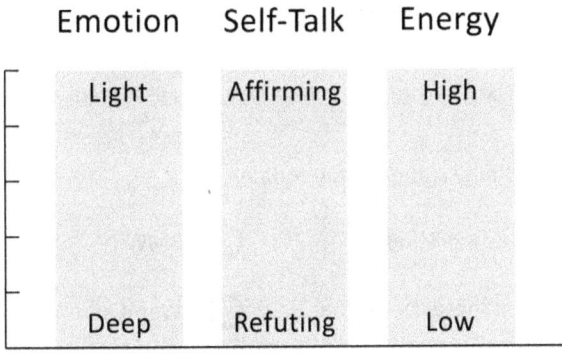

Emotion	Self-Talk	Energy
Light	Affirming	High
Deep	Refuting	Low

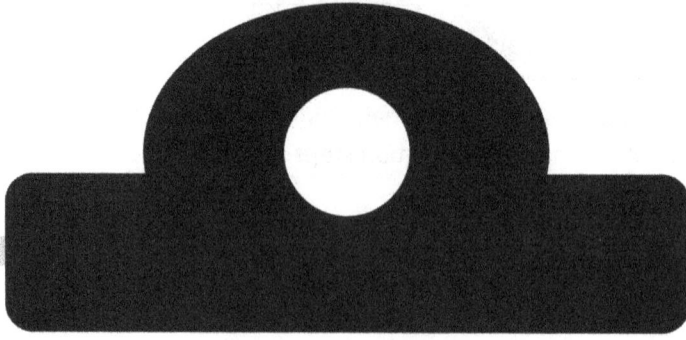

TODAY'S GAME PLAY CHECKLIST

Place a checkmark next to each completed game play:

☐ Today's principle card selected and engaged

☐ Fuel-up activities selected from your lightness and energy menu

☐ Intention statement—engaged and refined

☐ Feelings, self-talk, and appreciation entered in captain's logs

☐ The essence questions exercise

☐ Game plan actions entered

☐ Your state of being on the mood elevators assessed

☐ Select and play a mind game today:

    ◯ Abundant Mind   ◯ BMW

    ◯ Been There, Done That   ◯ Weed and Feed

    ◯ Freeing Your David

Day 67—The Reaping the Harvest Mind Game

One of the wonderful attributes of the inner conscious mind is that it is free from time and space limitations. We notice this in our dreams. People from the past and present can be in the same dream, even those who have left the physical plane of existence. Events can shift spontaneously yet, in that state, it all seems perfectly normal. The imagined house you live in within your dream is nothing like your "real" one, yet you don't question it at all. The rational mind is deep under, taking a lovely break from its usual business of analyzing and organizing, and so forth.

While awake, we are quite capable of using our imagination. Michelangelo did when he projected his imagination into the stone to free his David. In our mind game, you freed yours, seeing the end result of your intention fully realized in all of its exquisite glory. Now, at a highly suggestible state, on the edge of sleep, using metaphor, you will return to the garden to enjoy the harvest. Your magnificent, creative mind will align with Libby's frontier of emotion, and together they will stimulate further illuminations for Tex to organize. You will then verify and implement these insights into action, and bring your intentional outcomes to life.

This garden exercise follows the same ritualistic process. You will find a comfortable position, close your eyes, and enter that highly relaxing and impressionable state. You will project your imagination to the same room within your home, view and enter the imaginary door, go down the spiral staircase, through the torch-lit hall, kick off your shoes, and enter the brightly illuminated room through the door marked as your inner conscious mind.

Once again, you will be greeted by the friendly person who hands you the staff, and you will proceed to the table covered in white linen. You will look at the screen before you on the little puppet show-like stage, and open the curtains to see the image of the beautiful garden.

You will enter the scene, enjoy the color and fragrance of the flowers, feel the warmth of the sun, and hear birds melodiously singing in the distance and the rustling of the leaves stirred by the gentle breeze of nature's breath. Your seed has gone through all the stages of growth and within this lush setting before you stands a magnificent tree of grand stature, bearing ripe fruit.

You will behold the richness of the moment, freely sharing the savory fruit with all those you love, who are now present with you in the garden. Their presence reminds you of the valuable roles they have played in your life, and that this tree is theirs, as well as yours, and how the attainment of this outcome is pregnant with the treasures from the journey. The preparation of the soil, the tending, the feeding, and even the weeds played their part as guides for appropriate and dedicated nurturance.

Once again, your attention will be drawn to the awareness of many other fruit trees within your garden. Each tree represents the treasures already present within your fabulous life, the gifts you were given by your Creator, and what you have shaped from that raw material. As aware as you are that new seeds of intention will be planted and more fruit will be born, the ultimate fulfillment lies in the awareness of what is present, in the present. While in the garden, stimulated in the dynamism of it all, you are peaceful. You are tranquil.

Today's Great Day Game Planner

It's great to be alive and well! What will make today a fulfilling and satisfying day? Do the "write" thing, and jot down whatever action steps you'd like to take.

....

....

....

....

....

....

....

Highlight three priority actions. These priority actions will take precedence over all others. Then, time permitting, select others from the planner.

Mood Elevators

Draw a line or shade in each of the mood elevators to reflect your state of being in the moment.

Emotion	Self-Talk	Energy
Light	Affirming	High
Deep	Refuting	Low

TODAY'S GAME PLAY CHECKLIST

Place a checkmark next to each completed game play:

☐ Today's principle card selected and engaged

☐ Fuel-up activities selected from your lightness and energy menu

☐ Intention statement—engaged and refined

☐ Feelings, self-talk, and appreciation entered in captain's logs

☐ Reaping the Harvest mind game played

☐ Game plan actions entered

☐ Your state of being on the mood elevators assessed

Day 68—Reminders and Tips of the Week

Hanging Out in the Garden of Your Choice

We reap more robust harvests when repetition is in play. This is true at the outer world of action and the inner world of contemplation. We also know the impact the environment has on our attitude and perspective, effecting our emotions, thoughts, and behavior.

At this stage of the game, you can enter mind game-like states to reflect, project, or simply revel in the present moment. If you find the garden to be the place of choice, personalize it. Add a babbling brook; a comfortable place to sit, recline, or lie down; and perhaps a table and a few chairs for chats with your mental mentors. The more familiar you are with the environment, the more comfortable and relaxed you will be, and this inner world will become a very real world for you. As you return regularly to the same place and continue to embellish it, you'll notice that your imagery will become more vivid. Mental pictures, sounds, and textures will sharpen, enhancing the effectiveness of all of your mind games.

Some years ago, my favored place was at the beach with Joan beside me. I'd feel the sand running through the fingers of one hand while feeling the chill of a tasty piña colada in the other. I'd get up and notice the hot sand, almost too hot to handle, beneath my bare city feet, and notice how it would progressively cool as I walked toward the water's edge. The sound of the ocean got progressively louder as I first heard the crashing waves flow onshore and then the quieter tones as they receded rhythmically with every breath I took. Then, a seagull came into view, and I heard its call as it hovered on the shoreline supported by the oncoming breeze. In the distance, there were two guitarists singing and playing Hawaiian songs.

In more recent years, I shifted to my favorite little airport. Perhaps you're not surprised! For Persephone, her butterfly garden is the perfect match. Where will you go? It's your mind. Let your boundless imagination guide you to the optimal environment of your choice.

Follow the Leaders

Speaking of repetition, this is worth repeating. Earlier, I strongly urged players who were interested in strengthening their subjective abilities to take the Silva Method. You certainly will benefit from their audio programs. If you are fortunate to have a local Silva facilitator in your area, participating in their live training programs will accelerate your growth in developing command of your mental faculties.

What do award-winning neuroscientist Mark Robert Waldman, oncology research pioneer O. Carl Simonton, and best-selling authors Jack Canfield, Dr. Wayne Dyer, Shakti Gawain, and Richard Bach have in common? Aside from being leaders in their own fields, they all encourage you to take the Silva Method.

Millions of people in over 100 countries and in 30 different languages have taken the Silva Method. For more information, go to SilvaMethod.com.

Today's Great Day Game Planner

It's great to be alive and well! What will make today a fulfilling and satisfying day? Do the "write" thing, and jot down whatever action steps you'd like to take.

....

....

....

....

....

....

....

Highlight three priority actions. These priority actions will take precedence over all others. Then, time permitting, select others from the planner.

Mood Elevators

Draw a line or shade in each of the mood elevators to reflect your state of being in the moment.

Emotion	Self-Talk	Energy
Light	Affirming	High
Deep	Refuting	Low

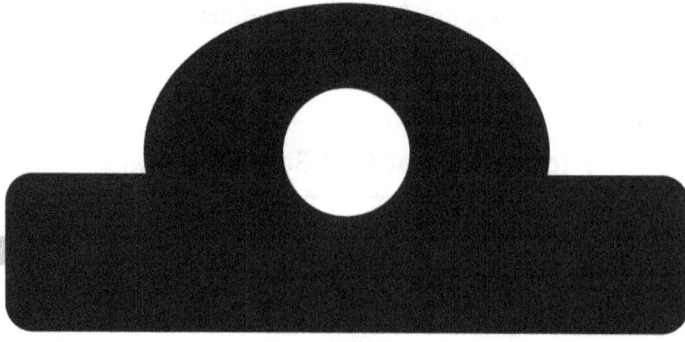

TODAY'S GAME PLAY CHECKLIST

Place a checkmark next to each completed game play:

☐ Today's principle card selected and engaged

☐ Fuel-up activities selected from your lightness and energy menu

☐ Intention statement—engaged and refined

☐ Feelings, self-talk, and appreciation entered in captain's logs

☐ Game plan actions entered

☐ Your state of being on the mood elevators assessed

☐ Select and play a mind game today:

   ○ Abundant Mind   ○ BMW

   ○ Been There, Done That   ○ Weed and Feed

   ○ Freeing Your David   ○ Reaping the Harvest

Days 69 and 70—Free Day Reminder

Understanding Personal Reality and the Bigger Picture

Day 71—Your Personal Reality

RE-inforced Assumptions Literally Imagined as True for You

Our brains have a love affair with the familiar. We'd really like to believe that reality is firm and all is universally true for all of us. This is the case for things like gravity but far from it when it comes to our personal reality.

Allow me to play with just one last acronym. Your perception of reality is a product of RE-ALITY (RE-inforced Assumptions Literally Imagined as True for You). We make assumptions all the time and, with the power of our imagination, perceive them as "the truth." We reinforce them over and over again in our self-talk and behavior.

Okay, I lied. Just one more acronym, I promise: REALITY (RE-inforced Assumptions Literally *Interpreted* as True for You). We know that our perspective and attitude have much to do with how we interpret our circumstances and the choices we make.

Throughout the game, we have worked with the appraisal principle to gain objectivity. We've dropped labels of "good" and "bad," knowing that these filters of judgment color our perspective. Instead, we've appraised our emotions, thoughts, people, and events objectively as valuable guidance information, and we've experienced the favorable shift this has on our view of things.

Dr. Hendrie Weisinger, author of *Emotional Intelligence at Work: The Untapped Edge for Success*,[29] stated, "It is the meaning we assign to events and to people we encounter that affects us for good or ill, not the events or people themselves." That is at the heart of the appraisal principle, and it is in exercising this principle that we discover how extremely flexible our personal reality is.

This is the case in all areas of life. Our political leanings and religious beliefs are two evident areas which some have fought to the death over. For those who disagree with us, we view them as mad or completely out of touch with reality and, of course, those same people believe that we are out of touch with reality as well. Both go beyond belief, convinced that what they believe is in fact the truth.

But beliefs can and do change. Just as one may believe in Santa Claus and no longer does—sorry, Santa—and with sufficient information, people do at times change their political leanings and religious views. This requires objectivity and a willingness to reconsider the assumptions we've invested in.

With all of that said, let's visit with Jenny and hear her story.

Jenny's Story

Jenny is four years old. She has just created what, in her mind, is an artful masterpiece. Excitedly, she goes to find Mommy to share her drawing. Running into the kitchen, she sees her beloved mother.

"Mommy, Mommy, look what I did!"

Her enthusiasm is promptly stifled by mommy's reactive behavior.

"Jenny! What's wrong with you? Can't you see I'm on the phone?"

Jenny was startled by her mother's sudden outburst. In this case, Jenny's shocking emotional reaction was appraised as a feeling of rejection. Another child may have interpreted this event differently. Another light-hearted youngster may have assigned the meaning that her mommy is simply busy, would think little of it, and go back to coloring.

Jenny's feelings of rejection opened up a new file within her folder of beliefs—beliefs that were subsequently reinforced over and over again in her self-talk. This inner dialogue, combined with feelings of rejection, deposited beliefs of "I'm not good enough," "I'm unimportant," and "I'm inadequate" into a belief folder, which she would continue to carry throughout life.

Jenny's memory of this event, whether consciously recalled or not, caused her to be tentative when preparing to make presentations at school and later on in life while at work. This triggered self-talk that she and her work may not be good enough, and she became fearful that her ideas might be rejected.

Her feelings and self-talk, paired together, created a convincing belief for Jenny and became a significant part of her personal reality. Time and time again, this tension had Jenny shy away from sharing her ideas. The few times she did step up, her ideas were often minimized because her lack of confidence led others to question the value of those suggestions. This was more "real" evidence, further reinforcing the beliefs she carried.

Because the evidence is so convincing and appears to be the truth, it makes perfect sense that she would act in alignment with her perceived reality. Although Jenny may continue to produce masterful works, her beliefs may hold her back from success with them. Jenny needs to cultivate belief in herself and her work in order to realize her potential and benefit from it. She needs to challenge the underlying assumptions or find another creative means if those assumptions are no longer within her conscious awareness. Einstein was believed to have said, "Reality is merely an illusion, albeit a very persistent one."

Whether or not I am attributing an accurate meaning to what he supposedly said, I do believe our assumptions and assigned meanings create our beliefs and perceptual illusions of our personal reality. Just look at how flexible our personal reality is! Does that make you uneasy, or does it stimulate possibilities within you?

On the one hand, we'd really like to know with great certainty what the truth is. If only it were in black and white, it would provide the stability that Amy and Libby long for; on the other hand, when we accept the malleable nature of our personal reality, we are empowered to mold it by our own intentional design.

Let's look at the anatomy of beliefs in a little greater detail, and see the impact this can have on your personal reality.

The Anatomy of Beliefs

Here are five key ingredients that set a fertile environment for belief formation:

1. Suggestibility
2. Authority figures
3. Emotional resonance
4. Interpretations
5. Reinforcement

By our nature, we are suggestible beings. Whether it's a survival instinct or a strong human desire, we want to be accepted by our tribes, be they family, friends, schoolmates, or associates, each with their own elected tribal leaders.

As young children, we rely on adults to provide our basic needs for food, clothing, and shelter as well as our emotional needs to feel protected, cared for, and loved. Emotion plays a major role. The more intense the emotion, the greater the impact it has on us.

With each experience, we assign meanings, which may or may not be accurate. People with different dispositions will interpret their experiences in accord with those dispositions shaped by their innate nature, environmental influences, and life experiences. With repetition—be it an event, emotional reaction, thought, or behavior—our belief in our interpretations are fortified and convinces us that our assumptions are accurate and, in fact, are the truth.

Jenny's story is a perfect example to illustrate the anatomy of a belief. Remember: Jenny was reveling in her masterpiece, which she was eager to share with her mother.

1. **Suggestibility:** Jenny's dominant brain state at the age of four is similar to the mental state hypnotherapists orient their patients and the state we are cultivating with our mind game exercises, a highly impressionable state.

2. **Authority figures:** Her enthusiasm for her masterpiece was shot down by the most important person in her world: the person she loves, honors, and depends on more than anyone else on the planet.

3. **Emotional resonance:** Jenny experienced a sudden shift from joyful exuberance to startling rejection. Here we see the principle of the law of resonance in play (see card deck or appendix). Within an instant, Jenny's mother's agitation triggered Jenny's agitation.

4. **Interpretations:** Jenny totally relies on her mother for all her needs and her very survival. She carries the belief that whatever Mommy says is, in fact, the truth. Amy's threatened, Libby's sensitivity resonates with rejection, and Jenny assigns meanings to the event: "Something is wrong with me. My artwork is unimportant. I am unimportant. My artwork is not good enough. I am not good enough. My artwork is bad. I am bad." Tex goes along for the ride and builds a rational case for Jenny's appraisals.

5. **Reinforcement:** Jenny is now tentative about her value and the value of her work. She is apprehensive about approaching family members, teachers, associates, and other people in her world, concerned about possible rejection, shame, and potential disappointment. In cases where she works through the discomfort, her insecurity comes through and her ideas are questioned, reinforcing her belief of her inadequacy with real-world evidence that she doesn't make the grade.

The belief is established ("I am not good enough") and perfectionist behavior becomes a way of being. When similar events occur, the emotional tone brings back the past event and reinforces the beliefs ("I'm not good enough," "I am unimportant," and "I am inadequate").

The meaning that Jenny assigned to this event is not the truth; it is an interpretation of the truth. At the age of four, Jenny had not yet developed the capacity to consider other equally valid interpretations of her mother's behavior:

- She could have finally gotten through to her doctor to get the findings of Jenny's blood tests.

- She could have been having a fight with Jenny's dad.

- She could have just gotten some terrible news.

- She may have been tense, stressed, or under pressure for any number of reasons.

- She may have simply had a rough day.

Jenny's mother may not have realized the impact her reactive outburst had on her daughter, and Jenny didn't have the scope to consider that her mom's outburst had little to do with her.

Jenny's a game player now and, by most standards, a well-adjusted woman. She intellectually understands that she assigned the meaning to this event a long, long time ago.

"It really wasn't my mom's fault. At the very least, she didn't mean any harm. Does that mean it is my fault?"

The trading blame game is not one we play in the 90-Day Game. Seeking fault, blame, weakness, defects, and deficits are all reactive judgments and come from a victim mentality. Instead, we return to paddling on course with our productive OARs. We observe our new understanding, appraise its value, and respond in ways that serve our intentions for the benefit of all. Now we have all we need to do just that.

The payoff for Jenny here is for her to revel in the awareness that she discovered a false assumption and that she can replace it with a more accurate appraisal. It's about the choice she has to assign new meanings and reinforce empowering beliefs. That is the rational thing to do, the emotionally intelligent thing to do, and the most practical thing to do in order to get on with living her fabulous life!

Jenny always knew that she lacked confidence and, although she has a better understanding of it now, she honestly admits that, at some level, she has anger. It is part resentment for her mom's reactiveness and part hostility with herself for letting her sensitive nature hold her back for all these years.

With some coaching, Jenny began to appraise her sensitive nature as a valuable asset, one which enables her to strongly relate to others with compassion. Like Jenny, each of our greatest strengths is coupled with our greatest challenges. So, when challenged, I invite you to take out your OARs and reappraise the challenge as an opportunity to identify more of your strengths and, by all means, add them to your talents, strengths, and skills list.

Jenny's a real player and, even though she recognizes that it is in her best interest to respond with objectivity, the emotions persist. Jenny will Rumi-nate on it, take it to court, and, with all of this precious insight, she will play another mind game. This one will soothe Jenny's Libby with compassionate love and make effective use of the five key ingredients that set a rich environment for belief formation. This is the Rewind, Review, Recreate mind game, to which you will be introduced tomorrow.

Today's Great Day Game Planner

It's great to be alive and well! What will make today a fulfilling and satisfying day? Do the "write" thing, and jot down whatever action steps you'd like to take.

....

....

....

....

....

....

....

Highlight three priority actions. These priority actions will take precedence over all others. Then, time permitting, select others from the planner.

Mood Elevators

Draw a line or shade in each of the mood elevators to reflect your state of being in the moment.

Emotion	Self-Talk	Energy
Light	Affirming	High
Deep	Refuting	Low

TODAY'S GAME PLAY CHECKLIST

Place a checkmark next to each completed game play:

☐ Today's principle card selected and engaged

☐ Fuel-up activities selected from your lightness and energy menu

☐ Intention statement—engaged and refined

☐ Feelings, self-talk, and appreciation entered in captain's logs

☐ Game plan actions entered

☐ Your state of being on the mood elevators assessed

☐ Select and play a mind game today:

○ Abundant Mind   ○ BMW

○ Been There, Done That   ○ Weed and Feed

○ Freeing Your David   ○ Reaping the Harvest

Day 72—From Judgment to Love: The Rewind, Review, Recreate Mind Game

We are not punished for our anger, we are punished by
our anger ... Let a man overcome anger by love.

— Gautama Buddha[30]

Clients and players report that the Rewind, Review, Recreate mind game is a most effective tool in releasing resentment, anger, and hostility through understanding, compassion, and love.

The above quotation has been attributed to Buddha in a variety of forms. Whether said by Buddha or not matters little. The point here is that, when we carry the burden of anger, resentment, and hostility, it is a weight that has impact on no other than ourselves. When we label these and many other emotions as "negative," we fight or guilt ourselves for having them or flee from them through some form of distraction.

Consistent with our theme, all emotions are to be honored and engaged. The so-called "negative" becomes the catalyst for "positive" action. Once again, engagement recaptures vital energy and leads us to the freedom of enhanced personal realities.

The first step is to reach a level of acceptance and embrace the past. With this in mind, let's take a moment to understand what we mean by "embracing the past" before beginning the exercise.

Embracing the past means that:

- We understand that the totality of all of our previous life experiences brought us to this precious, present moment, and to reject any part of it is tantamount to rejecting ourselves. Therefore, embracing our past is a loving act of kindness.

- Forgiveness is about cultivating greater understanding, compassion, and love. We accomplish this by releasing that which we are holding to ourselves too closely.

- Most inappropriate, hurtful behavior comes from an absence of self-love, a lack of awareness, and often a sense of unworthiness felt by the offending party. This helps us understand why sending love to the offending party is an obvious choice.

- At the spiritual, soulful level, the illusion of separateness is shattered, and we all have the same universal needs: to be appreciated, cared for, and loved. Therefore, forgiving another is forgiving ourselves and vice versa.

- As Deepak Chopra said, "Healing is the return of the memory of wholeness."

- By continuing to enter the deep peace found in mind games and meditation, we continue to develop an inner calmness and are less reactive, thereby enabling us to be more understanding of our own behavior and the behavior of others. Consequently, by being peaceful, we are less likely to cause harm or be harmed.

The Rewind, Review, Recreate mind game will allow you to make a good study of your interpretations of the past, and use the sacred gift of your imagination to release and replace resentment, anger, and hostility with understanding, compassion, and love.

If you have any challenges applying this process to your particular situation, send an email to Team@90DayGame.com, and we'll be happy to assist you.

Within this exercise, we capitalize once again on the fact that the brain does not know the difference between a "real" and a "vividly imagined" event.

Are you holding on to any resentment, hostility, or anger from the past? If so, let the Rewind, Review, Recreate mind game audio guide you through the process of releasing it. Understand, this is not psychotherapy nor medical advice. If you are experiencing significant, prolonged, or reoccurring sadness or depression, I strongly suggest you seek appropriate medical attention.

Today's Great Day Game Planner

It's great to be alive and well! What will make today a fulfilling and satisfying day? Do the "write" thing, and jot down whatever action steps you'd like to take.

....

....

....

....

....

....

....

Highlight three priority actions. These priority actions will take precedence over all others. Then, time permitting, select others from the planner.

Mood Elevators

Draw a line or shade in each of the mood elevators to reflect your state of being in the moment.

Emotion	Self-Talk	Energy
Light	Affirming	High
Deep	Refuting	Low

TODAY'S GAME PLAY CHECKLIST

Place a checkmark next to each completed game play:

☐ Today's principle card selected and engaged

☐ Fuel-up activities selected from your lightness and energy menu

☐ Intention statement—engaged and refined

☐ Feelings, self-talk, and appreciation entered in captain's logs

☐ Rewind, Review, Recreate mind game played

☐ Game plan actions entered

☐ Your state of being on the mood elevators assessed

Day 73—Intentions in Context: What Really Matters

When flying, it is important to keep an active scan out the window and on the needles and scopes of all the instruments inside the cockpit. In inclement weather, the instrument panel is the pilot's only reference. At times, a pilot can get fixated on one instrument, and the one that is not working optimally often gets the most attention. This could cause disorientation and significant consequences. In order for a successful flight, the pilot must keep this scan going to get the complete picture in order to maintain situational awareness.

As passionate as we are when living our meaningful intentions and all of the intentional outcomes we are bringing into life, we can get fixated on our mission. We don't want to be racehorses with blinders on, do we? It is important to view our intentions in the context of our entire lives, keeping in mind what really matters.

Jerry built a rather successful printing business with blueprints as his specialty niche. At age 22, I was arranging a health insurance plan for him and his employees. At the time, Jerry was in his early 60s, and he saw himself in me.

He said, "John, you are a highly motivated young man, just like I was when I was your age. I put all of my energy into this business, determined to make it a success. Today, I am divorced. My children are all adults, and I don't know them—actually, I never knew them. In reality, I was married to this business. As successful as this business is, I cannot buy any of that back. Don't do what I did."

Although Jerry was not an emotional type, I sensed that tears were not far behind the mask of his somewhat gruff appearance. To do my job well as a financial advisor, I had to ask a lot of questions, many of them highly personal. Consequently, I came to know him well. Jerry had high blood pressure and a couple of scares with his heart over the last decade. I could not help but equate his high blood pressure with the long-standing stress of his work. His cardiac issues mirrored his broken heart from the loss of his family. If he had a chance to do it over, he candidly admitted that he would have made different choices.

I heard these stories time and time again from the small business owners who honored me with the opportunity to advise them on financial matters. In turn, they advised me. They shared their life experiences with me: a young man with an even younger looking baby face.

Sometime back, in the early '90s, I recall attending a wealth creation symposium with a number of my associates from the New York office. My intended roommate was unable to make the trip, and I found myself sharing a room with a man known to be one of the most successful people in the business. In casual conversation, I mentioned how I enjoyed working from my home office because it enabled me to have breakfast with my kids and gave me the flexibility to go to school functions and so forth.

As I shared what I thought was casual conversation, I was more than surprised to see this man well up with tears. Divorced, no relationship with his kids, and yes, he too was a "highly successful" businessman. It was more than a dozen years, but my mind went immediately back to my client Jerry. Both of these men fell prey to fixation.

On a lighter note, I recall an initial session with a new coaching client who said he was so focused on his work that one day, he looked down with great surprise to see his massive belly asking, "Where did that come from?" Lighter indeed, but still troubling and risky too.

Is success in business worth the cost of family and health? Can we fully contribute to our work and our families if our physical health is impaired? Strained relationships are a major distraction to our work and will eventually impact our health as well. You see, it's all interconnected.

The Fabulous Five

The Fabulous Five offers us a variety of uses: for life balance, as a structure for our great day game planner, and as a mind game. The Fabulous Five areas are:

1. Health and wellness
2. Career and finance
3. Relationships
4. Recreation
5. Contribution

Health and wellness, career and finance, and relationships are pretty straightforward. Often overlooked, wellness includes spiritual, emotional, and psychological states as well as physical health.

Recreation, which you can also view as re-creation, is an important ingredient to revitalized energy. In the game, it has been highlighted in many ways: the lightness and energy menu, fuel to give you the energy needed to create what you want and to enjoy life now, enhanced creativity, and the Wallas model for *Eureka!* insights. Contribution serves as a touchstone and a reminder of the contributions you've made to others and to those who have contributed to your fabulous life, and contributions to contemplate going forward.

For Your Great Day Game Planner

Consider incorporating the Fabulous Five into your great day game planner. You can scan these areas as you select your practical actions for the day.

For those who enjoy mind mapping, you may use something like this as a template, extending branches from each area:

THE FABULOUS FIVE

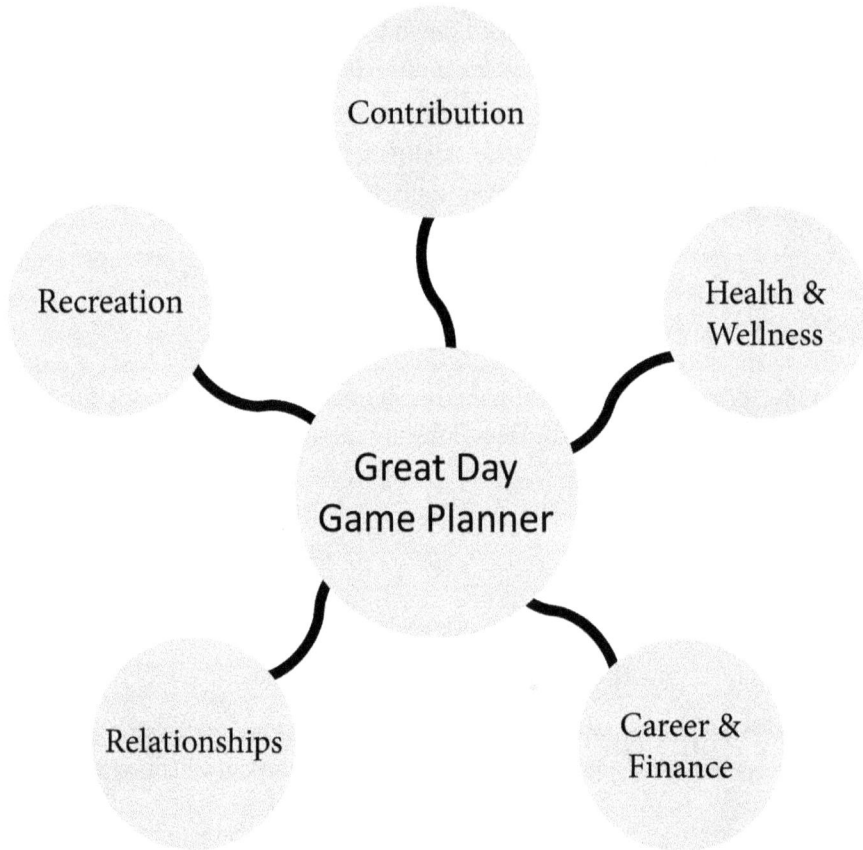

Let's keep in mind that the best format you can have for your great day game planner is one that is designed to meet your specific needs. With that said, consider the importance and value of being attentive to all five of these areas within your fabulous life.

The Fabulous Five Mind Game

Applied as a mind game, the Fabulous Five is very much akin to the Abundant Mind mind game. In this exercise, you will celebrate the riches and successes in all areas of your fabulous life, and identify practical actions you will take to enhance them all the more. I start most of my days with this one.

Now go ahead and play the Fabulous Five mind game.

Today's Great Day Game Planner

It's great to be alive and well! What will make today a fulfilling and satisfying day? Do the "write" thing, and jot down whatever action steps you'd like to take.

....

....

....

....

....

....

....

Highlight three priority actions. These priority actions will take precedence over all others. Then, time permitting, select others from the planner.

Mood Elevators

Draw a line or shade in each of the mood elevators to reflect your state of being in the moment.

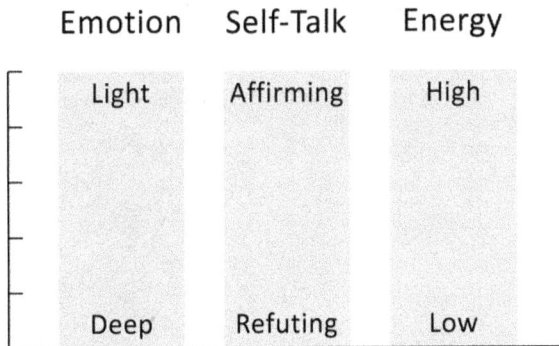

Emotion	Self-Talk	Energy
Light	Affirming	High
Deep	Refuting	Low

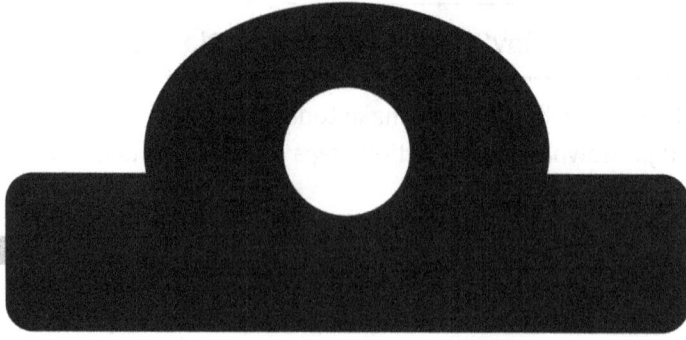

TODAY'S GAME PLAY CHECKLIST

Place a checkmark next to each completed game play:

☐   Today's principle card selected and engaged

☐   Fuel-up activities selected from your lightness and energy menu

☐   Intention statement—engaged and refined

☐   Feelings, self-talk, and appreciation entered in captain's logs

☐   Fabulous Five mind game played

☐   Game plan actions entered

☐   Your state of being on the mood elevators assessed

Day 74—The Great Day Debrief

Tony's Story

It is Friday, early evening, and Tony arrives home from his day at work, eager to greet his young family. In an excitable, rapid crawl from the family room toward the foyer come his twin daughters Dianna and Dylan, donned in diapers and geared up to welcome Dad home. Tony, so happy to see them, promptly discards his briefcase in favor of scooping the beloved pair into his arms to take pleasure in a warm embrace.

Carrying them back to the family room, he plops himself and his brood onto the couch. Dana, his wife, gets wind of her hubby's arrival and joins in. As Dana fills Tony in on the day's adventures, Tony's mind begins to drift to the recollection of his own recent events.

Catching himself quickly, he tunes back into Dana's voice. Within a few brief moments, Tony's mind chatter begins to invade his state once again. He shakes it off and becomes attentive, thankfully, before Dana can notice. This would not be the first time that Tony was accused of being married to his business—a rather raw, open wound that Tony is now committed to healing and that needs no further salt.

Dana wraps up the recap and, after a quick yet affectionate peck on the cheek, makes her exit to go upstairs to change, and Tony resumes his precious time with his sweet baby girls.

"Did I leave the application with Mr. Halligan? The office is expecting me to bring it in on Monday. Speaking of Monday, we have a breakfast meeting. Is this the meeting I am hosting? Is it at the Hilton or the Crowne Plaza?"

Sensing a shift in the environment, the little ones migrate from the sofa towards the television and the toys, which are resting on the plush carpet. Their movement wakes Tony up from his trance. Saddened by this, Dad sheds his suit jacket, pulls himself back to the present, and joins Dianna and Dylan on the rug.

"That can wait," he says to himself. "It's time for me to be here now! After all, the babysitter will arrive in just one short hour, and Dana and I will be going to the Miller's house for dinner and a schmooze-fest."

Climbing Mount Daddy, the twins revel, smothering him playfully, and Tony is back in kid heaven. With tickles and giggles at full force, Tony begins a vacant stare, once again haunted by loose ends and uncertainty.

"If that application is in my briefcase, I can scan it and send Halligan an email. Then I can swing by on my way to the Hilton ... or is it the Crowne Plaza?"

Frustrated by the distraction, he tells the tiny tots that he'll be right back, jumps to his feet, and, like a heat-seeking missile to its target, he dashes to his briefcase. Sure enough, no application is there, and he releases a sigh of relief. Startled immediately after, he remembers that he put it in his suit jacket pocket to have it handy to give to Halligan! Darting back to the couch, he grasps the garment and, sure enough, the pocket is empty. He recalls now that he did in fact give Halligan the document.

Finally freed from the distraction, he returns back to the floor. Like it or not, his mind chatter soon turns back to the loose ends of the day's events. His body may be home, but the rest of him has not yet punched the clock.

Do you relate to Tony's plight? Is he a self-centered, insensitive clod who puts his work ahead of his wife? Is he so self-absorbed that he'd rather immerse himself in his work than be with his beautiful little bundles of joy?

If you ask Tony, he will tell you that he wants, more than anything, to be fully present with his family and that all he does is for them! Although, at times, even he doubts himself, battles in self-judgment, and wonders, "If this were really true, perhaps I would behave differently." So much frustration and sadness, so much confusion and misunderstanding, and so much time and energy wasted, when so much useless suffering can easily be eliminated.

Gratefully, Tony's friend Mike clued him in and enrolled him as a game player. After some Rumi-nating on his emotions and taking some of those beliefs to court, he freed himself of judgment and took up the simple practice of this new great day game play, which you can add to your repertoire—the great day debrief.

Sometimes Tony debriefs before he leaves the office and at other times parked in the car, knowing that if he wants to be home with more than just his body, he needs to clear his mind of the loose ends in order to be fully present.

Tony refers to his great day game planner and reflects on the day's events. With great satisfaction, he checks off the actions taken and transfers any remaining key actions to a fresh plan for tomorrow. Taking a few relaxing deep breaths, he reminds himself of how grateful he is to have meaningful work and consciously connects the value it yields for his wonderful family. He reflects on activities he enjoyed, acknowledges his accomplishments, registers lessons learned, and objectively assesses areas that he chooses to enhance.

Tony is glad that he followed Mike's lead, and now enjoys a clear head when he arrives home. The loose ends are neatly tied together, and the next steps to be taken are off his mind and onto the next great day game planner. He is on course with his plans, feeling competent and confident.

By applying the power of directed attention, Tony now enjoys peace of mind, relaxing evenings with his family and restful nights' sleep. The sore spot between Dana and Tony is well healed. Although Tony loved Dana just as much before as he does now, Dana feels more cared for, appreciated, respected, and loved. In order to care for Dana and his girls, Tony first had to identify clear intent, and then honor what he truly wanted. He had to first care for himself, appreciate and respect his own needs, drop his self-judgment and doubt, and love himself enough to take action.

The Checklist and the Mind Game

Like a tasty sandwich, the meat of a great day is set between great day game plays in the morning and a great day debrief sometime in the late afternoon or evening. Due to the game plays' potentially stimulating energy, it is best not to debrief too close to bedtime. In the end, it's the player's choice.

You'll find this to be similar to the way you begin the day. Here's how you do it:

- Reflect on the principle of the day and how it applied to your experiences.

- Engage your intention, connecting the dots between the actions you have taken and how your behavior is supporting your intent.

- Check off the actions you have taken from your great day game planner, and transfer any remaining key actions to a fresh plan for tomorrow.

- Reflect on whatever revitalizing activities you selected from your lightness and energy menu and register how it enhanced your day.

- Select the Great Day Debrief mind game audio.

Once this debrief is complete, you are ready to have an enjoyable evening and a refreshing night's sleep.

Today's Great Day Game Planner

It's great to be alive and well! What will make today a fulfilling and satisfying day? Do the "write" thing, and jot down whatever action steps you'd like to take.

....

....

....

....

....

....

....

Highlight three priority actions. These priority actions will take precedence over all others. Then, time permitting, select others from the planner.

Mood Elevators

Draw a line or shade in each of the mood elevators to reflect your state of being in the moment.

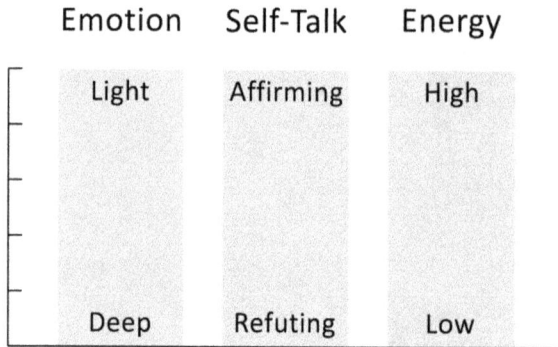

Emotion	Self-Talk	Energy
Light	Affirming	High
Deep	Refuting	Low

TODAY'S GAME PLAY CHECKLIST

Place a checkmark next to each completed game play:

☐ Today's principle card selected and engaged

☐ Fuel-up activities selected from your lightness and energy menu

☐ Intention statement—engaged and refined

☐ Feelings, self-talk, and appreciation entered in captain's logs

☐ Game plan actions entered

☐ Your state of being on the mood elevators assessed

☐ Select and play a mind game today:

○ Abundant Mind   ○ Weed and Feed

○ Been There, Done That   ○ Reaping the Harvest

○ Freeing Your David   ○ Rewind, Review, Recreate

○ BMW   ○ Fabulous Five

See next page for Great Day Debrief checklist

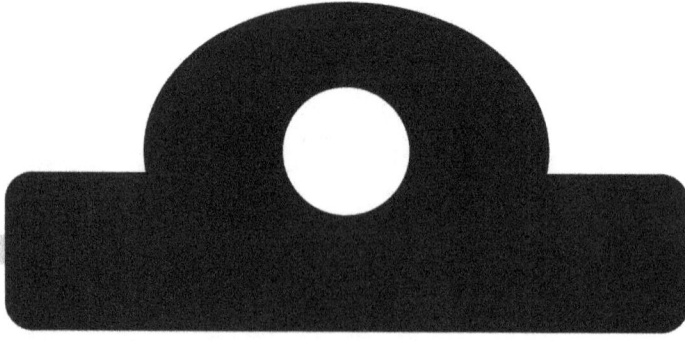

GREAT DAY DEBRIEF CHECKLIST

Place a checkmark next to each completed game play:

☐ Today's principle reflected

☐ Intention statement engaged

☐ Actions taken and checked off on great day game planner

☐ Remaining actions transferred to tomorrow's great day game planner

☐ Value from fuel-up activities acknowledged

☐ Great Day Debrief mind game completed

Day 75—Reminders and Tips of the Week

Rewind, Review, Recreate Revisited

While the main purpose for the Rewind, Review, Recreate mind game is intended to release resentment, anger, and hostility with understanding, compassion, and love, once understood, we can repurpose it in a variety of ways. Since the brain makes no distinction between a real or a vividly imagined event, this game play can restore order to what may remain as unconscious residue, which is restricting congruent, harmonious flow. Here are a few applications to consider.

Rewind a disturbing dream and review its content. Is there any valuable information to gather? During my career transition, I had a recurring dream. Dressed in a suit, with my briefcase in hand, I found myself in a dangerous place. It was an urban jungle of violence and drugs. Thugs, playing with switchblades and hand guns, inhabited the street corners. I felt like a likely target for assault, robbery, or worse. I could not find my way out but, when I did, I realized that I'd left my briefcase behind and needed to return to retrieve it.

My review of this dream led me to interpret that I was uneasy about my career transition. It was unfamiliar, uncertain, and risky territory. Although at a high threat, I still felt the need to return. The briefcase clearly held something that I deemed essential to retrieve. I appraised the briefcase as a symbol of the value I held for the mission.

In a mind game setting, I recreated the dream, got familiar with the territory, and befriended the locals, who helped me find what I was looking for. This eased my tension, the repetitive dream ceased, and my restful sleep was restored. Funny, as I exchanged some coaching and facilitating activities for writing this book, a similar dream resurfaced. With potential concern around lost revenue, I had a hunch that Amy was manning the projector of my dream machine in the dark of night. When the dawn returned, I rewound, reviewed, and recreated the dream, had a good chat to allay Amy's fear, and got back to advancing my intention.

How about unpleasant events? They too can be rewound, reviewed, and recreated. The review will provide valuable information that you can utilize when similar circumstances present themselves. In turn, this will increase your confidence to handle whatever may come down the pike.

How about accidents? I was in a car accident when I was 19 years old. I tore back muscles and had chronic pain for more than 20 years. My back would go out and, at times, I would find myself flat on my back. I would get around on my elbows and feet, arching myself from room to room. Although this doesn't sound very funny, my wife and I ultimately got a chuckle out of it.

In a burst of self-worthiness, I felt that it was time to get this pain and inconvenience out of my life. I had heard that every cell of the human body replaces itself over the course of seven years; some believe it takes even less time. Checking the web today, I found this on Stanford's School of Medicine website. Their research states that, "Every one of us completely regenerates our own skin every 7 days. A cut heals itself and disappears in a week or two. Every single cell in our skeleton is replaced every 7 years. The future of medicine lies in understanding how the body creates itself out of a single cell and the mechanisms by which it renews itself throughout life."[31]

Close to 20 years ago, I wondered why the consequences of accidental injury continue beyond this seven-year time frame. My conclusion was that the cells must have memory, and I would provide the cells with a new memory, one which would produce fresh, healthy cells.

In the replay of the accident, I imagined that I avoided the impact and checked to see if everyone else was okay. I repeated this imagery every time I had a twang of discomfort and, ever since, my elbows have not been exercised in that silly, inverse crawling manner.

I am not going to suggest that I have any scientific evidence for my success. If it makes sense to you and you want to try it, go right ahead. It couldn't hurt and, who knows, it just may help.

The Fabulous Five Pocket Primer

If the idea of living a more balanced life appeals to you, why not make it a habit? Grab an index card and jot down one key habit or outcome within each of the five areas you'd like to integrate into your fabulous life. Pop it in your pocket, take a look at it a few times a day, and update it when the spirit moves you.

Today's Great Day Game Planner

It's great to be alive and well! What will make today a fulfilling and satisfying day? Do the "write" thing, and jot down whatever action steps you'd like to take.

....

....

....

....

....

....

....

Highlight three priority actions. These priority actions will take precedence over all others. Then, time permitting, select others from the planner.

Mood Elevators

Draw a line or shade in each of the mood elevators to reflect your state of being in the moment.

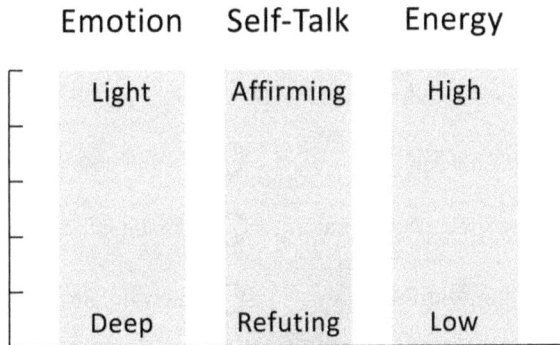

Emotion	Self-Talk	Energy
Light	Affirming	High
Deep	Refuting	Low

TODAY'S GAME PLAY CHECKLIST

Place a checkmark next to each completed game play:

☐ Today's principle card selected and engaged

☐ Fuel-up activities selected from your lightness and energy menu

☐ Intention statement—engaged and refined

☐ Feelings, self-talk, and appreciation entered in captain's logs

☐ Game plan actions entered

☐ Your state of being on the mood elevators assessed

☐ Select and play a mind game today:

    ○ Abundant Mind   ○ Weed and Feed

    ○ Been There, Done That   ○ Reaping the Harvest

    ○ Freeing Your David   ○ Rewind, Review, Recreate

    ○ BMW   ○ Fabulous Five

See next page for Great Day Debrief checklist

Days 76 and 77—Free Day Reminder

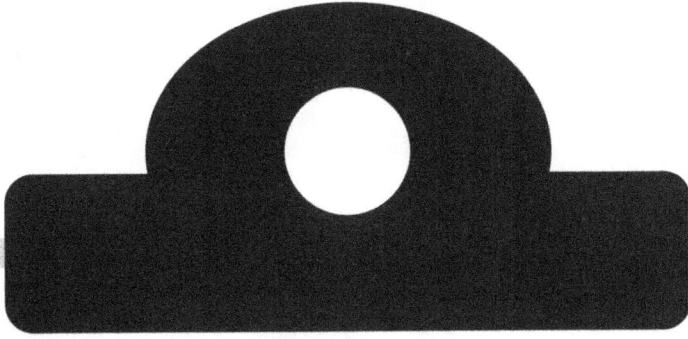

GREAT DAY DEBRIEF CHECKLIST

Place a checkmark next to each completed game play:

☐ Today's principle reflected

☐ Intention statement engaged

☐ Actions taken and checked off on great day game planner

☐ Remaining actions transferred to tomorrow's great day game planner

☐ Value from fuel-up activities acknowledged

☐ Great Day Debrief mind game completed

PART IX

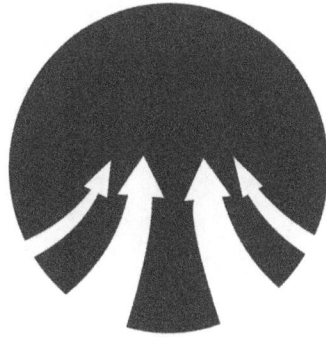

Living Your Fabulous Whole Life

WEEK 12

Interim Play

Days 78-82—Interim Play

Congratulations! All of the game plays and practices have been covered. Interim play will give you the opportunity to play with new game plays and practices recently introduced over the past few days. Continue playing with the great day game planner and the mind games of your choice.

Observe where you are at this stage of the game, *appraise* which strategies will be most appropriate to utilize in the moment, and *respond* by taking action. Ask yourself, *What game play or practice will most greatly support me in moving toward my intentional outcomes?* Is it more clarity? Emotional lightness? Confidence? Practical action? The 90-Day Game Resource Guide will be a helpful reference for you during interim play. For a strong game finish, challenge yourself to wrap up most of your days with a great day debrief.

Remember, you can access additional great day game planners and other forms by going to 90DayGame.com.

Today's Great Day Game Planner

It's great to be alive and well! What will make today a fulfilling and satisfying day? Do the "write" thing, and jot down whatever action steps you'd like to take.

....

....

....

....

....

....

....

Highlight three priority actions. These priority actions will take precedence over all others. Then, time permitting, select others from the planner.

Mood Elevators

Draw a line or shade in each of the mood elevators to reflect your state of being in the moment.

Emotion	Self-Talk	Energy
Light	Affirming	High
Deep	Refuting	Low

TODAY'S GAME PLAY CHECKLIST

Place a checkmark next to each completed game play:

☐ Today's principle card selected and engaged

☐ Fuel-up activities selected from your lightness and energy menu

☐ Intention statement—engaged and refined

☐ Feelings, self-talk, and appreciation entered in captain's logs

☐ Game plan actions entered

☐ Your state of being on the mood elevators assessed

☐ Select and play a mind game today:

○ Abundant Mind   ○ Weed and Feed

○ Been There, Done That   ○ Reaping the Harvest

○ Freeing Your David   ○ Rewind, Review, Recreate

○ BMW   ○ Fabulous Five

See next page for Great Day Debrief checklist

GREAT DAY DEBRIEF CHECKLIST

Place a checkmark next to each completed game play:

☐ Today's principle reflected

☐ Intention statement engaged

☐ Actions taken and checked off on great day game planner

☐ Remaining actions transferred to tomorrow's great day game planner

☐ Value from fuel-up activities acknowledged

☐ Great Day Debrief mind game completed

Moving Forward in the Present

Days 85-88—Interim Play Continued

Day 89—The Victory Lap

Celebrate Your 90-Day Game Successes

It's time to have our last visit with Carl. It is inspiring to see how his meaningful intention statement developed. He has come a long way from old and self-defeating habits, sadness, and a sense of incompetence to productive behavior, fulfillment, and confidence.

Carl writes:

I am celebrating my new life both personally and professionally, knowing that I have taken the right path—the one my soul guided me to take.

I am starting my days bright and early with great confidence and enthusiasm, eager to embrace the day. It is rewarding to kick things off with a morning team meeting before heading out to service my clients.

I hired one of my three interns, and she is now working with me full time. I am anticipating that I will have another employee on board soon.

My staff is handling administrative needs and customer support, utilizing systems we set up together. Things are well organized, and we are poised for significant growth.

By having this team, I am able to do what I do best. I am building strong client relationships and providing them with solutions to their business challenges. Referrals are at an all-time high, and new clients are coming on board at a consistent and comfortable pace.

I have learned to embrace change and now understand the transforming power love has.

I am honoring the strong value I hold to provide financial stability and emotional ease for my family. My wife and I are providing the things both of us want for our kids. We are building a financial reserve, and I am now turning a sufficient profit, which is enabling me to continue reinvesting in my business.

I am learning to maintain realistic expectations of what needs to be accomplished on any given day, and selecting priority actions has become a solid habit.

I now have the confidence and the tools to handle situations as they arise, and I am able to appraise them in ways that are in the best interests for all involved.

The career I am enjoying is providing immense satisfaction for me and better lives for us all.

This experience has made me discover two things that, at some level, I've always wanted: the ability to be present and to have a peaceful mind.

Yes, meaningful intention statements ultimately become gratitude statements. Like Carl and Persephone, some players will follow through on the original intention that brought them to the game, and others will discover deeper intentions as Karen did.

When you take a look at your earlier drafts, and compare them to the one you have now, you will see this progression. Maybe you crossed the finish line early, perhaps you are there now, or you may be approaching it. Outcomes will come and go, so what matters most is that you embrace this favorable movement and appreciate who you are, all that you have accomplished, and all that you have learned and will continue to learn, create, and enjoy.

Before we take a victory lap, we have one other piece of unfinished business, which I will begin to address with a brief personal story.

On January 18, 1976, I took my check ride for my private pilot certificate. The check ride is the flight that a student pilot takes with a Federal Aviation Administration examiner to demonstrate the required competencies to earn the right to fly—in this case, as a private pilot. As I was preflighting the airplane (that is, inspecting it for airworthiness), as all good pilots should, someone approached me. Without introduction or any pleasantries whatsoever, this person said, "Come on! Move it along! You're not a mechanic. Let's get going! I want to make it back to watch the Super Bowl!"

It was clear that he was my examiner, and I was in for quite a ride. The flight lived up to my expectations. He was a gruff and stern government man with a military background, which he wore on his sleeve with every step he took. He yelled at me throughout the flight and even shoved me in one instance. I assumed that he was testing how I'd perform under pressure, and that's what I kept my mind on because any other thought might have brought me either to tears or reactive anger. After all, I had a ticket to return home the next day, so I too was motivated to get this done, and I wanted to head home with my pilot's license.

We landed, and he headed back to the hangar without another word. As I shook off the distressing experience, trying to avoid thinking about the likely verdict that I did not want to hear, I tied down the airplane safely on the ramp and proceeded back to the hangar to get the news.

A flash of optimism came into my entire being as the examiner was typing. (Yes, there were still typewriters in 1976, and that is how they prepared your temporary certificate.) Of course, he could have been typing something else too. No words were spoken as his attention was solely on the typewriter and not me.

He stood up and pulled the paper from the machine. Then he turned to me and said, "Congratulations, and fly safely," and silently he left.

Beyond the huge relief and great sense of accomplishment, the experience confirmed that flight training gave me what I needed: the ability to keep a cool head under pressure, and that is exactly what I would need for future flights and in other challenging circumstances.

I'll now sit behind my imaginary typewriter and ask you to accept this certificate. This is more than a course completion certificate. This is a player-in-command certification.

Beyond acknowledging the commitment you have demonstrated to follow through, and the growth and development you have achieved, it is symbolic or your ticket to ride: to soar and enjoy a quality of life that will continue to grow and expand for the benefit of all.

What I want for you is to enjoy this achievement. Recognize and acknowledge the fact that you have all the necessary resources within you to live your life with a cool head and a warm heart.

Congratulations! Now, let's take that victory lap. Here are a few things you can do to celebrate:

- Take a look at where you began (Day 1) and your initial responses to the jumpstart questions.
- Compare your most recent meaningful intention statement with your original draft.
- Review your talents, strengths, and skills list, and see how aware you've become of the many talents and strengths you possess and the skills you have developed.
- Review your inspiring successes listed on your appreciation log.
- Ask yourself, *How have I grown?*

Run through this victory lap checklist, and check off the shifts that you have made. This is included in the playbook and available for download online, if you'd like to print it.

Make a list of any other shifts that you have made. Revel in your shifts and successes with yourself, your buddy, your coach, and, if you're playing the telegame, bring them to the victory lap call.

Victory Lap Checklist	
I have a greater sense of:	**I feel more:**
❏ Purpose	❏ Fulfilled
❏ Self-acceptance	❏ Content
❏ Worthiness	❏ Enthusiastic
	❏ Patient
I have more:	❏ Present
❏ Clarity	❏ Connected with others
❏ Empowering beliefs	❏ In command and less controlling
❏ Balance	❏ Intuitive
	❏ Guided
	❏ Faithful
	❏ Free to choose what is in my best interest
	❏ Comfortable with being uncomfortable
	❏ Successful
I am more:	**I am:**
❏ Appreciative	❏ Lighter
❏ Grateful	❏ Calmer
❏ At ease	❏ Able to see the perfection within the perceived imperfection
❏ Joyful	
❏ Graceful	❏ Seeing more of what's available rather than what's missing
❏ Focused	
❏ Creative	❏ Taking action
❏ Imaginative	❏ Less self-conscious more people-centric
❏ Confident	❏ Less judgmental and more accepting and compassionate
❏ Responsive and less reactive	
❏ Flexible	❏ Better at prioritizing
❏ Organized	

Victory Lap Checklist	
I am experiencing more:	**I now understand that my:**
❏ Possibility thinking ❏ Empowering beliefs	❏ Soul has complete awareness of who I am and my purpose for being here ❏ Emotions are how my soul guides me to meet my needs and honor my values ❏ Self-talk is how my soul makes me aware of the beliefs I am attending ❏ Behavior is how my soul navigates in the physical world

Today's Great Day Game Planner

It's great to be alive and well! What will make today a fulfilling and satisfying day? Do the "write" thing, and jot down whatever action steps you'd like to take.

....

....

....

....

....

....

....

Highlight three priority actions. These priority actions will take precedence over all others. Then, time permitting, select others from the planner.

Mood Elevators

Draw a line or shade in each of the mood elevators to reflect your state of being in the moment.

Emotion	Self-Talk	Energy
Light	Affirming	High
Deep	Refuting	Low

TODAY'S GAME PLAY CHECKLIST

Place a checkmark next to each completed game play:

☐ Today's principle card selected and engaged

☐ Fuel-up activities selected from your lightness and energy menu

☐ Intention statement—engaged and refined

☐ Feelings, self-talk, and appreciation entered in captain's logs

☐ Game plan actions entered

☐ Your state of being on the mood elevators assessed

☐ Select and play a mind game today:

    ○ Abundant Mind   ○ Weed and Feed

    ○ Been There, Done That   ○ Reaping the Harvest

    ○ Freeing Your David   ○ Rewind, Review, Recreate

    ○ BMW   ○ Fabulous Five

See next page for Great Day Debrief checklist

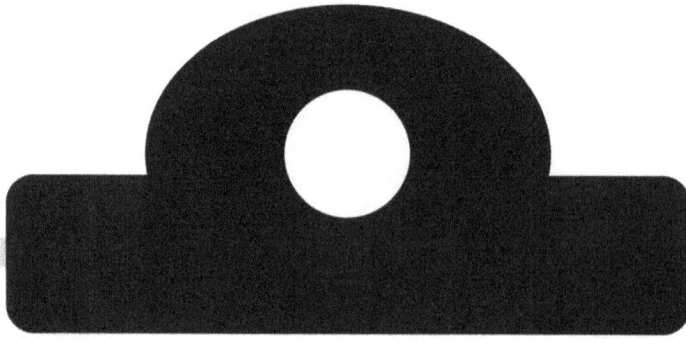

GREAT DAY DEBRIEF CHECKLIST

Place a checkmark next to each completed game play:

☐ Today's principle reflected

☐ Intention statement engaged

☐ Actions taken and checked off on great day game planner

☐ Remaining actions transferred to tomorrow's great day game planner

☐ Value from fuel-up activities acknowledged

☐ Great Day Debrief mind game completed

Day 90—Moving Forward in the Precious Present Moment

How to Revel in Your Fabulous Life Daily

Our opportunities for joy today as well as tomorrow lie nowhere else but supremely in this present moment. Here are a few suggestions on how you can utilize the elements of the 90-Day Game going forward to revel daily in your fabulous life. Let these ideas act as a springboard for your own creative play. After all, many of these suggestions have come from 90-Day Game players.

Great Day Game Plays

The majority of certified players-in-command continue to start their days with the great day game plays. Think of it as an athlete's pregame or a pilot's preflight briefing. The question to ask yourself is, *What morning routine will I establish to increase the likelihood of having satisfying and fulfilling days?* Here are a few ideas to help you answer that question.

The Principle Card Deck

Is there a guiding principle you want to live by that is not in the deck? Is there a value you choose to honor? How about a thought or emotion that sets an inspiring tone, a belief, or a habit that you want to fully internalize? If so, add them to the deck.

Lightness and Energy Menu

Having coached with hundreds of people internationally, when it comes to creating both lightness and energy, there are two behaviors that come as close as you can to a universal truth: physical and mental exercise. Like warming up a car on a frigid morning, they lubricate the gears of your body and mind, and get things moving smoothly.

One great intention to hold is to have all the Fabulous Five areas of your life ultimately show up on your lightness and energy menu, including your career. So much of our time is invested in our work. Aim to develop enjoyment in it, so much so that you'd do it for the love of it. Ask yourself, *How can I cultivate enthusiasm for my work, like the spirit a child has when they are going out to play? How can I ultimately add everything I do to my lightness and energy menu?*

Mind Games

Most players, including myself, begin the day with a Been There, Done That mental rehearsal and/or a Fabulous Five mental exercise. These two are easy to combine. You now have sufficient familiarity with the basics of mind games, so you can leave the audio behind. Acknowledge that you are now in command of this state. Deep belly breaths and a countdown from 10 to 1 will quiet all your SEMB resources. Reflecting on gratitude and successes opens your appreciative and creative mind, and then you can take it from there.

You can make use of the audio for other applications, if you'd like; however, as far as a routine start for the day, these two are simple to play. Make it easy and portable to do as part of your morning routine. Players report that the nominal time invested in mental prep is always more than recaptured from the resulting refined and purposeful action that these exercises yield.

Your Great Day Game Planner

Beginning the day with clear priority objectives increases the likelihood of getting them accomplished. When you get them done, you enjoy forward movement and that leads to the satisfaction and fulfillment we are seeking. Customize your great day game planner to suit your needs in the moment.

While developing this game book, my game planner helped me navigate through this writing project while attending to my coaching practice. I also incorporated the other Fabulous Five elements, tailored to my personal interests. Keeping this balance at the forefront of my awareness gave me the comfort of knowing that what really matters was not going to be obscured by obsessive fixation. Ask yourself, *How can I custom design my game planner to assure that I take priority actions while enjoying balance, rich relationships, and fun and fulfilling days?* Remember: Life is happening now, so enjoy it!

The Game Practices

Intention

Intention simplifies choice making. You can ask yourself, *Does this thought I am having or this action I am taking align with my intention?* If the answer is yes, proceed; if the answer is no, redirect your attention and behavior accordingly. Without an intention, you can neither ask nor answer this question.

You need not play a full 90-Day Game all the time. It's great when you have a strong urge and want to make a significant change. In the absence of such an urge, it still pays to have an intention for the day, the week, or maybe the month. Be flexible, yet keep the value of establishing mindful intent. Ships and airplanes need a rudder to keep them on course. Let intent be your metaphoric rudder.

Attention

If intention is your guidepost for both thought and action in the objective world, mind games are your guideposts for thought and action in the subjective world. There is a menu of 10 items from which to choose, and you can easily make more of your own. Investing time in mind games will produce emotional ease and increase intuitive insights, supporting congruent alignment with all of your SEMB resources.

Take Your OARs with You

Along with the rudder, keep your OARs handy. As intention simplifies choice making, OARs guide discernment. When you notice that you're a bit conjangled, it's often a simple matter of promptly observing your emotions, your thoughts, and the situation at hand. By appraising them objectively in a way that serves you and then realigning, you can respond with appropriate practical action. The gift is in the noticing, and employing your emotionally intelligent OARs rather than amplifying the challenge by weaving an intricate story around it. If you are more than a little rattled by any of it, you can always head to either the guest house or the courtroom. The tools are here for you in this game book and listed in the 90-Day Game Resource Guide following this day. Further support like Player's Clinics, coaching, and more can be found at 90DayGame.com.

Reflection

Wrapping up your day with a great day debrief is one of the most beneficial actions you can take. You capture your accomplishments and register lessons from the great teachings that life provides. When you customize these game plays and practices, you will design a game worth playing and a life worth living.

What I want for you is to recognize that the greatness does not lie in this or in any other book. Books, authors, coaches, and teachers can set a great environment, but the greatness lies nowhere else but within you!

May this game book be my contribution to setting a fruitful environment for you. I'll close by leaving you this final thought: The only difference between a fabulous life and something less than a fabulous life is one of perspective—yes indeed, one of attitude. When you realize this, you will know that you are already living your fabulous life. Enjoy!

Congratulations!

PLAYER IN COMMAND CERTIFICATE

THIS AWARD CERTIFIES THAT

_____

HAS SUCCESSFULLY COMPLETED

The 90-Day Game

_____ John Felitto CFP
DATE   SIGNATURE   TITLE

90-Day Game Resource Guide and Index

We've covered a lot of ground in these 90 days, learning and practicing a wide range of techniques, tools, and exercises. Their order in the game was designed to help you build and strengthen the perspectives and competencies needed to realize your meaningful intention and enjoy the process along the way. Moving forward, you now have a treasure house of resources that you can use in any number of ways, depending on your needs.

Are you looking for increased clarity, confidence, or objectivity? Seeking insights to develop or implement a plan? Want to refresh your perspective and attitude? Scan the list, which is organized by intentional outcomes. There are many tools from which to choose.

Enhance Clarity, Develop Sense of Purpose, Get in Touch with What Matters

Enhance Emotional Buoyancy, Ease, Resilience

Enhance Confidence in Yourself and Your Plans

Enhance Gratefulness, Abundance, Sense of Worthiness

Do the "write" thing (that is, express how you feel about yourself and the riches you have attracted into your life, and capture insights).

Enhance Creativity, Intuition, Idea Generation

Do the "write" thing (that is, express how you feel and capture insights).

Play the Abundant Mind mind game ....31-32, 102-106, audio

Take a lightness and energy break...21-25, 36, 136, 180, 182, 190, 257, 287

Project the end results in a Freeing Your David mind game ....123-125, audio

Play Reaping the Harvest mind game to stimulate intuitive insights............................ 239, audio

Utilize BMW mind game to trigger intuitive insights...................................... 182-184, 187, audio

Consult mental mentors 135-136, 242

Sleep on it 184, 190, 302

Enhance Productivity, Fulfillment, Satisfaction

Begin your day completing a great day game planner................................26-29, 36, 257-258, 288

Mentally rehearse your day with the Been There, Done That mind game..............117-120, audio

Play the Abundant Mind mind game ....31-32, 102-106, audio

Play the Fabulous Five mind game..256-258, audio

Review and update your talents, strengths, and skills list..78-79

Express your plans and get feedback and support from your buddy or coach 8, 11, 83, 190

Take action and cause yourself to have a new, successful experience 218

Complete your day with a great day debrief.. 261-263, 289

Play the Great Day Debrief mind game...audio

For support, contact us at Team@90DayGame.com.

Glossary of Definitions, Distinctions, Acronyms, and Idioms

PLEASE NOTE

The objective of this glossary is to create a common language for game players to communicate with each other easily and proficiently. In some instances, definitions found in the game book may differ from those found in dictionaries.

Definitions

affirm: to make firm, strong; to fortify, strengthen

affirmation: repetitive statement, which can reinforce both desirable and undesirable beliefs

alert witnessing: self-observation of emotions and self-talk; observing as a third party with a loving, supportive, and light attitude; having qualities of attentiveness, compassion, self-communication, and amusement

Amy: game character who serves the honorable role of protector; name derived from traits associated with the brain's amygdala, among other things, responds to stimuli that warn of danger, triggering emotional reactions like fighting, freezing, or fleeing; when presented with change, can overreact to events that pose no real survival threat; at her best when harmoniously teamed up with Libby and Tex

appraisal: estimate of the value of a situation, event, or thing; estimate of the value gained from an experience; thoughtful examination of an event or a belief

appraise: to assess the value or quality of

appreciate: to grasp the nature, worth, quality, or significance of; to raise or increase in value; to recognize with gratitude or thankfulness

behavior: manner of acting, which always follows the beliefs being attended

beliefs: reinforced assumptions that we confidently imagine to be true or interpret as the truth

Blue Chevy Theory: committed attention on an intention influences what we notice, bringing forth an increase in meaningful coincidences, synchronicity, and insights aligned with intent (see "coincidence, meaningful" and "synchronicity")

coincidence, meaningful: noticing of two of more concurrent incidences, often resulting from where one's attention lies; seasoned players utilize all coincidental experiences to support their intentions

congruence: harmonious alignment of the four resources of soul, emotion, mind, and behavior

congruent: in harmony

conjangled: discordant state of being; misalignment of the four resources of soul, emotion, mind, and behavior

data: information

desire: a wish; a feeling that accompanies an unsatisfied state; a craving, a yearning, or a longing

directed attention: intentional act and development of directing one's attention from one place to another

divine guidance: intuitive guidance information received from the soul through the channel of emotion

do the "write" thing: expression of encouragement for players to express themselves and capture their insights in the written form

empowering affirmation: self-created repetitive statement designed with the express purpose of internalizing a belief aligned with intent; contains material evidence from the player's direct experience

goals: (see "Intentions versus goals" under "Distinctions")

illumination: *Aha!* or *Eureka!* moments of insight, which often follow incubation

incubation: act of intentional disengagement from active problem solving

inner conscious: a term coined by José Silva, founder of the Silva Method, who discovered that we have access to states that heretofore were considered to be subconscious or beneath conscious awareness

intention: desire in action (see "desire")

intentional outcomes: goals with context; subjective targets and resulting outcomes derived from the active engagement of meaningful intentions

intention statement, meaningful: evolving statement filled with passion, purpose, love, and benefits for all, which incorporates the player's talents, strengths, competencies, and values; conduit for conversation between the game player and his soul; player's guidepost for thought and action; expressed in real time

Libby: game character who symbolically represents the aspect of the player's full range of emotions with capacities to feel and intuit; name derived from traits associated with the limbic system, the emotional center of the brain; at her best when harmoniously teamed up with Amy and Tex

mind games: subjective, dynamic mental exercises inspired from the work of José Silva

needs: that which is necessary in order to realize meaningful intentions; some are consciously known and others are to be discovered through the player's conversation with his soul; soul communicates needs through emotions and flashes of intuitive insights

negative: broad label used to express dissatisfaction with conditions, events, thoughts, and emotions

negative emotions: meaning one assigns to deep emotions; players appraise all emotions as valuable guidance information to meet needs and honor values

negative thoughts: meaning one assigns to challenging self-talk; players appraise all self-talk as valuable guidance information to identify and fortify beliefs in alignment with intent

objective: anything perceivable by the physical senses of sight, hearing, smell, taste, and touch; things of a material nature

observe: (see "alert witnessing")

principles: moral and ethical values; guidelines that support meaningful intentions; intentionally general in nature so they may apply to every situation that individuals are likely to encounter

react: (see "Response versus reaction" under "Distinctions")

real time: actual time during which a process occurs; present oriented

relaxation response: term coined by Herbert Benson, MD, and defined as "a physical state of deep rest that changes the physical and emotional responses to stress and the opposite of the fight or flight response"[32]; state is self-induced through techniques, such as passive and dynamic meditation and mental exercises, which we call "mind games"

repetition: recurrence of action needed to fortify or establish new insights, beliefs, emotional responses, and behaviors

resiliency gap: span of time between an emotional disturbance or sadness and the return to acceptance, understanding, and ease

resource: source of support; available supply to be drawn upon, either material or nonmaterial; source of information and/or action

respond: (see "Response versus reaction" under "Distinctions")

responsibility: ability to respond

sacred: expression of revered honor and respect

social hypnosis: collective state of consciousness derived from survival instinct and reaction to uncertainty; social attitudes perpetuated from fears and perceived risks; trance-like state of overreactiveness dominated with expectations of negative outcomes

soul: game concept; energy resource imbued with full awareness and a complete understanding of one's life purpose; player's main source of guidance, which communicates through emotions and thoughts

source: originator of a resource or resources

spiritual: of, concerned with, or affecting the soul

subjective: anything perceivable through inner states of emotion, feeling, thought, inner vision, imagery, imagination, visualization, self-talk, and intuition; things of a nonmaterial nature

success response: state of increasing responsiveness and decreasing reactiveness to emotions, thoughts, and events (see "Response versus reaction" under "Distinctions"); indications of success response growth include, but are not limited to, increased compassion for self and others, a building faith and confidence in one's self and in one's plans, and an attitude of gratitude

synchronicity: term coined by Carl Jung and defined as "an intimate connection between the internal image and the external world"[33]

Tex: game character who symbolically represents the aspect of the player's tendency to build rational cases from incomplete data; name derived from traits associated with the brain's neocortex; at his best when harmoniously teamed up with Libby and Amy

valuable guidance information: expression used to recognize, appreciate, and appraise the inherent value of all events, circumstances, thoughts, and emotions, and their capacity to be utilized to meet needs, honor values, and support meaningful intentions

values: our concept of the worth of things, of people, and of states of being that are valuable to us; strongly influence our level of persistence within our chosen actions

Wallas model: Graham Wallas's creative process model that involves the four stages: preparation, incubation, illumination, and verification

Distinctions

Abundant versus scarce mentality

- *Abundant mentality:* Where the dominant attention is on the riches already present and the opportunities available
- *Scarce mentality:* Where the dominant attention is on that which is missing and an expectation of misfortune

Appraisal versus assumption

- *Appraisal:* Examined belief
- *Assumption:* Unexamined belief

Assessment versus judgment

- *Assessment:* Evaluation of the nature, quality, or ability of someone, as in assessing someone's strengths, talents, skills, and unique abilities
- *Judgment:* Having or displaying an excessively critical point of view

Brain versus mind

- *Brain*: An organ that, among other things, interacts with consciousness
- *Mind*: Consciousness that interacts with the brain

Command versus control

- *Command:* Taking full responsibility for one's conditions, states of mind, and courses of action
- *Control:* Folly of believing one is solely capable of determining events and outcomes that involve external forces in the environment and the choices and behaviors of others (e.g., the pilot is not in control of the weather, crosswinds, or turbulence, but he is in command of navigating the airplane and his actions)

Creative behavior versus reactive behavior

- *Creative behavior:* Resulting state derived from congruent, harmonious, and aligned SEMB resources
- *Reactive behavior:* Resulting state derived from incongruent, conjangled, and mis-aligned SEMB resources

Effort versus struggle

- *Effort:* A healthy application of the four energy resources of SEMB directed toward a meaningful intention
- *Struggle:* An inefficient and excessive exertion of one or more energy resources; causes include fatigue, or a conscious or nonconscious attending of a limiting belief; relieved by disengagement, an alternate activity, a period of rest, or sleep, enabling the reengagement of appropriate effort

Emotion versus feeling

- *Emotion:* Spontaneous reaction one has to stimulus absent of analysis
- *Feeling:* Meaning one assigns to an emotion

Emotions versus moods

- *Emotions:* Spontaneous reactions one has to stimuli absent of analysis
- *Moods:* More generalized dispositions

Intentions versus goals

- *Intentions:* Process-oriented goals with the context of vision, purposeful mission, and values
- *Goals:* Outcome-oriented goals without the context of vision, purposeful mission, and values

Natural talents versus skills

- *Natural talents:* Innate aptitudes and capabilities
- *Skills:* Strengths acquired and developed through choice and life experience

Objective versus subjective

- *Objective:* Anything perceivable by the physical senses of sight, hearing, smell, taste, and touch; things of a material nature
- *Subjective:* Anything perceivable through inner state of emotion, feeling, thought,

inner vision, imagery, imagination, visualization, self-talk, and intuition; things of a nonmaterial nature

Present conditions versus future conditions

- *Present conditions:* Product that resulted from where your attention has been
- *Future conditions:* Product resulting from where your attention is now

Present-oriented versus future-oriented

- *Present-oriented:* Orientation utilized in meaningful intention statements, reflecting current conditions and actions being taken
- *Future-oriented:* Orientation utilized in mind games and other subjective exercises, employing imagination and visualization of outcomes

Rational mind versus creative mind

- *Rational mind:* Analytic, linear, limited to current known data; essential in organizing data and implementing actions; sometimes referred to as "left brain"
- *Creative mind:* Intuitive, nonlinear, imaginative; essential for the receptivity of new data; sometimes referred to as "right brain"

Response versus reaction

- *Response:* Thoughtful response that takes into consideration the implications of one's behavior
- *Reaction:* Exclusively stimulus-based reaction that does not take into consideration the implications of one's behavior

Rumi-nating versus ruminating

- *Rumi-nating:* Game practice inspired by the poet Rumi, which welcomes reflection of all emotions, both light and deep; when Rumi-nating, players honor the value of all emotions, appreciating them as a divine call for attention; when entertained, players obtain valuable guidance and greater clarity of their needs and values
- *Ruminating:* In psychology, defined as the compulsively focused attention on the symptoms of one's distress

Acronyms

BMW (Body-Mind Wisdom)

IMAGE (Illusions of Mind That Attract and Gather Energy)

OAR (Observe, Appraise, and Respond)

REALITY (RE-inforced Assumptions Literally Imagined as True for You)

REALITY (RE-inforced Assumptions Literally Interpreted as True for You)

SEMB (Soul, Emotion, Mind, and Behavior)

SOUL (Source of Unconditional Love)

Idioms

"Can't think straight": Inability to access logic or reason due to neural disconnections within the brain when highly stressed

"It dawned on me" or "It came to me": Instinctive expressions prompted from the experience of illuminations after incubation or active engagement

"Sleep on it": Instinctive expression used when one intuits the need to cease excessive effort; effective disengagement strategy; sleep states disengage the rational mind, allowing the creative mind to incubate with an expectation of illumination to follow

Appendix: Top 10 Spiritual Principles for Evoking Your Greatness

Within-state enlightenment leads to more realistic perception of the world and ourselves: consequently we can engage in more effective action that can eliminate much useless suffering.

—Charles T. Tart, PhD[34]

The observations we make with our five physical senses are so powerful they convince us that external reality is the only reality that exists. This false assumption causes us to incessantly push ourselves to DO more and to HAVE more. Our physical environment becomes filled with more things, but our inner BEING is left unfulfilled. This inner emptiness drives us to double our efforts to struggle and DO more.

Although less obvious, our inner world is another true reality that seeks the deeper fulfillment of calmness, ease, and peace. When fulfilled within your BEING, you tend to want less, need to DO less, and ironically attract and HAVE more! Furthermore, you have the presence of mind to more richly enjoy all of what you DO and HAVE.

So let's downshift from the incessant rushing and take a moment of mindfulness to review the following principles. If you are attracted to living these principles, avoid struggling to implement them. Exertion causes stress, which is counterproductive. Simply direct your attention on one principle a day. These principles are within you already. Your gentle attention will evoke these truths from within your heart and become increasingly present in your daily awareness.

Love

Love is the only true emotion; everything else is a reaction. Going beneath the roles we play (e.g., boss, coworker, sibling, and parent), we shatter the illusion of separateness and realize that we all have the same basic needs: to be cared for, appreciated, and loved. Being aware of this, we see the connectedness that unifies us all. This thing we call "love" goes beyond the romantic definition and speaks to all that is pure and positive. Call it God, universe, or higher self—it matters very little. The fact remains that this power is the ultimate expression of totally pure, unconditional love. It is within all of us, and we have access to it through the simple act of intent.

Appreciation

When you focus on what you have versus what is missing, you shift from a scarce to an abundant mentality. The universe is complete; nothing is missing. By appreciating what you already have, you increase your perception of its value, opening you up to noticing and attracting more and more to be grateful for.

Appraisal

Let go of the need to judge or label anything. This includes yourself, people, and events. Instead of judging people or things as good or bad, consider appraising it as valuable information. This information can then be applied toward whatever goals or intentions you have in your life. If a salesperson does not make a sale, he will ordinarily judge that as "bad" and will likely judge either himself, the client, the product, and/or the company as "bad." By removing the label and seeing the event as valuable information, the salesperson gains from the learning experience, which will bring him to the next level of professionalism. In doing so, one conserves an enormous volume of vital energy. When you cease to label the people you encounter, you become more compassionate and understanding of others and of yourself.

Present

Being fully in the "present" is truly a "gift." It is a gift to yourself as well as others. You literally create your future with your present thoughts and actions. When you are fully in the present, you have 100% of yourself involved and remain alert to the opportunities that are present. The people you encounter subjectively sense whether or not you are fully with them. This has a great impact on the quality of your personal and business relationships.

The Circle of Generosity

Giving and receiving form a circle of energy that is incomplete if either aspect is missing. Give whatever you want. If you want more money, help people make money; if you want more joy, create more joy for others. Know that, in order to fully give, you must be able to fully receive. Many spiritually minded people often shy away from receiving, particularly material wealth. Wealth is an aspect of this abundant energy circle of giving and receiving. The difficulty lies when you become overly attached to it or horde it; you stop the flow. By circulating your wealth, you create more and more for all to enjoy. Finally, open to giving to yourself. Honor your own worthiness to receive or no one else will.

Authenticity

Fully accepting, loving, and being yourself allows you to be 100% authentic. This means being fully responsible for yourself. Most of us think of responsibility as what we "should" be doing or living up to someone else's standards. "Responsibility" means having the ability to respond; trusting yourself and living your values. Realize that there is nothing to fix. Being authentic is simply being who you are. This authenticity is highly attractive and draws people to you who are "on the same page," so to speak. That means that your life will be filled with effortless relationships. When you stop doubting yourself and stop living up to the expectations of others, your inner self-talk shifts from "How am I doing?" to "How can I help?" There are over seven billion people on the planet, with plenty of candidates for personal and business relationships that are natural and effortless.

The Law of Resonance

Our essential nature is nonmaterial and composed of vibrating energy. If you had two pianos in a room, whatever chord you strike on one will cause the other to vibrate the same chord. Your thoughts and actions carry this truth. If you carry love within you, you attract love to you; if you carry pity, hatred, anger, or resentment, you attract that as well. Love everyone, including those who are difficult or who you sense have wronged you, and you will not only do that person a favor but everyone who encounters that person. Commit to loving everyone unconditionally, and you will find that, over time, your life will be totally void of disturbing relationships and filled with loving ones.

Worthiness

You are born deserving of all good things. Look at a newborn baby. Is it worthy and deserving of love and happiness? Of course. Are you worthy and deserving of love and happiness? Of course. Know that if you think not, you have accepted a false assumption within your belief sys-

305

tem; an interpretation from an external source. Connect within the source of your spirit, which is complete, and embrace your worthiness. If you still have doubt, look at your baby picture, and think this through again.

Grace and Ease

Struggling comes from fear and doubt and causes you to draw from the limited resources of your intellect. When you apply the principle of grace and ease, you draw from a much larger pool of resources: the creative faculties of imagination and intuition within your inner conscious mind. Struggling bypasses the natural processes of incubation and illumination where inspiration is drawn. "Grace and ease" means less tension, anxiety, and controlling and more ease, trust, and faith.

Faith

By "keeping the faith," you express trust in yourself and in something higher. You begin to surrender to process versus being impatiently obsessed with outcomes. It is a knowing that your desires and intentions, or something better, will arrive when they are meant to. Faith develops when you incorporate these principles into daily living. Only direct experience will reinforce this faith. Once experienced, you are released from the finite limitations of struggling and enjoy the infinite abundance of all that is already here. Then you will fully understand that less forcing attracts more.

Endnotes

1. http://www.quoteswave.com/picture-quotes/17228.
2. Although widely believed to be a direct quote from Albert Einstein, there is speculation that this is a paraphrase by writer Bob Samples from his book, *The Metaphoric Mind: A Celebration of Creative Consciousness* (Reading, MA: Addison-Wesley, 1976). In any case, this quotation embodies the great respect Einstein held for the coordinated application of imagination, intuition, and rational thinking reflected in numerous direct quotations. Therefore, I am comfortable using this quotation to illustrate points with the spirit of Einstein's sensibilities throughout this text.
3. Good Reads (accessed 2/5/2015), http://www.goodreads.com/quotes/13119-you-never-change-things-by-fighting-the-existing-reality-to.
4. "The Journal of Transpersonal Psychology, Volumes 1-4," Transpersonal Institute, 1969, p. 124.
5. See note 1 above.
6. Susan Corso, *God's Dictionary: Divine Definitions for Everyday Enlightenment* (New York: Tarcher/Putham, 2002).
7. http://www.susancorso.com/PDFs/SeedsArchive/SeedsVI-2004.pdf.
8. Mihaly Csikzentmihalyi, *Flow: The Psychology of Optimal Experience* (New York: Harper Perennial Modern Classics, 1990).
9. http://www.sciencedirect.com/science/article/pii/S0361923011001341; https://s100.copyright.com/AppDispatchServlet?publisherName=ELS&contentID=S0361923011001341&orderBeanReset=true.
10. Used with permission by David Rakel, MD, University of Wisconsin. http://abcnews.go.com/Health/video/relaxation-response-9362175; http://abcnews.go.com/Health/AlternativeMedicine/relaxation-response-ease-stress/story?id=9411762.
11. R. A. Vandell, R. A. Davis, and H. A. Clugston, "The function of mental practice in the acquisition of motor skills," *J Gen Psychol.* 29:243-250, 1943.
12. "Living Your Fabulous Life," radio show, 2002.
13. http://www.ncbi.nlm.nih.gov/pubmed/7792376.
14. Ibid.
15. Renos K. Papadopoulos, ed., *The Handbook of Jungian Psychology: Theory, Practice and Applications* (East Sussex: Routledge, 2006).

16. Stephen R. Covey, *The 7 Habits of Highly Effective People: Powerful Lessons in Personal Change* (New York: Simon & Schuster, 1989).

17. Jonathan Barnes, ed., *The Complete Works of Aristotle, The Revised Oxford Translation* (Princeton, NJ: Princeton University Press, 1884).

18. *The Essentail Rumi* (New York: HarperCollins Publishers, 1995).

19. Thomas J. Leonard, *The Portable Coach: 28 Sure Fire Strategies For Business And Personal Success* (New York: Scribner, 1998).

20. Ralph Edward Oesper, *The Human Side of Scientists* (Cincinnati: University of Publications, University of Cincinnati, 1975), p. 58.

21. See T. Ward, "Creativity." In *Encyclopaedia of Cognition,* edited by L. Nagel (New York: Macmillan, 2003); see Steven M. Smith, "Fixation, Incubation and Insight in Memory and Creative Thinking." In Steven M. Smith, Thomas B. Ward, and Ronald A. Finke. *The Creative Cognition Approach* (Cambridge, MA: MIT Press, 1995).

22. See note 3 above.

23. See note 4 above.

24. From the song "Tin Man," recorded and performed by American rock band "America," produced by George Martin, lyrics by Dewey Bunnell, released in August 1974 on the Warner Bros. record label.

25. From Franklin D. Roosevelt's first inauguration as the **32nd President of the United States,** which was held on Saturday, March 4, 1933, http://research.archives.gov/description/197333.

26. Jack Tempchin and Robb Strandlund, "Already Gone," recorded by the Eagles for their album, *On the Border* (1974).

27. Stan and Janice "Jan" Berenstain, *The Berenstain Bears and the Bad Habit* (New York: Random House Books for Young Readers, 1986).

28. Thomas Moore, *Care of the Soul: A Guide for Cultivating Depth and Sacredness in Everyday Life* (New York: HarperCollins Publishers, Inc., 1992).

29. Hendrie Weisinger, *Emotional Intelligence at Work: The Untapped Edge for Success* (San Francisco: Jossey-Bass, Inc., 1998).

30. Eknath Easwaran, *To Love Is to Know Me: The Bhagavad Gita for Daily Living* (Volume 3) (Tomales, CA: Nilgiri Press, 1984); *The Sacred Books of the East: Volume 10. Part 1. The Dhammapada, A Collection of Verses,* Being One of the Canonical Books of the Buddhists, translated from Pali by Friedrich Max Müller, Elibron Classics series (Boston: Adamant Media Corporation, 2005).

31. http://stemcell.stanford.edu/research.

32. http://www.bensonhenryinstitute.org/building-resiliency/2-uncategorised/34-faq.

33. http://oatd.org/oatd/record?record=handle%5C:10393%5C%2F9564.

34. Charles T. Tart, *Waking Up: Overcoming the Obstacles to Human Potential* (Boston: New Science Library, 1986).

JOHN FELITTO is a trusted coach, highly respected advisor, and thought leader to entrepreneurs internationally. He is the founder of Felitto Coaching & Consulting Associates.

For more than three decades, his practical methods have helped both individuals and business owners enhance the quality of their lives, guiding them to realize their intentions. John is renowned for his expertise in translating deep principles and concepts into practical strategies and steps for greater personal and professional fulfillment.

John's lifelong curiosity with mindfulness and its impact on human behavior developed into an insatiable thirst for learning. He calls upon 40 years of study in fields including esoteric consciousness to value-based principles, emotional intelligence, and analytic self-regulation strategies. Interviews with best-selling authors on his radio show, *Living Your Fabulous Life,* as well as in-depth experience with his many clients deepened and enriched his expertise.

Through deep listening and Socratic inquiry, he creates a powerful environment for his clients' self-discovery, thereby evoking their own inherent greatness. He is training other coaches, who are interested in working with his methodology, to expand his reach and enhance lives globally.

John lives with his wife of 34 years and their three children in Pearl River, New York. He strongly encourages his clients to play—both for the joy of it and for the rejuvenating qualities that lead to fresh insights. He walks his talk as a private pilot and avid electric guitarist.